DAUGHTERS OF THE KGB

Also by Douglas Boyd

Non-Fiction

April Queen, Eleanor of Aquitaine
Voices from the Dark Years
The French Foreign Legion
The Kremlin Conspiracy
Normandy in the Time of Darkness
Blood in the Snow, Blood on the Grass
De Gaulle: The Man Who Defied Six US Presidents
Lionheart
The Other First World War

Fiction

The Eagle and the Snake
The Honour and the Glory
The Truth and the Lies
The Virgin and the Fool
The Fiddler and the Ferret

DAUGHTERS OF THE KGB

MOSCOW'S SECRET SPIES, SLEEPERS AND ASSASSINS OF THE COLD WAR

DOUGLAS BOYD

This book is dedicated to all the political prisoners
and others who suffered in the Stasi prison
on the Lindenstrasse in Potsdam,
and to our predecessors there under the KGB 1945–1952
and under the Gestapo 1933–1945

'Those who do not remember the past are compelled to repeat it.'

George Santayana

Cover illustrations: © Londonstills.com/Alamy and iStock © gonullena.

First published 2015

The History Press
The Mill, Brimscombe Port
Stroud, Gloucestershire, GL5 2QG
www.thehistorypress.co.uk

British Library Cataloguing in Publication Data.
A catalogue record for this book is available from the British Library.

isbn 978 0 7509 5850 9

Typesetting and origination by The History Press
Printed in Great Britain

Contents

ACKNOWLEDGEMENTS

Despite the two and a half decades since the collapse of the USSR, a surprising number of people who assisted my research asked not to be mentioned as sources, some giving no reason and others pleading that there might be repercussions against family members still living in their countries of birth. Others still were helpful initially and then said, 'I'm sorry. I can't help you any more.' I never argued or tried to persuade them because it seemed this was not from personal guilt for anything, but rather that even thinking about those years will always be too painful for millions of people who lived through them. Who could blame them for that?

Among those I can thank for their help are Stella Dvořaková, William Sirben and Jiři Dubnička for insights into the Cold War period in Czechoslovakia; Nikolai Karailiev for reading the Bulgarian pages and Gabriele Schnell, whom I first met in the former Lindenstrasse prison in Potsdam, for the work she has done to document the experiences of the Stasi's victims in the so-called German Democratic Republic.

At The History Press, I can also thank commissioning editor Mark Beynon, project editor Rebecca Newton, designer Katie Beard and cover designer Martin Latham.

List of Abbreviations

AAP	Australian Associated Press news agency
ABLT	Állambiztonsági Szolgálatok Történeti Levéltára (Hungarian state intelligence archives)
ABW	Agencja Bezpieczeństwa Wewnętrznego (Polish counter-espionage service)
AK	Armia Krajowa (Polosh Home Army)
AL	Armia Ludowa (People's Army)
AVH	Allamvédelmi Hatósag (second name of Hungarian secret police)
AVO	Allamvédelmi Osztálya (first name of Hungarian secret police)
BA	Belügyminisztérium Állambiztonsági (Hungarian intelligence agency)
BfV	Bundesamt für Verfassungsschutz (Federal German security service)
BIRN	Balkan Investigative Reporting Network
BIS	Bezpečnostní Informační Služba (Czech post-Communist security service)
BKP	Bulgarska Komunisticheska Partia (Bulgarian Communist Party)
BND	Bundesnachrichtendienst (Federal German intelligence service)
BStU	Bundesbeauftragte der Unterlagen des Staatssicherheitsministeriums der ehemaligen Deutschen Demokratischen Republik (Stasi archives)
CIA	Central Intelligence Agency
CIC	US Counter-Intelligence Corps

CIO	Anti-Communist Czech Intelligence Office
CNSAS	Conciliul Naţional pentru Studearea Archivelor Securitâţii (Romanian post-Communist intelligence archives)
CPGB	Communist Party of Great Britain
ČSSR	Československá Socialistická Republika (Czechoslovak Socialist Republic)
DM	Deutsche Mark (West German currency)
DST	Direction de la Surveillance du Territoire (French security service)
EAM/ELAS	Left-wing Greek resistance
FDJ	Freie Deutsche Jugend (Communist equivalent of the Hitler Youth organisation)
GCHQ	Government Communications Headquarters
GDR	German Democratic Republic
GRU	Glavnoye Razvedatelnoye Upravleniye (Soviet military intelligence)
GZI	Główny Zarząd Informacji (Polish military intelligence)
HVA	Hauptverwaltung Aufklärung (East German foreign intelligence service)
IGM	Internationale Gesellschaft für Menschenrechte (International Association for Human Rights)
IM	inoffizielle Mitarbeiter (informer working for the Stasi)
IWF	Institut für wirtschaftliche Forschung (Institute for Scientific Research, a cover name for HVA)
KDS	Komitet za Darzhavna Sigurnost (Bulgarian Committee of State Security)
KdSBP	Komitet do Spraw Bezpieczeństwa Publicznego (Polish Committee for Public Security)
KGB	Komityet Gosudrarstvennoi Bezopacnosti (Committee of State Security of USSR)
KgU	Kampfgruppe gegen Unmenschlichkeit (West German anti-Stasi group)
KKE	Kommunistikó Kómma Elládas (Greek Communist Party)
KPD	Kommunistiche Partei Deutschlands (German Communist Party)
KSČ	Komunistická Strana Československa (Czechoslovakian Communist Party)
LSK	Luftstreitkräfte (East German air force)
MBP	Ministerstwo Bezpieczeństwa Publicznego (Polish Ministry of Public Security)
MDP	Magyar Dolgozók Párt (Hungarian Workers' Party, i.e. Communist Party)

MfS	Ministerium für Staatssicherheit (Ministry of State Security)
MI5	British Security Service
MI6	British Intelligence Service
MIG	Mikoyan i Gurevitch (names of two Soviet aircraft designers)
MKP	Magyar Komunista Párt (Hungarian Communist Party)
MNVK2	Magyar Néphadsereg Vezérkara 2 Csoportfőnöksege (Hungarian military intelligence)
MSW	Ministerstwo Spraw Wewnętrznych (Polish Ministry of Internal Affairs)
MSzMP	Magyar Szocialista Munkáspárt (Hungarian Socialist Workers' Party)
MVD	Ministerstvo Vnutrennikh Dyel (Soviet successor to NKVD)
NICSMA	NATO Integrated Systems Management Agency
NKVD	Narodny Komissariat Vnukhtrennikh Dyel (Soviet forerunner of KGB)
NSA	US National Security Agency
NSDAP	Nazionalsozialistische Deutsche Arbeiterpartei (full name of Hitler's Nazi party)
NVA	Nazionale Volksarmee (East German army)
OKW	Oberkommando der Wehrmacht (German General Staff in Second World War)
OSI	US Air Force Office of Special Investigations
OSS	US Office of Strategic Services (in Second World War)
PCF	Parti Communiste Français (French Communist Party)
PCI	Partito Comunista Italiano (Italian Communist Party)
PCR	Partidul Comunist Român (Romanian Communist Party)
PKSh	Partia Komuniste e Shqipërisë (Albanian Communist Party)
PKWN	Polski Komitet Wyzwolenia Narodowego (Polish Committee of National Liberation)
POW	Prisoner of war
PPSh	Partia e Punës e Shqipërisë (Albanian Workers' Party)
PSL	Polski Stronnictwo Ludowe (Polish Christian Democrat agrarian party)
PZPR	Polska Zjednoczona Partia Robotnicza (Polish United Workers' Party, i.e. Communist Party)
RAF	Royal Air Force
RBP	Resort Bezpieczeństwa Publicznego (Polish Department of Public Security)
RHSA	Reichssicherheitshauptamt (Chief Administration of Third Reich Security)
RIAS	Rundfunk im Amerikanischen Sektor (US-financed propaganda station in West Berlin)

RTRP   Rząd Tymczasowy Rzeczyoospolitej Polskiej (Provisional Government of Poland)

SB (MSW)   Służba Bezpieczeństwa Ministerstwa Spraw Wewnętrznych (Polish Security Service of Ministry of Internal Affairs)

SDECE   Service de Documentation Extérieure et de Contre-Espionage (French intelligence service)

SDP   Sozialistische Demokratische Partei (German Social Democratic Party)

SED   Sozialistische Einheitspartei Deutschlands (East German Communist Party)

SHAPE   Supreme Headquarters, Allied Powers in Europe

ShIK   Shërbimi Informativ Kombëtar (Albanian successor to Sigurimi)

ShISh   Shërbimi Informativ Shtetëror (successor to ShIK)

SIE   Serviciul de Informaţii Externe (Romanian post-Communist intelligence service)

Sigint   Signals intelligence (electronic eavesdropping)

SIS   Secret Intelligence Service

SOE   Special Operations Executive

SRI   Serviciul Rôman de Informaţii (Romanian post-Communist security service)

SSR   Soviet socialist republic

Stasi   Ministerium für Staatssicherheit (East German Ministry of State Security)

StB   Státní Bezpečnost / Štátna Bezpečnost (Czechoslovakian State Security service)

SWT   Sektor für Wissenschaft und Technik (HVA Section for technological espionage)

TVO   Trudovo-Vazpritatelni Obshchezhitiya (Bulgarian gulag)

UB   Urząd Bezpieczeństwa (Polish state security)

UPA   Ukraïnska Povstanska Armiya (Ukrainian underground army)

ZAIG   Zentrale Auswertungs und Informationsgruppe (evaluation department of HVA)

Part I

Setting the Scene

Through a Glass Darkly

Each year, 3 October is a German national holiday known as *der Tag der deutschen Einheit* – the day of German Unity. It celebrates the reunification of the country in 1989 after forty-four years of being split in two by the front line of the Cold War. The date is not an exact anniversary of any particular event, but was carefully chosen to avoid reminding people of embarrassing events in recent German history.

On 3 October 2008 several thousand people were celebrating the reunification at what had been the border crossing-point between Marienborn in the so-called German Democratic Republic (GDR) and Helmstedt in the Federal Republic when the country was divided roughly north to south by the Iron Curtain after the Second World War. Living conditions to the east of the 'inner German frontier' were so grim under the neo-Stalinist government implanted by, and controlled from, Moscow that a total of 3.5 million GDR citizens fled to the West between the end of the war in 1945 and the building of the Berlin Wall in 1961.[1]

By 1952 the population haemorrhage threatened the economic survival of Stalin's German puppet state and the green border was made increasingly escape-proof by barbed wire, watch-towers, minefields, searchlights, trip-wires connected to locked-off machine guns and SM-70 Claymore-type mines with a *lethal* range of 25m. There were also stretches where attack dogs roamed free and the foot patrols of border guards had orders to shoot to kill – the infamous *Schiessbefehl* that cost so many lives.

To the many thousand troops of the Western Allies who drove along the autobahn to Berlin during the Cold War, the Marienborn–Helmstedt crossing was known as Checkpoint Able; Baker was at the other end of the autobahn, where it entered West Berlin; the more famous Checkpoint Charlie was on the line where the American sector of 'the divided city' confronted Communist East Berlin.

On that sunny, rather windy, autumn afternoon in 2008 at Marienborn/Helmstedt family groups were picnicking on the grass and people of all ages queued to visit the small museum at this former flash-point where World War III might have begun. The motorway having been diverted once the checkpoint was redundant after the reunification of Germany, people wandered across the vehicle lanes that had often been clogged with Allied military convoys and commercial traffic deliberately delayed by Soviet troops or GDR border police. Others photographed a solitary watch-tower that had been left standing to remind visitors that Checkpoint Able had been one of the few tightly controlled gaps in the long internal German border stretching 866 miles from the shores of the Baltic all the way to the Czech frontier. Whereas two-thirds of escape attempts had previously taken place across this 'green border', the number of documented attempts there after the border was closed in 1952 plummeted to fewer than 100 per year, of which only about six were successful.[2] Many of the other would-be refugees paid with their lives.

For most of the Germans present on that day in 2008, the occasion was a pleasant family day out. Doubtless, some of the older visitors had unhappy memories, having lived *im Osten* – to the east of the border – under the most repressive Communist regime in Europe. I shared their mixed feelings, walking with my wife away from the crowds towards a small, rather temporary-looking building to the left of the traffic lanes. For other visitors curious enough to peer through the grimy windows, there was no evidence of the crushing bureaucracy of which this had been the westernmost outpost, but looking through that glass darkly took me back nearly half a century.

On 12 May 1959, aged 20, I was sitting in that office on a wooden chair facing an officer of the Ministerium für Staatssicherheit – the Ministry of State Security, usually abbreviated to 'Stasi' – who had been interrogating me for six long weeks. Also present were his escort of two Stasi heavies in ill-fitting suits and a distinguished-looking English lady in the smart blue uniform of the International Red Cross, who had come to escort me back to the free world. For twenty minutes, she fielded all attempts to get her to make any political remark by her ready stream of small talk about the weather, the pleasure of drinking tea as opposed to coffee and so on. As the clock on the wall showed the agreed handover time of midday, she rose to return to the Helmstedt side of the crossing, in what was then the British zone of occupied Germany.

With nothing against him personally, I shook hands with my interrogator. It was the Cold War that had made us enemies. If he had sometimes had me hauled out of my cell for questioning in the middle of the night or very early in the morning, it was not often enough to constitute harassment, but it did make me wonder whatever sort of life he led, if those were his normal working hours.

Walking with the Red Cross lady, whose name I never learned, out of the door and towards the western side of the checkpoint, time slowed down. It seemed a long walk, and I was frightened that this was a dream, a delusion or some kind of psychological trick that would end with a sudden shout of *'Halt! Stehenbleiben!'* at which I would turn round to see a frontier guard with his machine pistol levelled at me – and raise my hands, waiting to be taken back to my cell.

That whole morning seemed unreal. Woken in my cell at 6 a.m. by a prison guard bearing the usual breakfast of black bread, some brown jam of unidentifiable fruit and a mug of ersatz coffee suitably called *Muckefuck*, I had been marched along the echoing corridors of the political prison in Potsdam's Lindenstrasse, known ironically to its unfortunate inmates as *das Lindenhotel*. Instead of conducting me into the usual interrogation room, the guard escorted me to a small courtyard just inside the main gate of the prison. There my Stasi interrogator, Lieutenant Becker – I learned his name fifty years later – stood by an ancient black Mercedes saloon with the two heavies. Without a word being exchanged, they got into the front seats, with Becker and me in the rear. The double gates of the prison swung open, the driver accelerated though the archway and, with tyres screaming on the cobbled street, drove out of Potsdam and headed westwards along the autobahn, overtaking every other vehicle because there were no speed limits for a car belonging to the Stasi.

'Where are we going?' It seemed a normal enough question to ask, for a prisoner who had been in solitary confinement for six weeks with only a few brief sorties for exercise in a prison yard surrounded by walls 5m high, topped by a sentry post, in which stood a guard with loaded sub-machine gun. No answer, but Becker did produce from his plastic briefcase a paper bag containing a sandwich of sliced garlic sausage on pumpernickel, which tasted like manna to me after six weeks of bland prison food.

'*Hat's geschmekt?*' he asked. I replied that the after-taste of garlic was delicious, which led to a surreal discussion in which Becker explained that the German word *Nachgeschmack* means a *bad* after-taste. It is strange, the details that stay in the memory.

But, at midday, there was no challenge as my elegant lady escort and I crossed from the Marienborn side to the Helmstedt checkpoint. In 2008 I could see that my 'long walk' had only been about 200 yards. Safely on the British side of the crossing, I looked back to see Becker and the two other Stasi men getting into their car for the return to Potsdam. The Red Cross lady was thanked for her help by two men in civilian clothes standing by an unmarked car, and then she left us. One of the men was from the British security services; the other said, 'Welcome back, Boyd. I am Flight Lieutenant Burton of the RAF Police.'

He could have said, 'You are guilty of high treason and we are going to shoot you.' I was so dazed, I would probably not have protested.

During my debriefing interrogations by Flight Lieutenant Burton and others in the British occupation forces' headquarters at München-Gladbach, I had to admit that the first days and nights of my solitary confinement in Potsdam were – and still are – burned into my memory. The last few days were also clear, but the long and occasionally terrifying weeks between, during which I was held incommunicado, were mostly just a blur. As it was entirely possible that I had been injected with a truth drug and betrayed classified information about the top secret work on which I had been employed in the Signals Section at RAF Gatow, there was some talk during my debriefing at München-Gladbach of sentencing me to several years' imprisonment on my return to the UK.

I was instead flown back to Britain and debriefed for a second time by the very perceptive Air Chief Marshal Sir Hubert Patch, who rightly considered that, although I had been criminally foolish to get myself caught on the wrong side of a hostile frontier, I had to some extent redeemed myself by foiling an attempt by the KGB to get their hands on me. He also gave me a reference for my first job application. Was that goodwill, or a way of keeping tabs on me? In addition, Burton gave me a London telephone number belonging to the security services. He said I was to 'ring it and ask for Mr Shepherd, if contacted by any peace-loving people' as the Soviets called their sympathisers and undercover agents in the West.

As a Russian linguist, trained for real-time interception of VHF transmissions of Soviet fighter pilots over-flying the GDR and Poland, I had signed the Official Secrets Act and undertaken not to visit any Warsaw Pact country. Not only had I been into the GDR – a hostile police state, where I had no right to be – but I had been arrested on the wrong side of the border in the middle of the night by Grenzpolizei border troops and Soviet soldiers pointing loaded guns at me on the otherwise deserted railway station of Albrechtshof, a north-western suburb of Berlin.

Several hours after my arrest, the heavy door of cell No. 20 in the Stasi interrogation prison on Potsdam's Lindenstrasse closed behind me, leaving me to reflect on my situation. I was a prisoner, held in solitary confinement in a political prison in a country with which the United Kingdom had no diplomatic relations. There were no consular or other British officials to visit me and advise me about my rights. Not that it made much difference. Nobody in that prison had any rights. The reader who has grown up in a Western democracy, however imperfect in some aspects, will find it impossible to understand what it feels like to have no rights at all.

In 2006, seventeen years after the collapse of the so-called German Democratic Republic, Florian Henckel von Donnersmarck's award-winning film *Das Leben der Anderen – The Lives of Others –* was acclaimed as a shatteringly accurate portrayal of the four decades of grey and depressing life in the GDR. Its central character is Georg Dreyman, a highly privileged playwright. After the fall of the Berlin Wall, he goes to the Bundesbeauftragte der Unterlagen des Staatssicherheitsministeriums der ehemaligen Deutschen Demokratischen Republik – the office of the Federal Commissioner for the Archives of the Ministry of State Security of the Former German Democratic Republic, understandably abbreviated to 'BStU'. The fall of the Berlin Wall spurred hundreds of anxious Stasi officers to burn and shred thousands of files containing details of their own activities and those of their undercover agents in the West. Also, thousands of the surveillance files covering most of the population of the GDR were destroyed by delirious crowds invading the Stasi's offices and prisons after the fall of the Wall, but Dreyman is hoping to find his file intact. He wants to examine it for clues why his lover killed herself. In the BStU reading room, a clerk wheels in a trolley piled high with 2in-thick dossiers.

'Which one is mine?' Dreyman asks.

The clerk replies, 'They all are.'

And so are all the files piled high on two more trolleys. That brief scene lasting only a few seconds is a measure of the relentless spying on *everyone* in the GDR, for Dreyman had belonged to the elite stratum of society, being a personal friend of Margot Honecker, whose husband, Erich, ruled the GDR. Even that had not saved him from the Stasi's scrutiny.

Watching Donnersmarck's gripping film gave me the idea of requesting my own Stasi file.

On the day before my 2008 trip to Marienborn–Helmstedt I visited the former political prison in which I had been held in solitary confinement, to find that it is now a memorial to the 4,000 people sentenced there to forcible sterilisation in the Nazi era and the thousands imprisoned there by the Gestapo prior to 1945, by the KGB 1945–52 and by the Stasi 1952–89. Fortunately, during my incarceration I was unaware of the appalling suffering of many inmates because I was held in a separate wing as a pawn to be traded in due course for some political advantage. Had I then known how brutally the Stasi treated citizens of the GDR undergoing interrogation elsewhere in the prison, I should have been far more frightened.

Revisiting the interrogation room where I had verbally fenced with Becker at all hours of the day and night, I clearly recalled one episode towards the end of my spell in 'the Lindenhotel'. One morning, I was shown into the interrogation room and there found, instead of Becker, two men and a woman seated at the desk. As soon as the door was closed behind me, the woman said in Russian, '*My predstaviteli praviteltsva sovietskovo soyuza.*' The sentence meant, We are representatives of the government of the Soviet Union.

Until then I had succeeded in bluffing Becker and his masters that I was a clerk in charge of a bedding store in Gatow. As I read in my Stasi file fifty years later, Becker's *streng geheim* telex dated 31 March 1959 announcing the arrest and detention of the author was sent over a secure teleprinter link from Potsdam District Office to Stasi Centre in Berlin. It included this passage: '[Boyd] explained that his work (in RAF Gatow) consists of filling in forms for catering supplies and equipment and making tea, polishing floors, etc.'[3]

The three Russians from the KGB or GRU – Soviet military intelligence – confronting me in the interrogation room knew very well what went on in the Signals Section of RAF Gatow. I tried to keep from showing on my face the fear that the Russian words inspired. The interpreter repeated the introduction in English. For the next couple of hours, the two men fired questions at me in rapid succession. From time to time, she pretended to forget to translate a simple question and simply repeated it in Russian. '*Zanimayetyes sportom?*' Do you play sport? '*U vas skolko let?*' How old are you? And so on. Each time, pulse racing, I smiled as though it were all a joke while I waited for her to put the question into English.

By the end of the 2-hour grilling, I pretended to believe they had a plan to 'spring' me from the prison and release me on the border of the British sector of Berlin, to make my own way back to Gatow. They said they would do this because our countries had been allies during the Second World War. I was warned that I must on no account tell Becker that they had talked to me, in case he spoiled the plan.

In the West, we thought at the time that all the Warsaw Pact countries were united against us, but I took a chance in the belief that the Russians' warning meant that even the neo-Stalinist Stasi did not like being pushed around by the Soviet forces, whose HQ was at Karlshorst outside Berlin. I kicked up such a fuss with the guards after being returned to my cell that Becker made a visit, to see what was wrong. His angry reaction when I informed him of the Russians' intrusion told me that I had guessed right and that the half-million Russian troops stationed in the GDR were regarded as occupation forces, not brothers-in-arms.

My Stasi file indicates that, to spite the KGB team for its intrusion, Department 3 of the Stasi's 7th Directorate recommended on the day after their visit that I be handed over through the East German Red Cross to the British Red Cross – a back-channel used by the two governments from time to time. But I was not informed. As the days and sleepless nights passed without any further visit from Becker, I became increasingly uneasy, and stayed on an adrenalin high until my release.

On the day prior to my return to Potsdam in 2008, I collected my Stasi file, reference Allg/P 11626/62, from the BStU in Berlin's Karl-Liebknecht-Strasse, near the Alexanderplatz. At last, after all those years of wondering, I could check how much, if anything, I had given away. And there it was, in black and white: '[Boyd] gave no further information about his work [in RAF Gatow] or his unit. Even the little [personal] information was given reluctantly because it is forbidden [for him] to give military information.'[4]

At the time of my unsought adventure, most people believed that there was no political censorship in Britain, whereas the system introduced in 1912 and still in force today enabled Admiral George Thompson, then Secretary of the D Notice Committee, to drop a note to the press and broadcasting organisations 'requesting' no mention be made of my youthful misadventure. Thus, few people had any idea that I had been through the Stasi mill and was fortunate enough to come out in one piece. Nor did I volunteer the information, even to my own family, because during the debriefing I had been told not to talk about it to anyone until I had grandchildren. Now I do have that blessing. In any case, the collapse of the USSR makes it all irrelevant today – or does it?

On return to civilian life, the desire to find a job using my fluency in several European languages led me into the international film business, where my Russian and German brought frequent contacts with representatives of East European state companies like Film Polski, Hungarofilm, Československý Filmexport and Moscow's Sovexportfilm. When I moved on to head the BBC Eurovision office, my contacts there included officials of the Eastern European television services. Since, during the Cold War, all these privileged visitors to the West were routinely debriefed by their national security services on their return home and some were full-time intelligence officers working under commercial cover, this could have been awkward. It never was, so there was no need to call the mysterious telephone number and 'ask for Mr Shepherd'. Many a pleasurable evening was spent with these colleagues from behind the Iron Curtain, drinking their wine, vodka and *slivovitz* and eating their national delicacies in smoky restaurants filled with the smells and the sounds of their homelands: folk music and voices arguing.

Did we talk politics? Never. I think they enjoyed being off-duty with someone who could speak their languages, or at least a common tongue more familiar to them than English. I certainly enjoyed their company and kept in touch with some of them for years. Thus, from a little hint here and another there, I experienced the Cold War from both sides. As I had sensed during my time in 'the Lindenhotel', they were pursuing the difficult path of occupied peoples who did not love their Soviet occupiers, but had to comply with Moscow's orders most of the time or risk dire consequences.

Douglas Boyd,
South-west France, March 2015

Notes

1. E. Sheffer, *Burned Bridge*, Oxford, OUP 2011, p. 67
2. For a more detailed breakdown, see Sheffer, *Burned Bridge*, pp. 175–8
3. Scans of the file may be found in D. Boyd, *The Kremlin Conspiracy*, Hersham, Ian Allen 2010, pp. 9, 10
4. Ibid

2

LIFE IS A GAME OF CHESS

The Russian term *vozhd* corresponds with *der Führer* in German. As *vozhd*, or dictator of the USSR, Josef Vissarionovich Djugashvili, aka Stalin, had every reason to feel pleased with himself after the German surrender in May 1945. Despite his pre-war purges that decimated the senior ranks of the Soviet armed forces, Russia had come out of the war in a stronger geopolitical position than before it. That this was largely due to massive American supplies of materiel shipped on the dangerous Arctic convoys to Murmansk and delivered through British-occupied Iran, and to the second front opening with the Normandy invasion in June 1944, did not allay his satisfaction that Russian armies had penetrated farther west than since Cossack troops had pursued Napoleon's defeated Grande Armée all the way to Paris after the war of 1812. In the process of forcing Hitler's retreat, Stalin's armies had repossessed the Baltic states and steamrolled a path through Poland, Czechoslovakia and Hungary to occupy more than a third of the Third Reich, in which Austria – renamed Ostmark after the Anschluss of 1938 – had been reduced to the status of a province. The presence of eight entire Soviet armies on German and Austrian soil changed the political map of Europe. But this was far from being the only change since 1939.

Enjoying a break in the mild Crimean weather at Sochi that autumn, Stalin called for maps after a dinner at which his Foreign Minister Vyacheslav Molotov was present. 'Dinner' was at any time he chose, usually late. Although the bluff Georgian peasant who ruled the vast Soviet Union by terror had little else in common with the late Führer of the Third Reich, he too enjoyed forcing his close associates to stay up far into the night as an audience for his lengthy monologues, ignoring their need to be at work in their offices early next day while he slumbered on.

Gloating over the enormous expansion of territory overrun by Soviet forces during the war, he used the stem of his favourite Dunhill pipe as a pointer. 'In the North,' he said, 'everything's okay. Finland wronged us, so we've moved the frontier further back from Leningrad.' *Wronged us* was a typically paranoid way of putting it: the far outnumbered Finns had fought courageously for months to repulse the Red Army's massive invasion of their country in November 1939.

'The Baltic states,' Stalin continued, 'which were Russian territory from ancient times, are ours again. All the Byelorussians are ours now, Ukrainians too – and the Moldavians [by which he meant Romania] are back with us. So, to the west, everything's okay. [In the Far East] the Kurile Islands are ours and all of Sakhalin. [In] China and Mongolia, all is as it should be.' He prodded the Dardanelles at the bottom of the map with his pipe. 'Now, this frontier I don't like at all. We also have claims on Turkish territory and to Libya.'

The 'claim on Turkish territory' was a reference to a centuries-old obsession of Russian rulers: to grab control of the Dardanelles and Bosporus, so that the Russian Black Sea fleet could freely come and go into the Adriatic and Mediterranean without having the agreement of the Turks who lived on both sides of the narrow waterway.

Molotov's own wife was shortly to be sentenced by Stalin to five years *incomunicada* in a prison camp. He already knew how dangerous making a joke with the *vozhd* could be, yet was unable to resist quipping, 'And I wouldn't mind getting Alaska back.'[2]

Had they been compiling an alphabetical gazetteer, the next country to be mentioned would have been Albania. This primitive, largely mountainous, country was ruled by Enver Hoxha, son of a prosperous cloth merchant in the southern city of Gjirokastër, who had become a Communist activist during studies in French universities after being sent there by his father, aged 18.

Although Britain had supported with arms deliveries and liaison officers Hoxha's partisans fighting the Italian occupiers of their country during the Second World War, the Soviet Union had contributed little. Hoxha was, nevertheless, an admirer of Stalin, whom he was taking as a model for his post-Liberation policies. In his capacity as secretary-general of Partia Komuniste e Shqipërisë (PKS), the Albanian Communist Party, he was pushing through agrarian reform in line with Bolshevik collectivisation policy of 1917. 'All land to the peasants,' Lenin had proclaimed, before dispossessing them along with the landlords. Hoxha was also ruthlessly eliminating all political opposition. The country's monarch, King Zog I, had spent most of the war exiled in England with a large amount of his nation's gold reserves. Britain's post-war attempt to restore him to the throne by smuggling in armed anti-Communist resistance groups was to end in disaster when MI6 mole Kim Philby betrayed to Moscow not only the plan but the actual timing and coordinates of each group's arrival, resulting in at least 300 returning Albanian patriots being rounded up at gunpoint, arrested, tortured and executed shortly after setting foot on their native soil.

In neighbouring Greece, the Communist Party – Kommunistikó Kómma Elládas (KKE) – was controlled by Nikos Zachariadis, an alumnus of the Comintern's Lenin School who had spent most of the war in Dachau concentration camp. In his absence, KKE members under the umbrella of EAM/ELAS – the Greek Liberation Front – fought a guerrilla war against the German, Italian and Bulgarian occupying forces. They had overrun the whole country after the withdrawal of Axis forces in October 1944, and then gone underground after British intervention to restore King George II of the Hellenes to his throne in December 1944. Freed when US troops liberated Dachau in late April 1945, Zachariadis resumed control of KKE. He fought a subsequent bloody civil war with atrocities on both sides, in which the KKE looked likely to come out on top after the departure of the British interventionist forces.

On the eastern border of Greece lies Bulgaria. During the country's inter-war political unrest, lifelong Communist activist Georgi Dimitrov had been exiled under sentence of death after an attempted coup in 1922. After fleeing to Moscow, this shrewd operator was appointed by Stalin to head the Central European office of the Comintern, based in Weimar Germany. There, after the Nazis came to power in January 1933, Dimitrov was accused of complicity in the Reichstag fire, together with two other émigré Bulgarian Communists and Ernst Torgler, chairman of the German Communist Party – Kommunistiche Partei Deutschlands (KPD). At the trial in Leipzig before judges of the Reichsgericht – the Imperial German Supreme Court – Dimitrov refused counsel and conducted his own defence brilliantly. His calm and measured courtroom cross-examination of police supremo Hermann Göring, whom he reduced to shouting invective and insults, won Dimitrov international acclaim and so angered Reichskanzler Adolf Hitler that he decreed future such cases be tried by a new court, the Volksgericht, whose judges would be fanatical Nazis. Freed, Dimitrov returned to the USSR, took Russian citizenship and was made boss of the Comintern world-wide by Stalin from 1934–43; he survived the purges with impunity.

Bulgaria had not formally declared war on the USSR but was invaded by Soviet forces anyway in October 1944. After twenty-two years in exile, Dimitrov returned to Bulgaria as a protégé of the Red Army, to be appointed prime minister of a Communist-dominated coalition government. He was already assuming dictatorial powers, including the ruthless purging of *all* political opponents. So close was their relationship that Stalin had as near total confidence in Bulgaria's new ruler as was possible for so paranoid a man as the *vozhd*.

Romania was the missing link between Bulgaria and the Soviet Socialist Republic of Ukraine. In 1940, when France and Britain had ceased being able to guarantee the country's independence and territorial integrity, the Romanian government of King Carol II turned to Nazi Germany as a replacement guarantor, only to find that the German–Soviet Non-Aggression Treaty of 1939 had given back to the USSR large Romanian-speaking regions in the north and east of the country that had been awarded to Romania after the First World War. After King Carol was deposed by pro-German Mareşal Ion Antonescu, then supported by the anti-Semitic Iron Guards, Antonescu appointed Carol's son Prince Michael as puppet monarch in his stead. Declaring for the Axis powers, Romanian forces that peaked at 1.2 million men joined Hitler's Operation Barbarossa – the invasion of the USSR in summer 1941. Their contribution to the long and ultimately unsuccessful siege of Stalingrad was to cost the country dearly after the Axis surrender.

Since one-third of Hitler's oil came from the heavily defended oilfields at Ploeşti, these attracted massive Allied bombing raids in 1943. The retreat of Romanian forces from occupied Soviet territory in the summer of 1944 led naturally to the invasion of Romanian territory by the pursuing Red Army. This in turn led to a coup d'état that nominally put young King Michael on the throne. One of his first acts was to declare war on the Axis powers, but this was too little and too late to deflect Stalin's understandable lust for revenge – and for the oil at Ploeşti. The indigenous Communist party Partidul Comunist Român (PCR) was not popular among Michael's Russophobe subjects, who knew that Moscow would exact a terrible revenge for the country's role in Operation Barbarossa, but the Soviet intervention brought it to power under hard-line Stalinists Gheorghe Gheorghiu-Dej and Anna Pauker, who had spent the war years in Moscow preparing for this moment.

Thus, with eastern Germany and Austria occupied by Soviet soldiery, a *cordon sanitaire* had been established from the Baltic Sea all the way to the Adriatic and Black Seas, leaving Hungary, Czechoslovakia and Poland geographically cut off from the West and vulnerable to Soviet takeovers, whether by military power from outside or domestic political parties controlled by Soviet protégés – with nothing, or very little, that the Western democracies could do to interfere.

In the Balkans – an area coveted by the tsars for several centuries before the October Revolution – Stalin could also be pleased that Major James Klugman, a pre-war member of the Communist Party of Great Britain (CPGB), had managed to get himself parachuted into German-occupied Yugoslavia as deputy head of Churchill's Special Operations Executive (SOE). Once in-country, he and other SOE officers there persuaded the British Political Warfare Executive, MI6 and the Foreign Office in London that the predominantly Serbian royalist irregulars known as Četniki should not receive any arms drops. As a result, Allied weapons and supplies went exclusively to their bitter enemies, the predominantly Croatian bands commanded by lifelong Communist Josip Broz, a former officer of the Comintern and member of the Narodny Komissariat Vnukhtrennikh Dyel (NKVD) secret police who had taken the *nom de guerre* Tito. The result was that, after the Axis retreat from the Balkans, Russia had an apparently secure foothold in Yugoslavia, where the Communist-dominated Federal People's Republic was about to be proclaimed by Tito, a man Stalin thought at the time would be an obedient, even manipulable, puppet.[3]

However, ever since the October Revolution that brought Lenin, Trotsky and Stalin to power in 1917, the Kremlin's aim had been a *worldwide* expansionism of Soviet power under the pretence of liberating the working classes in the capitalist countries. Much had been achieved during the inter-war years, especially through the Comintern's campaign of espionage, massive financing of dissident factions and manipulation of industrial unrest, but Stalin was now preoccupied with continuing that expansion by exploiting the huge industrial problems of the European states whose infrastructure had been severely damaged in the war.

Italy seemed almost certain to fall under Soviet influence since the Partito Comunista Italiano (PCI) under Palmiro Togliatti had been the strongest single faction among the anti-German partisans. Togliatti was another European Communist who had spent many years in exile from his native land and passed the war safely in Moscow. Although a general election was planned for the following summer, the several centrist and right-wing Italian political parties were too busy squabbling with each other to concert their opposition to the PCI.

Similarly in France the Parti Communiste Français (PCF) had been the most numerous and best-disciplined armed element in the resistance, preparing to seize the reins of government in the power vacuum after the German retreat. After the liberation, although the other political parties resumed their internecine struggles that had weakened the country during the Third Republic and laid the foundation of the French defeat in 1940, the PCF's strategy had been foiled by General Charles de Gaulle, the country's first post-war head of government.[4] He had amnestied Maurice Thorez, General Secretary of the PCF, a deserter under sentence of death who had spent the war safely in Moscow, and allowed him to return to France as a *quid pro quo* for the PCF's temporary 'good behaviour'.

De Gaulle was perfectly aware that the PCF had obeyed the instructions of Dimitrov's Comintern to be pro-German for the first twenty-two months of the war, including the first year of German occupation of France – this in accordance with the Nazi–Soviet Non-Aggression Pact. The party's daily newspaper, *L'Humanité*, printed editorials that were saccharinely pro-German: 'It is particularly comforting in these times of misfortune to see numerous Parisian workers striking up friendships with German soldiers.'[5]

Articles in the paper urged PCF members to remember that German soldiers were workers like themselves who just happened to be in uniform. Party members should invite them into their homes and organise works' picnics, to make them feel welcome.

Only after Hitler launched Operation Barbarossa in June 1941 did the PCF go underground and launch a campaign of assassinations of off-duty Wehrmacht personnel in France. This had nothing to do with the French war effort and everything to do with obliging the occupation authorities to take reprisals that alienated the previously passive mass of the population, encouraged resistance in all its forms and forced the Oberkommando der Wehrmacht (OKW; German General Staff) to keep in France on garrison duty whole divisions that could otherwise swiftly have been transferred to the eastern front. Since the liberation, the PCF had reinvented itself as *le parti des fusillés* and claimed 75,000 martyrs shot by German firing squads, causing satirical journalist Jean Galtier-Boissière to remark scathingly, '*Tiens!* Of the 29,000 French victims (of the occupation), we now learn that 75,000 were apparently PCF members!'[6]

Notwithstanding the *volte-face* of 1941 and the transparent lie of 1944, both Moscow and the PCF placed their faith in the shortness of most people's memories and the power of the oft-repeated lie. So, the party was still a powerful force in French politics.

Stalin prided himself on being a chess-player of Grand Master level. In the geopolitical game he was playing, he knew that his next move must be to isolate *permanently* the liberated territories of Poland, Czechoslovakia and Hungary – each of which had good historical reasons to mistrust and resist Russian moves – from the influence and support of the democratic countries of Western Europe, and particularly from American interference. Then, he could take them out of the game, one by one, while their shaky post-war coalition governments were grappling with the social problems of reintegrating their demoralised populations and facing the challenge of rebuilding their much-damaged industrial and commercial infrastructures.

The best way to do that without alerting the Western democracies too early was to impose on the Russian-occupied eastern regions of Germany and Austria superficially democratic governments in which the real power lay with pro-Soviet factions that would gradually assume the same total control over their citizens as had the government of the USSR. Perversely, Hitler's dictatorship would make this easier: for twelve years in Germany and seven years in Austria the populations had been habituated to a slavish obedience to authority, with any sign of dissent brutally suppressed by the Gestapo.

It was no secret that the democratically elected British, French and US governments were under great domestic political pressure to demobilise the men who made up the bulk of the armies occupying their zones of Germany and Austria – a problem that did not arise in the USSR. In Stalin's mind, free and secret elections were among the many weaknesses that would ultimately bring down the democracies.

At the Big Three summit conferences during the Second World War, he had taken the measure of the Western leaders and planned his moves accordingly, dividing the UK–USA alliance by bringing US President Franklin D. Roosevelt completely under his thrall and thus isolating the junior partner of the Atlantic Alliance, Britain's wartime premier Winston Churchill, who certainly had no illusions about Soviet long-term aims. Roosevelt had for years been confined to a wheelchair as a result of polio, but was by this time also suffering from a complex of other health issues that seriously impaired his judgement, while leaving him convinced that he could 'handle Stalin better than the [British] Foreign Office or my State Department.'[7] This was a dangerous delusion.

A shrewd, although usually silent, observer at the wartime summit conferences was Churchill's Scotland Yard-trained bodyguard Walter Thompson. He saw clearly what was going on at the Teheran Conference in November–December 1943 and the Yalta Conference in February 1945:

> [Roosevelt's] view of Stalin was emphasised on the occasion he remarked to Mr Bullitt, the American ambassador in Moscow, 'Stalin doesn't want anything but security for his country, and I think that if I give him everything I possibly can and ask for nothing in return, he won't try to annex anything and will work for a world of democracy and peace.'[8]

Roosevelt's ignorance of Russian history, which is a tale of constant expansion for the past thousand years, was to cost the inhabitants of Central and Eastern Europe and the Balkans dearly. The Russian term *blizhneye zarubezhye* translates as 'the near abroad'. Although the expression may be modern, the idea that neighbouring states are the natural space which Russia – under tsarist, Soviet or post-Soviet governments – has a right to control and expand into, has been the motor of this millennial expansionism. A retired US diplomat, given a copy of the author's history of Russian expansionism,[9] commented that the implied right to independence of Poland and the other states falling within this area should be disregarded by Western leaders in order 'not to rattle the bars of the bear's cage.'[10]

Konstantin Rokossovsky, although a Soviet general, had a Polish father. Arrested during Stalin's purges, he was lucky not to be shot along with many fellow officers. Instead, he suffered nine teeth knocked out, three ribs broken and his toes smashed by hammer blows in torture sessions during thirty months of imprisonment in Siberia before being released at Stalin's whim to command six Soviet divisions that helped surround and force the surrender of General Friedrich Paulus's 6th German Army at Stalingrad. Subsequently, when the men and women of the Polish Home Army or Resistance were fighting for their lives in summer 1944, while German troops razed Warsaw to the ground around them, Rokossovsky commanded the Soviet forces to halt on the opposite bank of the Vistula. Obedient to orders from the Kremlin, he made no serious attempt to interfere, and his forces did not enter what remained of the devastated capital until January 1945.

Roosevelt might have rethought his conciliatory policies in August 1944 when RAF and USAF aircraft flew from airfields in Italy at the limit of their range to drop arms to the beleaguered Polish Home Army men and women fighting for their lives in Warsaw. After one flight of American aircraft was allowed to refuel behind the Russian lines, Stalin refused further refuelling facilities. On 18 August the official reply to a British request from the Soviet Commissariat for Foreign Affairs contained the following statements:

> The Soviet government cannot, of course, object to English [sic] or American aircraft dropping supplies in the region of Warsaw, since this is an American and British affair. But it decidedly objects to British or American aircraft, after dropping arms in the Warsaw region, landing on Soviet territory, since the Soviet government does not wish to associate itself either directly or indirectly with the adventure in Warsaw.[11]

A Polish-born colleague of the author's BBC years named Andy Wiseman, then flying in RAF uniform, was forced to land in Soviet-occupied territory. To the amazement of the aircrew, they were not only refused refuelling facilities by their Russian 'allies', but saw their aircraft impounded and found themselves locked up behind the wire in a concentration camp. Wiseman had no way of knowing at the time that it was only his British uniform which saved him from being shot, as had happened to so many thousands of fellow Poles in Stalin's deliberate campaign to emasculate the Polish nation so that the troubled country could more easily be controlled by its Soviet 'liberators' after the war.

Few people in the West knew at the time that, after the Russian invasion of Poland in 1940 and the occupation of the eastern half of the country under the German–Soviet Non-Aggression Pact, Stalin had decided to kill some 26,000 Polish officers and civilian intellectuals, held in three concentration camps after being taken prisoner while fighting in uniform against Soviet troops during the invasion. His decision was partially implemented at Katyn, near Smolensk, during April and May 1940, where 4,443 Poles held in the Kosielsk concentration camp on the Polish–Russian border were herded to the edge of mass graves and machine-gunned into them. A further 3,896 officers held in a camp at Kharkov/Kharkiv in Ukraine were also murdered by security troops of the NKVD, one of the several forerunners of the KGB.[12] In a way, the most gruesome executions of the captured Poles was effected at the camp of Ostrakhov, where Stalin's favourite executioner, Vasili M. Blokhin, dressed in a slaughterhouse apron, rubber boots and leather gauntlets before arming himself with a 9mm Walther automatic pistol to shoot up to 250 Polish prisoners in the back of the head inside a specially soundproofed killing room *on each of twenty-eight consecutive nights*. For the shocking total of 6,287 murders in his month's work, Blokhin was awarded the Order of the Red Banner and given a small cash bonus. Also executed at this time were 7,800 other Poles – some for no other reason than being *osadniki* or settlers, whose parents had moved into formerly Russian-occupied regions of their country that were awarded to Poland after the First World War. Tens of thousands more were imprisoned and tortured for no obvious reason at all.[13]

As far as the Western Allies were concerned, any help that enabled the Poles in Warsaw to hold at bay the German forces razing their city to the ground during August 1944 was also a way of tying down divisions that Hitler could otherwise employ against the advancing Allies in France or the Soviet forces on the eastern front. Churchill therefore desperately tried to gain Roosevelt's support in the matter, having put in writing to Foreign Secretary Anthony Eden in 1942 that permanent Soviet occupation of Poland would be a violation of the principles of freedom and democracy set forth in the Atlantic Charter signed by Roosevelt. Cold-shouldered by the US president, the British prime minister was obliged instead to inform the Free Polish leader General Władysław Anders that Britain could not longer guarantee the territorial integrity of the country on whose behalf it had declared war in 1939.

Like most Poles, Anders had no illusions about Stalin's intentions after the war, having already personally suffered as a prisoner in Moscow's Lubyanka prison. He warned Churchill that the Red Army advancing into Poland was systematically arresting all Poles in the occupied areas who had shown any resistance *to the Germans* on the grounds that they might also resist the Russian occupation of their country. Many of them were never seen again. Churchill then assured Anders that Britain would not abandon its Polish allies. It was a promise that was not kept by Britain's post-war governments.[14]

So, Stalin had good reason to think that, after the withdrawal of the British, French and US troops from the western zones of occupied Germany and Austria, the Soviet-occupied zones under their Communist governments controlled in Moscow were bound to subvert, and come to dominate, the western zones when reunified with them, changing the political shape of Europe for ever.

On that balmy autumn night in Sochi, it seemed to the *vozhd* that he was bound to be the victor in the most momentous game of chess to be played out in the twentieth century.

Although it was too late to save the European satellite states from a half-century of state terror, Stalin's intention to grab Turkish territory and the Dardanelles was blocked by President Truman's secretary of state informing the Kremlin that such a move would be resisted by the Western Allies even at the risk of starting a third world war. Similarly, when Stalin announced that he was not going to withdraw Soviet occupation forces from northern Iran, he was told in plain language that this would not be accepted by the West. On both occasions he gave way. As Winston Churchill remarked at the time, 'There is nothing [the Soviets] admire so much as strength.'[15]

Notes

1. S. Sebag Montefiore, *Stalin, the court of the Red Tsar*, London, Phoenix 2004, p. 524
2. Russia sold its North American colony to the United States in 1867 for $7.2m
3. For more detail see Boyd, *Kremlin*, p. 174
4. The full story is told in D. Boyd, *De Gaulle, the man who defied six US presidents*, Stroud, The History Press 2014
5. Quoted in D. Pryce-Jones, *Paris in the Third Reich*, London, Collins 1981, p. 64
6. Boyd, *De Gaulle*, p. 176
7. L. Rees, *Behind Closed Doors*, London, BBC Books 2008, p. 130
8. T. Hickman, *Churchill's Bodyguard*, London, Headline 2005, pp. 167–74
9. Boyd, *Kremlin*
10. He wished, understandably, to remain anonymous
11. Rees, *Behind Closed Doors*, p. 345; also Boyd, *Kremlin*, pp. 160–2
12. There were several, of which the longest lived were the Cheka, from the initials of Chrezvychaynaya Kommissiya or Special Commission for combating counter-revolution and sabotage 1917–22; Obedinyonnoye Gosudarstvennoye Politicheskiye Upravleniye (OGPU) or United State Political Administration 1922–34; Narodny Komissariat Vnutrennykh Dyel (NKVD) or National Commissariat for Internal Affairs 1934–46; Ministerstvo Vnutrennykh Dyel (MVD) 1946–54 and Komityet Gosudarstvennoi Bezopasnosty (KGB) or Committee of State Security 1954–89
13. Boyd, *Kremlin*, pp. 159–64
14. Rees, *Behind Closed Doors*, pp. 294–5
15. M. Copeland, *The Real Spy World*, London, Sphere 1978, p. 201

Part 2

The Stasi in German Democratic Republic

3

DEUTSCHLAND UNTER RUSSLAND

Most European national anthems invoke the protection of the Christian God for a sovereign, or declare the ideals of a revolutionary state. Since 1841, the German national anthem, set to music by Haydn, was a claim to own territory west to east 'from the Meuse to the Memel' and south to north 'from the Adige to the Belt'. This has something to do with the origin of the German word for war, *Krieg*, which is the root of *kriegen*, meaning 'to get' [territory for expansion of the Fatherland, called *Lebensraum* under Hitler]. However, since the first line is *Deutschland, Deutschland über alles*, meaning, 'Germany above all', it ought to have been changed in May of 1945 to *Deutschland, Deutschland unter Russland,* at least for the vast stretches of the former Third Reich that lay under Soviet occupation.

Before the guns had fallen silent, on 27 April 1945 Soviet aircraft flew the 'Ulbricht Group' of several dozen Moscow-trained German Communists led by Walter Ulbricht to an airfield inside the perimeter of Marshal Georgi Zhukov's First Byelorussian Army Group to the east of Berlin. A few days later the 'Ackermann Group' of German Communists were flown to the First Ukrainian Army Group south of Berlin, commanded by Marshal Ivan Konev. These several dozen puppet functionaries had orders not to set up immediately a Communist government to rule the Soviet Zone of occupation – which would have alarmed the Western Allies – but to lay the ground for the installation of an apparently democratic government, after the Russian zone of occupation had been completely purged by the Soviet administration. On 9 May 1945 – one day after the official end of the war in Western Europe – peace was officially declared between the USSR and those, mostly bombed-out, bewildered and hungry, inhabitants of the Reich who had survived the consequences of Operation Barbarossa, Hitler's ill-timed decision to invade the USSR in June 1941.

Three million Wehrmacht, Waffen-SS, Luftwaffe and Kriegsmarine personnel were held in Soviet camps, thousands of miles away from their homeland, in Siberia and the Soviet Far North. These POWs lived under appalling conditions that were partly a revenge for the German camps in which between 1.3 million and 1.65 million Soviet POWs[1] had been deliberately starved to death by their captors or allowed to die of exposure since the outset of Barbarossa. In addition, an estimated 600,000 surrendered Soviet officers and uniformed political commissars taken prisoner had been executed in defiance of the rules of war.[2]

German manpower was further reduced by the thousands more POWs held in other Allied countries. A half-million were in the USA. Some of those taken prisoner by British troops were in Canada and other faraway countries of the British Empire, but 162 camps in Britain held another quarter-million men. The author recalls his parents inviting two unrepentantly Nazi POWs to spend Christmas Day of 1946 in an English home, sharing the family's very limited rations in response to an appeal by the local authorities. France held a quarter-million German prisoners and demanded more to be used as slave labour for repairing damage suffered during the occupation and liberation. Although Supreme Allied Commander General Dwight Eisenhower and General George C. Patton had reservations about handing over German POWs who were almost certainly going to be ill-treated in revenge, the US Provost Marshal's department found a legal loophole by classifying 750,000 men taken prisoner after the end of hostilities not as POWs, but as 'defeated enemy personnel', who were not covered by the Geneva Convention of 1929. The men were taken from camps in the American zone and handed over to France, largely to excuse their captors from having to feed them from US resources. Held in wire cages with no shelter and grossly inadequate rations, thousands died from malnutrition, hypothermia and untreated disease.

The atrocities committed in Soviet territory by the Waffen-SS, the Allgemeine-SS and some Wehrmacht units killed thousands of civilians for no military reason. How many hundreds of thousands? There is no complete record. In addition, the non-combatant Einsatzkommandos massacred hundreds of thousands of Jewish and other civilian men, women and children. No records of this were kept, unlike in the Nazi concentration and death camps, where meticulous record-keeping was the order of the day. However, just now and again, information did leak out. For example, when a column of the armoured SS Division Das Reich hanged ninety-nine hostages in Tulle, France, on 7 June 1944, Major Kowatsch, the commanding officer, actually said to the Prefect of the town, 'We hanged more than 100,000 at Kiev and at Kharkov. What we are doing here today is nothing for us.'[3] It was therefore understandable, albeit deplorable, that the conduct of Soviet personnel in the final months of the drive into the Reich should include summary executions of soldiers and civilians of both sexes. Rape has always been, and still is, a ubiquitous feature of war between different ethnic groups. Its victims in this case were an estimated 2 million German females ranging in age from infants to grandmothers; one in ten was estimated to have died during, or as a consequence of, the act.[4]

Many British-held German POWs did not return home until 1949, but few held as POWs in the USSR would return before 1953; hundreds of thousands of others never returned, although were known to have survived being taken prisoner.

In addition, even before the end of the shooting came the looting, both official and unofficial, throughout the Soviet-occupied regions of Germany, designated by the Four Powers 'the Soviet Zone of Occupation', as agreed by the Big Three conference at Yalta. Whole towns were emptied of household furniture, including flush toilets and electric radiators, which were loaded onto horse-drawn wagons destined for homes in villages without running water or electricity. Westerners attending the last three-power summit meeting at Potsdam in July–August 1945 blinked their eyes on seeing heating stoves, cookers and mattresses being loaded onto wagons by Soviet troops returning home. Under the *official* reparations programme approved at the Potsdam Conference, between a third and a half of East German industrial capacity was dismantled by German forced labour under Soviet supervision[5] and removed to the USSR between the cessation of hostilities and the end of 1947, with 4,500 entire factories transported there. Some sixty major manufacturing companies were left intact, but under Soviet control.[6] Although the justification was to replace industrial equipment destroyed in the fighting on Soviet territory, the machinery of many entire factories was still rusting beside remote sidings one and two decades later because nobody in Russia had the technical know-how to reassemble it and get it working – or because nobody knew where it had been dumped. The industrial viability of the Soviet zone and the German Democratic Republic, as it afterwards became, was seriously damaged by the excessive reparations. According to some sources, they represented between 15 and 16 billion dollars in value at the time.[7]

Yet, the satisfaction of revenge is so much greater when suffering is inflicted on sentient people, rather than inanimate things. Long after the initial killings and rape had ended, human victims continued to be hunted down in all four occupation zones. High on the list were Wehrmacht and Waffen-SS personnel who had gone to ground, members of the Allgemeine-SS, civilians who had held office in the administration of occupied territory, members of the Nationalistische Deutsche Arbeiterpartei[8] (NSDAP) – although this had been compulsory for many people – and grandfathers of 60 years and older who had been forcibly conscripted into the Volkssturm[9] under threat of execution for foot-draggers. Sent into the front lines often without uniforms or weapons, the gallows humour of the last weeks of the war portrayed them as Germany's most precious resource because they had 'silver in their hair, gold in their teeth and lead in their legs'. Hitlerjugend youths of 16 and younger, accused of being 'werewolf' stay-behinds, were sentenced to between ten and twenty-five years in prison.[10] German friends of the author in Wedding, a working-class and traditionally Communist *Stadtviertel* of Berlin, recounted how two terrified unarmed boys aged 15 had been chased by Russian soldiers up five flights of stairs in their apartment building and onto the roof before being flung to their deaths in the street below during the fighting of May 1945.

In any war, these things happen in the heat of battle. What was different about the Soviet occupation of Germany was that, following at a safe distance behind the combat troops were detachments of Laventi Beria's NKVD troops, whose function was to arrest, imprison, torture and/or execute *any* German persons who might resist Stalin's plan to assume total power in the Soviet Zone. Perhaps surprisingly to readers unfamiliar with Kremlin paranoia, this included members of the KPD – the German Communist Party – who had endured years in Nazi hard-labour concentration camps as punishment for their political sympathies. The 'crime' for which they now had to be punished again was their suffering under the Nazis for membership of the KPD, which might enable them to return to political life, usurping positions of authority which Stalin reserved for his puppets who had spent the war years under strict control inside Russia.

After spending more than a decade in the USSR, where he survived Stalin's purges that claimed the majority of KPD refugees, the veteran communist Erich Mielke returned to Berlin in 1945 with NKVD General Ivan Serov, based in the Soviet occupation forces' HQ at the south-eastern Berlin suburb of Karlshorst. The chaos of the country to which he returned cannot now be imagined. In addition to all the men locked away in POW camps, some 13 million German-speaking people, mainly the elderly, women and children who had been expelled from East Prussia, Poland and Czechoslovakia were homeless refugees in what remained of the Reich.

Neither then nor later was much divulged about the way Mielke had spent the war years. It seems that this is because he was a much-decorated NKVD commissar attached to Soviet partisan bands, whose function was the interrogation and execution of captured German personnel – a story that would not win any votes in eastern Germany. Although initially given the comparatively lowly rank of police inspector, Mielke was ordered by Serov in 1947 to set up a secret police force closely modelled on the NKVD, which he knew so well. Called Kommissariat 5, it tracked down and arrested so many thousands of people with no Nazi connections, yet who *might* resist the implantation of a Stalinist state, that it was necessary to reopen eleven of the Nazi concentration and death camps, including Sachsenhausen and Buchenwald, less than three months after the Allgemeine-SS guards had left. According to Soviet records the 122,000 Germans incarcerated there included many members of the anti-Nazi German political parties, over a third of whom died of starvation or disease during confinement.[11]

But where could all these people be 'investigated' and forced to confess at show trials, to terrify the rest of the population? Totalitarian states like to centralise everything but, after the carpet bombing by British and American air forces, the centre of Berlin was a wasteland of shattered buildings and piles of rubble – the rubble had gone but it was still a wasteland when the author was posted there during his military service thirteen years later. However, a couple of miles north-east of the devastated city centre at Hohenschönhausen a large complex of buildings was still standing, more or less intact. It had been used by the NSDAP Volkswohlfahrt welfare organisation as a canteen where thousands of bombed-out families were supplied with a hot meal every day.

Requisitioned by the NKVD and swiftly surrounded by a 3m-high palisade erected using forced labour, and with this topped by barbed wire and punctuated by searchlights and watch-towers, the site was designated Special Camp No. 3. At various times it held over 4,000 inmates, crammed into inadequate facilities with insufficient food or even blankets in the unheated buildings. The living conditions, the violence of the interrogations and the prisoners' knowledge that a painful and unpleasant fate awaited them combined to kill off an estimated 3,000 people.[12] Cartloads of bodies were dumped daily into bomb craters with no identification. Survivors were put to hard labour constructing a partly underground detention facility, known as 'the U-boat', where suspects could be held in extremely stressful solitary confinement whilst being 'investigated' under torture. The unheated cells had no windows and some were bare of any fittings except a high threshold so that they could be flooded with cold water, in which the prisoners had to sit or lie when no longer able to keep on their feet. Around the perimeter, bilingual notices in German and Russian warned passers-by that this was a forbidden zone, near which they should not linger.

Since all authority in the Soviet Zone was vested in Stalin's occupying forces, these measures did not need to be sanctioned by any German law. Instead, NKVD proclamation 00315 dated 18 April 1945, required Soviet-occupied German territory to be 'cleansed of spies, dissidents, terrorists, Nazi party members, police and secret service operatives, officials and other hostile elements'.[13]

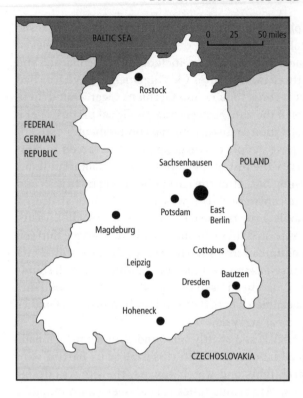

The Russian zone of occupation that became the German Democratic Republic.

Hohenschönhausen was the ideal place to extract false confessions from people who had committed no crime, but were considered 'hostile elements' by the NKVD, after which military tribunals sentenced them to from ten to twenty-five years' hard labour – or death in some cases. The victims included some ex-Nazis, but also activists of German political parties including KPD – and also Soviet personnel accused by their own commissars of failing to toe the party line. Most were cleared of any crime after the German reunification in 1989. A fresh wave of arrests took place when the Soviet occupation authorities decided to eliminate the most popular left-wing party, the Socialist Democratic Party of Germany (SDP), by merging it on 21 April 1946 with the KPD in a new party called the Sozialistische Einheitspartei Deutschlands (SED) or Socialist Unity Party. It was thought that the relabelling would avoid the embarrassment of Moscow being seen by the world as imposing a Communist government on its German satellite. In the ensuing elections, closely overseen by the Soviets in a very undemocratic manner, the SED claimed a massive majority, leaving a few seats in the new parliament for other parties, in a pretence of democracy. However, in Berlin, which was under Four-Power occupation after France was also allocated a sector of the capital and a zone of occupation carved out of the American and British sectors and zones, this manipulation was not possible. There, in free and secret votes, the SED polled less than half as many as the SDP.

The three western zones of occupied Germany became the Bundesrepublik or Federal Republic on 23 May 1949, prompting Moscow on 7 October 1949 to change its zone of occupation into 'the German Democratic Republic' (GDR), to which entity authority over eastern Germany was gradually transferred. The GDR was officially an independent state although transparently controlled by the USSR, which kept its armies of occupation there for more than four decades, facing off the NATO[14] forces in the West. On 8 February 1950 responsibility for internal security was vested in the newly created Ministerium für Staatssicherheit (MfS) headed by another Moscow appointee, Wilhelm Zaisser, with Erich Mielke as his deputy. Their massive headquarters building on the Normannenstrasse in Berlin-Lichtenberg is now a museum to the Stasi's reign of terror that lasted until the fall of the Wall in 1989. In 1951 the MfS took over from the NKVD its interrogation and imprisonment premises including Hohenschönhausen and 'the Lindenhotel' prison in Potsdam.

What sort of person chose to work for the MfS? Hans-Joachim Geyer was a former NSDAP member employed by the West German intelligence agency Bundesnachrichtendienst (BND) as a courier when arrested in East Berlin. Instead of resisting interrogation, he volunteered to become a double agent for the Stasi and betray all his contacts. Released, he was well remunerated by his new masters in addition to his BND salary for betraying more than 100 BND agents in the GDR from December 1952 for twelve months until the scale of his betrayals blew his cover. He continued to draw his Stasi salary in consideration of past services. After his death, the MfS paid his wife a pension and put his two sons through extended education, including medical school. Geyer was summed up as a family man with no political beliefs, no drink problem and no other vices, either. Exactly the sort of man of whom the Stasi management approved.[15]

In the Soviet Zone, the predilection for show trials shared by the Nazi and Soviet regimes during the 1930s was taken to new heights. A typical example was in June 1952, when a group of students who had been helping refugees escape from the GDR were put on trial and labelled 'cold-blooded terrorists and border provocateurs' in *Neues Deutschland*, the official newspaper of the SED.[16] The intention of the show trials was to demonstrate to the population and the world that the SED had total control of the GDR and could punish any resistance to its regime.

The SED Central Committee – which was effectively the government of the GDR – decided to tackle the severe economic problems caused by the crippling reparations to the USSR and the SED's rigid planned-economy approach to reindustrialisation of the GDR. Higher taxes were imposed, many state-controlled prices rose abruptly and a 10 per cent increase of work norms was announced, without extra pay. By June 1953 even the Soviet government was so alarmed at reports of unrest in the GDR that its president Walter Ulbricht was summoned to Moscow and ordered by the new chairman of the Council of Ministers, Georgi Malenkov, to release the pressure on the suffering population of the GDR before it exploded in open unrest.

Malenkov's *Diktat* came too late. On 16 June eighty building workers downed tools in protest on the Stalinallee – one of East Berlin's main thoroughfares, where the impressive facades of buildings had been erected to make a background for filmed and televised parades, but with no premises behind them – rather like the main street of a western town in a cowboy film. Strikes were forbidden in the GDR, where they were labelled 'sabotage'. The downing of tools was reported immediately on the American-financed radio stations RIAS Berlin and Radio Free Europe, which beamed Western news across the Iron Curtain. What part these broadcasts played in the escalation is open to debate, although a number of Western sources list some very high-ranking US politicians and military 'coincidentally visiting' the divided city at the time. The fact is that by the following morning, nearly a half-million striking workers were in the streets of Berlin and 150 other towns and cities,[17] waving banners and chanting demands for the government to resign. They believed their safety was guaranteed by the US, British and French garrisons in the Allied sectors of Berlin and the presence there of Western reporters and camera crews. Hundreds actually crossed into the western sectors to plead for armed support that was not forthcoming, despite recommendations of a number of Allied officials that arms be supplied.

Soviet High Commissioner Vladimir Semyonov and Marshal Andrei Grechko, who commanded the occupation forces, despatched middle-rank SED functionaries to several cities in an attempt to calm things down while Ulbricht and the other SED top brass spent 17 and 18 June cowering under Russian protection in the Red Army HQ at Berlin-Karlshorst. Some 20,000 Soviet occupation troops with T-34 tanks and armoured personnel carriers, plus 8,000 men of the GDR's Volkspolizei-Bereitschaften or paramilitary riot police, were deployed to suppress the demonstrations with water cannons, rifle butts and bullets. In Karlshorst, Russian intelligence operations now lay with the Ministerstvo Gosudarstvennoi Bezopasnosti (MGB) or Soviet Ministry of State Security. The senior MGB officer commented, '[The unrest in the GDR] was the reaction of people to the blunders of the country's leadership. Moreover, it was inadmissible to use tanks in such a situation.'[18] In fact, tanks were in the streets to fight the demonstrators but the gunners usually fired over their heads. Semyonov also picked up a broadcast from RIAS to the effect that there was no longer a viable government in the GDR, and commented to Ulbricht and the other nervous leaders of the SED that this was almost true. The background to this is that Stalin's death three months earlier had left Beria, Malenkov and other Party heavyweights arguing that they should solve one problem by abandoning the GDR. When Khrushchev gained control of the Praesidium, that was one of the charges levelled against Malenkov.[19]

Armoured personnel carriers of the paramilitary Bereitschaft units of the Volkspolizei equipped with water-cannons were used, but the Russian edict meant it was forbidden to machine-gun the demonstrators within sight of Western observers, although many were shot elsewhere. Some Volkspolizisten panicked and used their handguns. Official casualty figures alleged twenty-one deaths, although a West German report in 1966 alleged there had been 383 people killed during the demonstrations in which 1.5 million people took part all over the country. A further 106 were executed under martial law and 5,100 arrested, of whom 1,200 were sentenced to a total of 6,000 years in hard-regime labour camps. Party functionaries, who at first had thought the demonstrators in Berlin were alone in their protests, learned to their horror that a mob in Görlitz, near the Polish border, had sacked the local party HQ, the Stasi regional office and the prison.

The left-wing poet Bertolt Brecht, who had returned to Berlin after being expelled from the USA, suggested a solution in verse to the essential problems of the GDR:

> After the rising of 17 June, the Secretary of the Writers Union
> had leaflets distributed in the Stalinallee, stating that the people
> had forfeited the confidence of the government
> and could win it back only by redoubled efforts.
> Would it not be easier, in that case, for the government
> to dissolve the people and elect another?[20]

What happened was not, in effect, so very different. The flight to the West of hundreds of thousands of discontented GDR citizens,[21] many of them qualified professionals, was causing severe economic problems in the GDR. The SED's solution was to make even thinking about 'flight from the Republic' a crime punishable with several years' imprisonment. Although the long, so-called 'green' border between the GDR and the Bundesrepublik had already been sealed off, it was still possible in Four-Power Berlin for a GDR citizen to board an S-Bahn overhead railway train in the Russian sector and get off at a station in one of the western sectors. A single person travelling without baggage might well get away with this, but family groups or individuals unwise enough to take a suitcase with them were liable to be hauled off the train at the sector boundary and face interrogation, leading to automatic arrest.

So, after the uprising of June 1953 the Stasi's interrogation prisons were full to bursting with arrested demonstrators, would-be border-crossers – and Jehovah's Witnesses, who had been similarly persecuted for years by the Gestapo and Allgemeine-SS in Hitler's concentration camps. SED paranoia also created a number of VIP prisoners. Paul Merker was a member of the GDR Politburo and was arrested for daring to voice his disapproval of SED policy. The GDR's Minister of Trade, Karl Hamann, and Minister of Foreign Affairs, Georg Dertinger, were also arrested for similar reasons. On Moscow's orders, Dertinger was sentenced to fifteen years' imprisonment and his child forcibly fostered out under another name in a family considered loyal to the SED.

But Moscow's alarm over the riots of 17 June caused Zaisser to be sacked and replaced by a man who was called behind his back 'the walking pancake'. Ernst Wollweber's brief was to tighten the screws of the MfS in repressing the population of the GDR and especially escalate the clandestine war against agents of West German intelligence, the Bundesnachrichtendienst, controlled by Reinhard Gehlen. Described as fat, bald and frightening – physically the very opposite of Gehlen's slim frame and disciplined manner, although a fair match in deviousness after a lifetime as Comintern agent and saboteur – Wollweber first hit the headlines as a seaman who caused a mutiny in the Kaiserliche Marine during the First World War. In between his sabotage operations in the 1920s and 1930s, directed mainly against British and French ships, he took over the International Seamen's Union and pushed his way into the World Federation of Trade Unions. Elected to the Reichstag, he ran for his life when the NSDAP took over in 1933 and set up a Soviet spy network in the Baltic countries. When the Wehrmacht invaded Denmark in 1940 he abandoned the Comintern office there, moving to neutral Stockholm, a good base from which to organise sabotage of Nazi shipping – except that, to avoid being repatriated to Hitler's Germany, he had to accept a prison sentence.

In 1944 he was granted Soviet citizenship and returned to his homeland on the heels of the Red Army, to be appointed Director General of Shipping and Transport for the Soviet Zone of Germany. It was the ideal cover for sabotage schools, whose alumni caused much damage when taken aboard British and other Western ships. Aged 55 in 1953, Wollweber's great opportunity had finally come. How long his reign might have been is anyone's guess, but the habits of a lifetime of deceit and treachery caused him to conspire against First Minister Otto Grotewohl and eventually Walter Ulbricht himself. In 1957, after only four years in office, he retired 'on grounds of ill-health' and was divested of all his offices, replaced at the head of MfS by Erich Mielke and put out to grass, although not imprisoned. He died ten years later.[22]

After the far bloodier Russian suppression of the Hungarian uprising in 1956 a wave of revulsion swept the GDR, providing the Stasi with another crop of VIP victims, in addition to which it kidnapped 'hostile' figures from West Berlin. Tricked into insecure rendezvous and in many cases drugged with knock-out drops, journalists, lawyers and officers of the BND and the internal security organisation Bundesamt für Verfassungsschutz (BfV) – literally Federal Office for the Protection of the Constitution – were bundled into the boots of cars that drove at speed through the sector crossings and delivered them into Stasi interrogation prisons. With the head of the victim being concealed in a sack until he or she was locked into a cell in a windowless 'Minna' prison van, the victims had no idea where they were by the time they were locked into their prison cells.

By the end of the 1950s, convict labour had been used to expand the Hohenschönhausen facility with a further 200 cells and interrogation rooms, plus two cells whose walls were padded with slabs of rubber, where prisoners who had gone insane after prolonged torture were finally locked up.[23] All prisoners forfeited their identities, being required, when a guard entered the cell, to face the wall with hands behind the back and identify themselves with the number of the cell and their bed number, if the cell had more than one bunk. It was also obligatory in all the interrogation prisons to sleep during the hours when this was permitted – although prisoners were frequently interrupted by exhausting nocturnal interrogations – with both face and hands outside the scant bed coverings, so the guards could check them through the Judas-hole. Their rounds were frequent and unpredictable because they wore felt slippers so that no sound of footfalls should alert the prisoners. The overall effect of this strict regime was to impress on every detainee that he or she was helpless in the grip of an all-powerful state apparatus. It took exceptional willpower not to be broken and confess to whatever the interrogator wanted and suffer the consequences at a trial in the Volksgericht, or people's court, where the 'defence lawyer' was a government employee who was not permitted to defend the client, nor was the accused allowed to speak.

As to how many people underwent this treatment, the figure for prisoners in Hohenschönhausen alone from its inception in 1951 to 1989 is close to 20,000 people of both sexes.[24] In addition, the MfS used forty-nine other interrogation prisons and the Innenministerium or Interior Ministry operated forty-four prisons for convicted persons, where political prisoners and convicted criminals were detained for long periods in harsher conditions than anywhere in Western Europe. As more and more citizens were tracked down and sentenced, the MfS personnel manning the prisons of the GDR doubled every ten years. To feed the prisons with more victims, the Stasi increased its staff to an eventual 91,000 officers. Each day 90,000 letters were opened and read and 20,000 telephone conversations listened in to. Ironically, the enormous budget of the totally unproductive MfS rose by 1989 to 4 *billion* Marks, which contributed significantly to the economic collapse of the GDR.

In addition, there were nearly 200,000 *inoffizielle Mitarbeiter*, or regularly used but unpaid informants, most of whom were coerced into spying on colleagues, neighbours, friends and relatives, so that parents betrayed their own children and children betrayed their parents. Promoted in 1957, the Minister for State Security with the rank of lieutenant-general, Erich Mielke called the latter *meine Hauptwaffe* – his most important weapon in the unrelenting war against his own people. His organisation required, in addition to the headquarters in Berlin, fifteen regional HQs and 209 outstations. By comparison, under Nazism the Gestapo terrorised the entire Third Reich – not just the part that became the GDR – with a maximum of 13,500 officers. With an official ratio of one full-time MfS officer for every 180 citizens, as against one KGB officer for 600 citizens in the USSR in the 1980s, the Stasi was the most powerful and oppressive secret police force in the world, working with varying degrees of closeness with Soviet 'advisers'.

A new member of staff who arrived at the KGB district office in Dresden in August 1985 was Major Vladimir Putin, nicknamed 'Little Volodya' by his five colleagues in this most westerly KGB outpost, where much attention was concentrated on reporting political developments inside the GDR. The Dresden outpost was also tasked with identifying potential agents to work in the West, particularly targeting US bases in the Bundesrepublik, like that of the Green Berets special forces in the Bavarian town of Bad Tölz. According to a colleague in Dresden named Major Vladimir Ussoltsev, Putin's job was mostly trolling through exit visa applications received from the Stasi's Dresden office in the hope of finding would-be emigrants with relatives living near the bases. Curiously, at that time the Stasi was distancing itself from its Russian comrades in their office 100m away. Stasi General Horst Böhm, a personal friend of Honecker, actually barred the Russians from entering his HQ building.

There were also a number of other KGB outstations in the GDR. Ussoltsev wrote later that the paranoia in the GDR was 'like an Orwellian fantasy, a leftover from the Stalin era. The Stasi employed more people in the Dresden district alone than did the KGB in all of Byelorussia.'[25] In the Soviet Union a joke had it that there were three kinds of people: those who had been in prison, those who were in prison and those who would later be in prison. Although the GDR was often referred to in Western media as a police state, it could more accurately have been called a prison state after the erection of the Berlin Wall on the weekend of 13–14 August 1961, physically dividing the western sectors from the Russian sector. On the Monday morning, thousands of workers trying to cross the sector boundary to reach their places of work were told they could no longer do so. Elsewhere, the entire country was fenced off from the Western democracies with barbed wire and minefields, inside which every GDR citizen was liable to arrest and imprisonment on trumped-up charges without anything approaching normal legal process.

At this crucial moment in the isolation of the GDR, the exchange rate was one Westmark to four Ostmarks. Far from ending the economic decline, in the next twenty-eight years the exchange rate tumbled to 10:1 before the Wall was breached on 9 November 1989.

Notes

1. Depending on the source
2. K. Lowe, *Savage Continent*, London, Penguin 2013, p. 38 and end notes thereto
3. The full story of the Tulle massacre may be found in Boyd, *Blood in the Snow*, Stroud, The History Press, pp. 102–13
4. Some estimates of the rapes put the figure twice as high, the difference being accounted for by women who concealed what had happened to them
5. Sheffer, *Burned Bridge*, p. 25
6. A. Applebaum, *Iron Curtain, the Crushing of Eastern Europe*, London, Penguin 2013, pp. 36–7
7. H. Kierstein, ed., *Heisse Schlachten im Kalten Krieg*, Berlin, Verlag Das Neue Berlin 2008, p. 83
8. The correct title of the Nazi party
9. An auxiliary 'army' raised by Josef Goebbels for a last-ditch defence of the Reich.
10. Sheffer, *Burned Bridge*, p. 26
11. H. Knabe, ed., *Gefangen in Hohenschönhausen – Stasi-Häftlinge Berichten*, Berlin, List 2012, p. 10
12. Visitor's guide to Gedenkstätte Berlin-Hohenhausen
13. Knabe, *Gefangen in Hohenschönhausen*, p. 9
14. Formed in April 1949
15. Applebaum, *Iron Curtain*, pp. 414–15
16. *Neues Deutschland*, 29 June 1962
17. Stasi figures quoted in F. Taylor, *The Berlin Wall*, London, Bloomsbury 2007, p. 129
18. D.E. Murphy, S.A. Kondrashev and G. Bailey, *Battleground Berlin*, New Haven and London, Yale University Press 1997, p. 163
19. P. Brogan, *Eastern Europe 1939–1989*, London, Bloomsbury 1990, pp. 27–8
20. Leaflet picked up in the street
21. Murphy et al., *Battleground Berlin*, p. 149
22. C. Dobson and R. Payne, *The Dictionary of Espionage*, London, Grafton 1986, pp. 334–5
23. Knabe, *Gefangen in Hohenschönhausen*, p. 13
24. Ibid, p. 14
25. Article by C. Neef in *Der Spiegel*, No. 43, 2003

4

CREATING A NEW CLASS
OF CRIMINALS

At some point, the reader has the right to ask why the GDR was the most repressive state in the communist bloc during the Cold War – more so than even the Soviet Union itself. A West German general named Jörg Schönbohm had the task of unifying the GDR's Nazionale Volksarmee and the West German Bundeswehr after the fall of the Wall in 1989. Since these two armies with a common tongue had been trained for half a century specifically for war against each other, it was not a job one would wish on a best friend. Schönbohm reasoned that, while Poles still lived in Poland, Hungarians in Hungary and so on – all having their own languages, culture and history – the GDR 'could explain its identity as a second state on German territory only through Communist or Socialist ideology – there could be no GDR without [the justification of] Communism.'[1]

The political philosophy clumsily labelled Marxism–Leninism was therefore effectively a state religion in the GDR, whose hierarchy was as blindly savage in its retribution against non-believers as the Catholic Inquisition had been in its time. In addition, in 1945, when Communist rule was first imposed on the 18 million Germans living in the Soviet Zone, they were for the most part bewildered people who had been regularly assured by Josef Goebbels, the high priest of Nazism, right up to the last week of hostilities, that they were bound to win the war. For twelve years, from the Nazi takeover in 1933, any overt dissent from Goebbels' state religion had been punishable by harsh internment, family disgrace and death sentences. With the top Nazis all dead and their creed of racial superiority totally discredited by people their followers had been taught to describe as *Sklaven und Untermenschen* – slaves and sub-humans – it was relatively easy for the Moscow-imposed hierarchy of the victorious new state religion to keep the conquered population in continuing fearful obedience to its new rulers.

British author George Orwell,[2] a sincere left-winger appalled at what he saw as the perversion of communism under Stalin, spent the winter of 1943–4 writing *Animal Farm*, a brilliant satire on the Soviet Union. Because the far-from-avuncular 'Uncle Joe' Stalin was a wartime ally at the time, Orwell's publisher, Victor Gollancz, and several other British and US publishers rejected the book, and continued to do so until its truths were accepted and the phrase 'Cold War' was on every tongue.[3] In 1948 Orwell produced another satire on totalitarian rule entitled *1984*. In it, all citizens of the fictitious society which he described were spied on each minute of their lives by the Thought Police. When Stalin created the GDR in 1949 the Ministerium für Staatssicherheit was the incarnation of Orwell's Thought Police. Its main function was to root out and punish any deviant actions *or thoughts* in the population of the GDR.

It is one thing to read statistics, but figures of so many spies, so many refugees and so many prisoners are unsatisfying. The mind wants to know what happened to the individuals caught in the Stasi's net. How *exactly* did they suffer? Were men treated differently from women? What happened if they were, for example, single mothers with small children? How many lives were ruined? How many families destroyed?

Hubertus Knabe is the director of Gedenkstätte Berlin-Hohenschönhausen. The former Stasi interrogation prison is now a memorial to those who suffered there, visited by 170,000 people a year. Knabe has published many personal stories of prisoners interrogated there after the prison was taken over from the NKVD by the Stasi.[4] What follows is a small sample.

Fritz Sperling was the 40-year-old deputy president of the KPD, elected to the executive committee of the SED on the merging of the two parties in the Soviet zone. Leaving a hospital in the Soviet sector of Berlin on 26 February 1951 after treatment for his heart condition, he was tricked by a friend into getting into a car with three Stasi operatives and driven to Hohenschönhausen. As a Moscow-trained Communist who had been imprisoned by the Nazis pre-war and interned in Switzerland throughout the Second World War, he was not at first alarmed, having no idea that he would be held under interrogation for the next two years and eight months:

Arriving at the prison, I was forced to strip to my underclothes and shown into a cell containing only a rough wooden plank on which to sleep and a latrine bucket. The guard explained that in daytime I could sit on the plank bed, but not lean against the wall on either side. It was forbidden to lie down during the day and at night I must lie with face and arms visible through the spy-hole, which meant being unable to cover my chest despite my severe heart trouble. During my illegal activities [for the KPD before the Second World War], when I was both imprisoned and sent to labour camps, I had had a heart attack. After the war, my condition worsened.

Erich Mielke came in person to warn me that I had been arrested for anti-Party activities, which he advised me to confess and 'sacrifice myself for the good of the Party'. My protests that I had never betrayed the Party were unavailing. From February 1951 until December 1952 I was interrogated by Soviet intelligence officers, 'helping the German comrades'. They repeatedly punched me on the ribs over my heart while my hands were cuffed behind my back. Sometimes, senior officials of the GDR were present.

[After my long interrogation in Hohenschönhausen], for nine months in Bautzen II, I was not permitted to lie down in the day, although suffering from severe sleep deprivation. My cell was unheated, with no daylight or fresh air.[5]

The NKVD men in Bautzen frequently beat prisoners for no apparent reason and prisoners were not allowed toilet paper or sanitary towels as a form of humiliation. Sperling's health deteriorated rapidly until he had a further heart attack in September 1952. Denied medical help for five weeks, he was sentenced to seven years in prison as a war criminal, fascist and 'agent for crimes against peace'. In the political thaw that followed the 20th Conference of the CP of the USSR, in which Nikita Khrushchev denounced a selection of Stalin's crimes – excluding those in which he had himself participated – Sperling was pardoned but not rehabilitated, and died two years later at the age of 46 from the aggravation of his heart condition during detention.

Karl Fricke was a 27-year-old journalist working in West Berlin. On 1 April 1955 he received a telephone call from a man called Rittwagen, who had been imprisoned in the Soviet Union for five years pre-war and handed back as a known Communist to the Nazis – as were many others – under the German–Soviet Non-Aggression Treaty of 1938. He was immediately sent to a Nazi concentration camp.

Fricke had no suspicions that Rittwagen had subsequently become an undercover agent of the Stasi, despite all this. Although the journalist had written articles critical of the SED, he considered himself of far too little importance to be at risk when invited to visit Rittwagen's apartment, to borrow a book otherwise unobtainable in the West. There, he was drugged by a knock-out cocktail of Atropin and Scopolamine that Frau Rittwagen put into his glass of brandy. Fricke recovered consciousness seven hours later in a brightly lit room, surrounded by four or five Stasi officers, who proceeded to insult and swear at him. After being twice beaten up, he was thrown into a cell and left to recover.

Although he had no idea where he was imprisoned, Fricke was to spend 455 days and nights in Hohenschönhausen. For fourteen days, nothing happened to relieve the boredom and fear. Interrogations for the next seven days, every afternoon and from 10 p.m. to 6 a.m., with sleep in the daytime forbidden, left him weak and confused. His interrogators offered him rewards for cooperating and warned him that he was liable to a sentence of a dozen years' imprisonment if he did not. To reduce his resistance, the interrogations were suspended from August to October. What the Stasi called 'leaving the prisoner to stew'[6] was one of the most effective ways of wearing down a prisoner's resistance. Much later, Fricke described this:

We were 'shaved' every three or four weeks with a hair trimmer and had a shower every twenty days, when we also got fresh underwear. I began to stink because I could not wash my pants regularly. Generally, we were given one piece of toilet paper per day. It was a problem if you needed to go twice and I developed a severe infection in that area after six weeks. When I told the medical orderly at shower time, all he said was, 'Hurry up. In thirty seconds I turn the water off.' And that's how it was. We had hardly got wet when the tap was turned off.

No prisoner was allowed to see another when being taken to interrogation. At every corner of the corridors was a traffic light. If it was red, I had to stand in an alcove with face to the wall until another prisoner had been escorted past by his guard. When the light was green, and the way was clear, I was led on. In the interrogation room were two Stasi officers in civilian suits. I had to sit in the corner on a stool with hands visible on my knees.

Every week or so, I had 'open-air exercise' in a yard five metres by six with walls five metres high, on which stood a guard with machine pistol, as though I could jump that high.

After giving an unsatisfactory answer in one interrogation, I was locked into a mini-cell no more than fifty centimetres square. For four hours, I could not sit or change position to relieve the discomfort. This happened again when a guard saw through the Judas-hole that I had prised a splinter off my wooden bunk, with which to try and mend my shoe that was losing its sole. I was charged with 'damage to the people's property' and placed in the 'standing-only cell' for several long and painful hours.[7]

Many detainees were required to spend their initial interrogation sessions seated on a special chair, with hands beneath their thighs, an unnatural position which swiftly becomes uncomfortable. They were unaware that the chair had a false seat cover, under which was a special pad to absorb the odour of the nervous perspiration in their crotch. Immediately after the interrogation, the pad was placed in a hermetically sealed glass jar, to be sniffed by tracker dogs in the event that the prisoner was ever the object of a manhunt – as Dieter Hötger was to find out in 1967.[8]

Walter Janke was the 32-year-old head of the East Berlin publisher Aufbau, who was arrested in December 1956 and questioned in Hohenschönhausen until July 1957:

> I was made to strip naked in this brightly lit room before a huge portrait of Stalin – this was three years after Khrushchev had denounced him at the 20th Party Congress. Someone took my clothes and watch into another room, leaving me bollock-naked in front of Stalin. Another officer with an inspection lamp ordered me to open my mouth and checked it and my throat. Both arms had to be lifted high while he inspected my armpits with a magnifying glass. The officer with the lamp ordered, 'Bend over! Lower! Now pull your buttocks apart with both hands.' He inspected also my arse with the lamp.
>
> At my first interrogation, I was taken to an office where I found four men and Erich Mielke. He informed me that I was guilty of counter-revolutionary activities, which I denied. He screamed that the Stasi had broken stronger men than me and came so close that his spittle landed on my face. I asked him to step back because I didn't like being spat on. He and two of the other men left after the screaming, and the interrogation continued until seven o'clock next morning, when I was confronted with an indictment seven pages long.[9]

After the rapid erection of the Berlin Wall on 13–14 August 1961, many people were cut off from their families and loved ones. One such was 27-year-old Sigrid Paul, mother of a baby son she had been visiting daily in a West Berlin clinic where, for the past five months, he had been receiving medical treatment not available in 'democratic' East Berlin. It took nine weeks of form-filling and rejected requests for her to be allowed to visit him again and hold him in her arms – at which point she had to decide whether to stay with her baby in the West or return home to her husband. Believing that her child would soon be better and able to come home too, she returned to East Berlin but was not allowed to visit her child again. After eighteen months of anguish about the baby's progress, she and her husband were invited by some students in February 1962 to escape via a tunnel being dug by them underneath the Wall. Unfortunately the Stasi had infiltrated the student group and was already aware of the plan:

> On 28 February 1963 I was on the way to work when two men grabbed me and forced me to get into a black car. I was so shocked that I fought back and a bus driver stopped his vehicle and opened the door so that I could get away, but the men were too strong. I was virtually kidnapped and delivered to the Stasi interrogation facility at Berlin-Lichtenberg.

After my watch, handbag, belt and shoelaces had been taken away, I was questioned by several men at the same time about the students. I had not been told anything about their arrangements, but they did not believe this. It was very frightening and lasted all day and the whole night. The interrogators were changed every four hours or so, but I had no rest for twenty-two hours.

I was then placed in an unlit cell inside a closed prison van. After a long drive, it stopped and I was let out in a garage, so brightly lit that it hurt my eyes. I was taken into a room, made to strip naked and bend over in a crouch so that a grinning guard could check that I had not hidden anything in any bodily orifice. The humiliation continued when I was given men's underclothes, coarse socks and felt slippers, and taken into an unheated cell where I was told my name was now 93/2 – 93 for the cell and 2 for the number of my plank bed.

The cell window had been replaced by a double thickness of glass bricks, through which nothing could be seen: no clouds, no birds. Every ten minutes I was spied on through the Judas-hole. The cell light was kept on night and day. I had no idea where I was being held. Even my toilet things were kept outside the cell. With little or no sleep, after two weeks I was so weak, exhausted, lonely and desperate for news of my family that I signed everything that was put in front of me.

From time to time I heard knocking and realised that this was some kind of code. Letter A was one knock; B was two knocks and so on. I took the chance to join in, although this was totally forbidden, and punished by worse conditions. In May of 1964 I had to clean away the blood and excrement in a 'rubber cell', where they locked up prisoners who had gone out of their minds. Down there, there was no plank bed nor toilet can.

In July 1963 I was transferred to the Stasi prison in Rostock. Informed that I was at last about to be tried, I asked for a defence lawyer, to be told by my interrogator, 'You could have three defence lawyers, but it wouldn't make any difference.' Before the trial, at which I was sentenced to four years in prison for 'conspiracy to flee the Republic', I was not allowed to see the indictment, nor meet a lawyer.

Once sentenced, life was easier. I was allowed a quarterly visit from my mother and a monthly 30-minute meeting with my husband, who was serving time in a male working party at the same prison. Working alone in my cell, I still had a terrible yearning for my son. Day and night, I tried to imagine how he looked now. How big was he? Could he talk yet? What did his voice sound like? Had his teeth grown? What did he know about his parents? Did he even understand what a father and mother were? I could open the ventilation flap in the blocked-up cell window just a little, to let in some fresh air. Sometimes, I heard men's voices outside and, just now and again, my husband's unmistakable laugh.[10]

Sigrid was interned from March to August 1963 and from October 1963 to October 1964. Then:

> One day I was taken out of my cell very early and escorted into a prison van. I took courage in both hands to ask the guard where I was going, but he did not reply. I was taken to a prison in Berlin-Rummelsburg and put into a filthy, cold cell without plank bed or stool, where I was kept waiting for about twelve hours. In the evening, I was conducted to the gate office, given back my things that had been taken away when I was arrested – and found myself outside on the street.
>
> I don't know for how long I stood there, trying to think clearly as the sun went down in a wonderful orange sky. Very, very slowly I realised that I was free again. After all the privations and worry about my son, it was indescribably beautiful. Tears ran down my face.[11]

By an administrative oversight in the BStU after the end of the GDR, Sigrid eventually learned the name of her main interrogator. Many years later, she tracked him down, but he refused to talk to her.

By the 1980s even *asking* for a legal permit to leave the GDR could result in imprisonment. Waltraud Krüger was forcibly confined in a Stasi psychiatric hospital, on the logic that a communist state was as near heaven as one could get, therefore anyone wanting to leave it was clinically insane. Shown into a cell, she was brought a nightdress and some supper by a nurse, but was not hungry. Then came a psychiatrist in a white coat, who ordered her to eat, threatening her otherwise with forced feeding, which would be very painful. He told the 38-year-old detainee that she was in the medical wing of a Stasi interrogation prison. Since she still refused to eat, he called the nurse and ordered an injection. She asked what it was for, since her medical record indicated allergy to some medicines:

> No reply. An orderly came with a syringe. The injection was to be made in my buttocks, so I had to lie face down on the bed. When I refused, the doctor said, 'Don't forget, you are a prisoner under interrogation. You have to do everything we tell you to.' I still refused. Two more orderlies were called. They forced me down onto the bed and one of them did the injection. The nurse undressed me and I did not recover consciousness until next morning. When I was in prison in Magdeburg, I had used the knocking code to communicate with other cells, but when I tried it here, the doctor appeared and said, 'You're not in Magdeburg now. No knocking here.'

A medical doctor came and asked me questions about my health. The shrink said they were going to treat me with drugs. When I asked what for, he said that the state prosecutor had ordered it. The treatment started the following day: injections in the morning, at midday and in the evening of the anti-epileptic drug Luminal, which had been used to kill people in the Nazi euthanasia programme. [It also has sedative and hypnotic properties.] A declaration was put in front of me, saying that I wished to remain in the GDR. I refused to sign and went on hunger strike, so they tied me down on the bed and put in a drip.

Soon, I was no longer aware if it was day or night. After I tried to hang myself with a strip of the bed sheet, my nightie was pulled up. One guard wrenched my hands above my head and kneeled on them and the orderly held my legs down, so they could put needles into my thighs for a drip. With the first drops, I felt the most terrible pain – as if my legs were being torn off. Tears ran down my face. I begged the doctor to stop the infusion, but he said he would do so when I ate and drank and signed the declaration he was holding out. I still refused and he continued the drip for three-quarters of an hour. When he pulled out the needles, I screamed. I could hardly recognise my legs. It was agony to move them, and where the needles had gone in was raw and swollen. When I pleaded for some painkiller, the guard called from outside, 'Get yourself some from the West.'

I was warned that my sentence for refusing to sign the declaration would be not less than five years' imprisonment. Sometimes I could not understand the interrogations, but the questions were always the same, about my contacts with the West. Since I still refused to eat, my weight declined each day until I was taken into a room with several orderlies. They made me sit on a stool, cuffed my hands behind my back and fastened them to the stool. An orderly pulled back my head and the doctor inserted a tube in my nose so that the nurse could pour fluid in through a funnel. The more I struggled, the harder they pulled my hair, until even the interrogator was fighting me and I lost the last shred of human dignity by soiling myself.

Back in my cell, I begged for some release from my suffering, but God did nothing. The interrogator said my family would pay for it if I did not retract my request [to leave the GDR]. Then came the day I feared, when he told me that my daughter Anita had also been arrested. They showed me a letter in her handwriting, in which one sentence stood out: *Dear Mummy, Please find a solution for us all.* I was so confused, I had to ask the interrogator what it meant. He said she had confessed to having written 'all the letters' to the West. I asked to see that in writing, but in vain. To reply to my daughter, I was given paper and a pencil. I was weeping so much, I could hardly write, but managed a few sentences, imploring her to stick to the truth and not be squeezed like a lemon into uttering falsehoods.

My thoughts were all with my daughter. When had she been arrested and why did she have to atone for what I was supposed to have done? Then I was told my husband was also in the prison hospital because he and my daughter were considered accomplices in my 'crime'. The doctor came and pleaded with me to end the hunger strike, so my husband and daughter could be released and only I would be punished. But I was determined to continue until either I died or was given an exit visa. At my next interrogation, I was offered the same deal by the interrogator, who warned me that in the Bundesrepublik sick people like me received neither medical care or money. 'In which case,' I retorted, 'why don't all the people in the West come and live in the GDR?'[12]

By now many people in western Germany had taken an interest in Waltraud's problems. Every week, she was shown a list of their letters, on which she was supposed to mark the names she knew, which would be proof that she had contacts in the West. She was also told her husband and daughter had signed statements that they did not want to leave the GDR, but when she asked to see the statements, they were not produced. Although it pained her greatly to think of her daughter undergoing Stasi interrogations, what had happened to Anita was even more Machiavellian. A young IM (Stasi informer) called Michael Schilling had been tasked by the Stasi with seducing and marrying her – all to convince Anita to stay in the GDR.

Although Waltraud was now a shadow of the woman who had been arrested, it was the interrogator who eventually cracked and admitted that things were 'not wonderful, here in the GDR'. After his small admission, Waltraud agreed to end her hunger strike if she was given assurances that nothing would happen to her husband and daughter. A cup of broth was brought from the prison kitchen, but she was able to swallow only a little before being taken back to her cell. Although she now ate, the Luminal injections continued. On 14 July, after five weeks of this treatment, Waltraud was given back her clothes. She dressed and staggered in great pain to the main doors, where she was placed on a stretcher, which was lifted into an ambulance for an unknown destination. Seated beside her was her husband, who had been similarly mistreated in the prison hospital, but they were forbidden to speak to, or touch, each other.[13]

Suddenly, in January 1981 the family was given permission to leave the GDR legally with Anita, after their liberty was purchased by the Bundesrepublik. Welcomed by friends in the West, their relief and joy can be imagined from a photograph taken at the time. However, after being temporarily accommodated in a reception camp, they were informed that the quota of refugees for Bavaria, where they wanted to live, was already full. Settled in a rented apartment in Lower Saxony, where they knew nobody, they found themselves ostracised by neighbours as 'troublesome Ossies'.

In September 2000, just before the expiry of the legislation covering all SED and Stasi crimes except murder, the Berlin county court heard the trial of neurologist Horst Böttger for his treatment of the Krügers. Defended by a former Stasi legal officer and calling as defence witness a former KGB psychologist from Moscow, Böttger was found not guilty after pleading that Waltraud's suicide attempt justified his use of Luminal.

As to how many GDR citizens were arrested for attempting the crime of Republikflucht – flight from the GDR – they totalled 64,000 individual cases between 1958 and 1966. In the last years of the GDR, the figures were nearly 6,000 in 1987 and more than 9,000 in 1988.

Notes

1. J. Schönbohm, *Two Armies and one Fatherland*, Oxford, Berghahn Books 1996, p. ix
2. The pen name of Eric Blair
3. See Knabe, *Gefangen in Hohenschönhausen*
4. Ibid
5. F. Sperling in Knabe, *Gefangen in Hohenschönhausen*, pp. 147–53
6. Knabe, *Gefangen in Hohenschönhausen*, pp. 166–73
7. H. Fichter in Knabe, *Gefangen in Hohenschönhausen*, pp. 152–63 (abridged)
8. An example is displayed in the Normannenstrasse museum. The modus operandi was shown in the film *Das Leben der Anderen/The Lives of Others*, dir. von Donnersmarck
9. W. Janka in Knabe, *Gefangen in Hohenschönhausen*, pp. 174–91 (author's italics)
10. S. Paul in Knabe, *Gefangen in Hohenschönhausen*, pp. 236–47
11. Ibid
12. W. Krüger in Knabe, *Gefangen in Hohenschönhausen*, pp. 303–7
13. Ibid

5

FEAR AS A POLITICAL TOOL

Many of the Stasi prisoners interrogated in Hohenschönhausen ended up like Fritz Sperling, serving their sentences in one of the two long-term prisons at Bautzen in Saxony. A hundred miles south-east of Berlin, close to the Czech and Polish frontiers, the city now promotes itself as a medieval tourist attraction although, to Germans who lived in the GDR, the name was a synonym for political persecution and inhumane prison conditions. The high-security prison designated Bautzen II had been a political prison under the Nazis, was taken over by the NKVD/MGB after the war and run by the GDR Innenministerium from 1956 to 1989. The guards wore not Stasi uniforms, but the blue uniforms of the Interior Ministry prison service. Most of the prisoners were political victims of the regime, but convicted criminals also served time here. Among the politicals were many former members of the state, party or military systems, sentenced for 'treason' or simply for *Nestbeschmutzung* – literally, soiling the nest, i.e. criticising the SED, the GDR, some political or official figure, or simply telling an indiscreet joke. There was also a significant number of foreigners, particularly West Germans and convicted 'spies and saboteurs' from the West.

For these to be arrested, it was not necessary even to set foot in the GDR. By 1950 approximately 700 people had been drugged and/or kidnapped in the West like Karl Fricke, and then driven across the border in the boot of a car driven by Stasi thugs – as in a novel by Len Deighton or John Le Carré. Both methods ended in the same way, with the victim delivered to a Stasi interrogation prison, forced into a real or false confession and sentenced to long periods of imprisonment. Particularly targeted were members of Western intelligence services, print and media journalists who had been critical of the SED, and anyone involved in helping refugees escape to the West. These political prisoners were subject to especially severe detention.

The work they were allotted was unpleasant and/or hard; they had fewer privileges than convicted criminals; they were more likely to be given additional punishments and were generally harassed and spied on in various ways throughout their detention.

Extra punishments were regularly meted out to political prisoners. These included *Arrest*, which took the form of up to twenty-one days in a small, barred cell – which the victims called 'the tiger cage' – on reduced rations and with no bedding. When Werner König was sentenced to this, he was shackled by one foot and one hand to the bars and thus unable to reach the toilet. This obliged him to wet and soil himself, for which he was abused as a 'filthy pig' by the guards.[1]

Because everyone in the GDR was spied on, at Bautzen II this applied also to the guards. Documentary proof exists that regular reports on what they did and said were supplied to the Stasi and were used against them in some instances. In the ubiquitous paranoia of the GDR, even the informers who compiled these reports were themselves spied on.[2]

Even the word 'paranoia' is insufficient to describe the all-pervading fear. As late as August 1987, when it must have been obvious to many people that the SED regime was economically unsustainable and would soon collapse, the GDR Defence Ministry issued a formal order to all service personnel that their television sets must be 'sealed up to block the transmissions of the enemy on Channel 25' – i.e. West German television.[3] Personnel who chose to ignore this ran the risk of their children reporting them in school. Even colleagues who were childless took to hanging lights on the outside of their houses to blot out the give-away glow from the television screen, so that neighbours would not see it after the GDR television transmissions ended early in the evening.[4]

For those in prison, of course, there was only one state channel of television to watch. In an echo of the duplicitous slogan over the main gate at Auschwitz, *Arbeit macht frei* – work will make you free – every prisoner in the GDR long-term prisons was obliged to work as 'rehabilitation'. Some prisoners worked with others in workshops, assembling transformers and electric motors; those in solitary confinement were obliged to work alone. Female prisoners in isolation were put to sewing hand towels or sticking together the two halves of pencils – an activity that had been performed by machines in the West for 100 years and more. Others worked in groups, cleaning and polishing floors and fittings, or in the kitchen. Theoretically, there was a minimum wage, paid in Wertscheine, or prison currency, but because 82 per cent of earnings was deducted for 'food and board', and some of the remainder was kept back as savings, little was left to spend in the prison shop. Failure to keep up with work norms led to loss of earnings.[5]

An otherwise unknown man called Dieter Hötger was the only prisoner ever to escape from Bautzen II. Sentenced to solitary confinement, he was locked alone into work cell No. 19 at the corner of the main building between 5 a.m. and 3 p.m. each day. There, he succeeded in slowly removing twenty-three bricks from the external wall, where it was hidden behind a cupboard. Each evening, he replaced the loose bricks and the cupboard, and flushed the cement dust down a toilet. When he finally broke through his 50cm-wide hole in the 65cm-thick external wall, he found that it was 5m above the ground. He climbed through anyway and dropped down, to scramble over the outer wall and get away. There was little outside security since it was believed that Bautzen II was escape-proof.

Although in prison clothes with high-visibility yellow stripes on the sleeves, Hötger set out to walk the 100-plus miles to the frontier in Berlin. His escape triggered a nationwide manhunt, with hastily printed posters offering 1,000 Marks – the equivalent of two months' average wages – for his recapture. Yet, for nine days Hötger managed to evade all the forces mobilised against him, until he was tracked down only 17km away from the prison. Here again, the paranoia that ruled the GDR came into play. Oddly, there was no laid-down penalty for his escape, if it really was a solo effort. So, all the weight of the Stasi system went into trying to prove that he had had accomplices, because a conspiracy was punishable. When this failed, in March 1969 he was accused of 'espionage, collection of information, systematic hostile agitation, attempted illegal border-crossing and damage to socialist property' – i.e. the hole in the wall. For this idiotic collection of trumped-up charges, with only the last having any semblance of reality, he was sentenced to eight *additional* years' imprisonment. In September 1972 Hötger was freed after he was 'bought' by the Bundesrepublik.[6]

The Kampfgruppe gegen Unmenschlichkeit (KgU) or 'combat group against inhumanity' was regarded in the GDR as a terrorist organisation and any members who fell into the hands of the Stasi were treated as violent criminals. When the author was serving at RAF Gatow, an off-duty pleasure was sailing boats of the British Berlin Yacht Club on Lake Havel, but club members were warned not to stray too near the line of buoys at the southern end of the lake, which marked the border with the GDR. On one Sunday afternoon, a West Berlin lawyer who was a member of the KgU was sailing his yacht on the Havel well inside the British sector boundary when a Stasi high-speed launch crossed the boundary. The lawyer was dragged aboard it, next stop interrogation in Potsdam.

The inhumanity which the KgU was fighting is exemplified by what happened to a 22-year-old West Berlin girl named Sigrid Grünewald. In 1977, while visiting relatives in Thuringia, where she had been born, she fell in love. After her boyfriend's request for an exit visa was predictably turned down by the MfS, Sigrid paid a *Fluchthilfeorganisation* – professional people smugglers – to bring him out of the GDR, but the attempt failed. Aware of the risks, if caught, the boyfriend made another request for an exit visa. Meanwhile, the Stasi had been interrogating one of the people smugglers and learned of the failed rescue attempt. The next time Sigrid visited her boyfriend, both of them were arrested. In March 1982 she was sentenced to five and a half years' imprisonment in Bautzen II for 'attempted treasonous human trafficking'; her boyfriend was sent to serve his sentence in another prison. In this case, love triumphed after all. In September 1982 their liberty was purchased by the Bundesrepublik and they married in West Berlin a year later. The same court that had condemned Sigrid quashed her conviction in 1991.

It must have taken exceptional courage to be a civil rights activist in the GDR, but there were some, all closely watched by the Stasi. Vera Lengsfeld was 36 when arrested and treated more delicately than most of her co-detainees:

I was thrust into a metal cell near the door of the blue prison bus. A female officer clapped handcuffs on me. They were the sort that tightened if you put any pressure on them. Then a male officer removed the cuffs. The bus set off and stopped after being backed up very close to a brightly lit garage – all lights and uniforms. A young, attractive woman with a nice face in the uniform of a wardress took me into a cell, where I had to undress, so she could check my mouth and ears and other bodily orifices. As I was crouching with legs apart for this, I noticed someone looking through the spy-hole in the door. When I protested, the nice girl took no notice. Given some horrible jail clothes, I was so relieved to have clean underwear that I made no complaint, and was escorted to a cell measuring five metres by three.

My interrogator demonstrated how much the Stasi knew about me by playing my favourite piece of music by Mendelssohn during our first session. It was interrupted by the arrival of the judge, who was accompanied by a young and pretty secretary with long hair, whom I should never have suspected of working for the Stasi. The accusation was that I had 'participated in a forbidden meeting'. Before he could start taking down my statement, I informed him that before I had even been charged someone had spied on me while I was naked, which I considered an insult to my feminine dignity. The secretary looked at the judge, uncertain whether she should write this down. He said the conduct of prison staff was not his concern, but I insisted until he gave way. I then refuted his charges.

After a week, I was moved to another cell, with a 19-year-old East German girl who had been arrested trying to get on a plane at Budapest airport and locked up in a filthy Hungarian jail for two weeks, during which she had to take her shower watched by the all-male guards. She was now facing three years' imprisonment.[7]

Vera Lengsfeld had been arrested as a warning, and was released after two months' interrogation. Since several other civil rights activists connected with the Evangelical Church were imprisoned for exactly the same period, it is safe to assume that the Stasi was sending a warning to all civil rights workers. Arrested in her own home, Freya Klier, a 38-year-old mother, managed to compile a rough diary after her release:

The senior Stasi man said, 'Your daughter must undress. She'll be examined by a doctor and sent to a children's home.' But I had given fellow activist Ralf Hirsch a legal power of attorney to act as her guardian in just this situation. Trying to delay the awful moment when I would have to awaken Nadja, I went into the bathroom. The female officer who had searched the house the last time came with me and studied herself in the mirror while I used the toilet. I took my 'jail clothes' from the cupboard: a long dress and a pullover of Stephan's.

Then I could not put off the awful moment any longer and asked the woman to leave me alone with my daughter. She refused. Nadja slowly woke up, could not understand what was going on, and clung to me, crying. I cried too, whispering that she was not going into a home, just to the doctor and then to Ralf, where Grandma would visit her soon – and that I loved her. It was the most wretched hour of my life.

In the Stasi car driving through the morning rush hour, I built a psychological wall around myself. The first trial was getting undressed and letting them peer into my arse-hole [sic]. That humiliation lasted a hundred years. But I refused to change into the prison clothing. The wardress screamed at me but, with the exception of my tights (with which I could have hanged myself), I was allowed to keep my own clothes.

In the Magdalenenstrasse interrogation prison, Dr Schnur, the lawyer who acted for us, brought news from my husband, who was shattered by the arrest. Schnur also told me the Church leaders had suggested I take up a previous offer of study leave in the West. I refused.

My interrogator was a pleasant, intelligent man of my own age, which made me wonder why he had chosen such a hateful job.

Taken back to my cell I was given a copy of Neues Deutschland [the daily newspaper that was the official organ of the SED], in which I was horrified to read that my husband and all the others, including Ralf, had been arrested, allegedly for treason. The letters and names danced in front of my eyes. My brain was spinning. On Sunday I had this terrible dream where they brought Stephan into the exercise yard blindfolded. I screamed and ran down the steps to him but, when I got there, they had already hanged him.

I thought of Nadja all the time, wondering whether the parents of the other pupils at her school had told their children not to have anything to do with her. When I was much younger, I had put up with many months in jail, but now, after only a few days, I thought I was going mad.

On the way to interrogation on 28 January, I saw a female Stasi officer in the corridor carrying a pair of boots and a fur coat, which I recognised as belonging to Vera Lengsfeld. So she too was in the prison...

On 30 January it was Nadja's birthday – a day blacker than any nightmare. Walking round the exercise yard, I suddenly heard Stephan's voice, calling my name from a cell. I cupped my hands and called out as loudly as I could towards the barbed wire above the yard, 'Stephan, I love you!'[8]

Although Freya and her coreligionists did not wish to be expelled from the GDR, where they felt there was much work still to do, they were divested of their GDR citizenship and delivered to the border, where Nadja was reunited with her mother. Freya described the lawyer Dr Schnur as 'a good soul' because he represented many people accused of political crimes. She later learned that he was a Stasi informer, betraying his clients' confidences.

A similar case that year concerned Renate Persich, a 34-year-old nurse. Because she and her husband were practising Christians, their children were denied any formal education as punishment, which meant they would be unqualified for any profession or trade. Even the children of nominally Christian parents were denied education to Abitur level, and could thus never attend university. The Persich parents therefore requested an exit visa for the whole family, which unleashed a full-scale Stasi operation. Both parents and their two children were subjected to threats, harassment and questioning, to make them withdraw the visa application. After they turned to religious contacts in the West for help, Renate and her husband were accused of 'repeated treasonable intelligence activities' and sentenced to three years and seven months' imprisonment – in her case at Bautzen II. Ten months later, the couple were bought free by the Bundesrepublik and their children were allowed to follow four weeks later. In 1992 the court that had condemned the two adults quashed the conviction.

Does that matter? Strangely, given the numbers of GDR citizens who were falsely accused, or accused under punitive laws of 'offences' that would have passed unnoticed in the West, many detainees found after release that they were regarded as in some way criminal, and spent years ostracised by neighbours and workmates. Others were unable to find suitable jobs because most industrial and commercial enterprises in the GDR were *volkseigene Betriebe* – state-owned factories or companies run by works committees controlled by party members.

It is strange, in the context of twentieth-century Europe, to read of people being bought and sold by legal government agencies. Yet, between 1963 and 1989 human trafficking was openly practised in the two Germanies: the Bundesrepublik purchased the freedom of some 34,000 prisoners and 215,000-plus other GDR citizens, who were deprived of their GDR citizenship and transported to the inner German border. Once in the West, they were helped to find work and accommodation. Payments for these prisoners totalled 3.4 billion Deutschmarks, paid to the GDR in the form of food and other non-strategic materials goods. Full details of this 'trade' are still secret, but it was no secret that, at an average price of DM 96,000 per person, this traffic became a vital subsidy for the SED's 'planned economy', which would otherwise have collapsed sooner.[9] After many thousands made legal escapes from the GDR in this way, some dissidents deliberately made themselves targets for the Stasi – with all the unpleasantness that involved – in the hope of being bought out once imprisoned.

This traffic in misery made Dr Wolfgang Vogel the richest man in the GDR. He practised law in East Berlin, but was also recognised by the West Berlin legal system because he was a very discreet back-channel for the two German governments, which claimed to have no diplomatic relations. With the confident air of a prosperous businessman, he negotiated high-profile spy swaps, including that of U2 Pilot Francis Gary Powers and US citizen Frederic Pryor, traded for the top-level Soviet spy Vilyam Genrikhovich Fisher, aka Colonel Rudolf Abel. It is estimated that Vogel arranged more than 150 spy swaps, usually with handovers at the Glienicke bridge between Potsdam and West Berlin. He also arranged transfer to the Bundesrepublik of the 34,000 political prisoners and nearly a quarter-million other GDR citizens. The biggest spy swap took place on 11 June 1985, when Vogel arranged for a whole coachload – twenty-nine passengers – of CIA and other imprisoned agents to be handed over in exchange for just four eastern bloc agents. An ARD television documentary about this swap, which includes an interview with Vogel, can be seen on YouTube under the title *Tausche Ostagent gegen Westagent (2/2) Endstation Glienicke Brücke.*[10]

After German reunification, evidence from Stasi archives was used to accuse Vogel of extortion and tax evasion. The extortion charge centred on him pressuring would-be emigrants, whose cases he was handling, to sell their houses at knock-down prices to SED-approved purchasers. Convicted after the reunification of Germany in 1996 on five counts and briefly imprisoned, Vogel proved that lawyers always win. On appeal in 1998 the German Supreme Court dismissed two of the charges and the others were withdrawn by the prosecution, leaving Vogel to live out his natural term with his second wife in some luxury in a villa at the end of a quiet cul-de-sac in Schliersee in Bavaria, a few metres from the Schlierach river. There, he died aged 82 of a heart attack in September 2008. The funeral service was attended by 150 mourners, still divided by the Cold War polarisation of Germany. On the left of the aisle sat various Western public figures and an American diplomat; on the right sat an equal number of important former VIPs from the Stasi and SED. Only after the service, walking to the cemetery, did the two sides mingle.[11]

One of the 34,000 prisoners whose liberation enriched Vogel had a story so heart-rending that a television reconstruction was made of it, under the German title that translates as *The Woman at Checkpoint Charlie*.[12] In the summer of 1982, less than a year after divorcing her husband, Jutta Frick travelled with her two daughters and her new companion, Günter Silvio, from their home in Dresden to Bucharest. There, she visited the West German embassy in the hope of obtaining temporary travel papers under an assumed name that would enable them to cross into Yugoslavia and reach the Bundesrepublik from there. The papers were not accepted by the Romanian Securitate, which took the family into custody and returned them at the beginning of December to Dresden, where they were separated. Jutta was placed in a Stasi interrogation prison and her daughters were sent to spend six months in a children's home, after which they were given into the care of their father, a law-abiding citizen of the GDR.

Condemned on 4 January 1983 to three and a half years' imprisonment in Hoheneck – a medieval castle converted into the largest women's prison in Germany, where thousands were locked away behind the 4m walls topped with razor wire – Jutta was allowed to receive letters from the girls and to reply three times a month. Before the end of her sentence, Jutta and her companion were included in a group of prisoners who were bought out through the intermediary of Dr Vogel, the catch being that she had to sign away her rights to her daughters before leaving the GDR. Their father did not prevent them writing to his ex-wife, but in 1984 she could no longer bear to be separated from them. She went on hunger strike, asked the pope for help on two occasions and once chained herself to some railings outside an international conference, hoping Federal Foreign Minster Hans-Dietrich Genscher would support her plea for the release of her daughters. Among the many organisations she contacted was the Frankfurt-based Internationale Gesellschaft für Menschenrechte (IGM), or International Association for Human Rights.

Starting in October 1984 she repeatedly stood at Checkpoint Charlie with a large piece of cardboard on which was written a plea for help to obtain the release of her daughters and Silvio's son from the clutches of the Stasi. By 1986 Silvio could no longer stand the separation, and left Jutta to return to the GDR and his child. It took two further years of standing at Checkpoint Charlie on most days, whatever the weather, holding up signs in German or English with messages like *Give me back my children* or *My children are held captive in the DDR* [*sic*] for Jutta to finally embarrass the GDR government into handing over her daughters, then aged 15 and 17 – through Dr Vogel's office, of course. As their mother said, this release had nothing to do with high-level political contacts, but was brought about exclusively by her unrelenting campaign of vigils at the checkpoint, her hunger strike and petitions she had signed. For once, an individual had publicly faced down the GDR dictatorship – but at what cost!

To say that she was lucky seems incredibly insensitive, yet the fate of many of the women in Hoheneck before her is far worse. In 1946 a 20-year-old woman named Ursula Hoffmann, whose 56-year-old mother had been raped by two Soviet soldiers, was arrested by the NKVD/MVD and sent to Sachsenhausen concentration camp, where she fell in love with a Russian guard. How they managed to be alone in such an overcrowded place of misery is impossible to imagine, but Ursula found herself pregnant and, when this could not be hidden, she was put into interrogation. She refused to reveal the name of the father but he confessed to the crime of sexual relations with a German woman in order to save her further suffering. For this, he was sentenced to seven years in the Siberian Gulag.

Ursula gave birth in Torgau prison to a son she named Alexander. The child had no legal existence, no birth certificate, no ration entitlement and there were, of course, no provisions for feminine hygiene in Torgau. Even what children's clothes existed had to be made by the mothers from rags. But Ursula's life deteriorated further when a number of mothers with children and babies were transported in nightmare conditions to Hoheneck, where they were soon separated from their children, even those still at the breast. Under an arrangement piloted by Elle Kurtz of the Saxony SED administration and approved by State Secretary of the Interior Ministry Hans Warnke and Käthe Kern of the Ministry of Work and Health, the children were first placed in a hospital, which could not obtain rations nor clothing or shoes for them because they did not legally exist. From there, most were despatched to children's homes to be brought up as 'proper SED socialists' while some were given away to politically reliable couples for the same purpose. No contact was allowed between the mothers and their lost children. It was seven years before Ursula was reunited with her son, but their time together was limited as she died at the age of 41 from the consequences of her imprisonment.[13]

Notes

1. S. Hattig, S. Klewin, C. Liebold and J. Morré, *Stasi-Gefängnis Bautzen II 1956–1989*, Dresden, Sandstein 2008, pp. 152–3 (abridged)
2. Ibid, pp. 137–8 (abridged)
3. Schönbohm, *Two Armies*, p. 162 (author's italics)
4. Ibid
5. Hattig et al., *Stasi-Gefängnis Bautzen II*, p. 172 (abridged)
6. Hattig et al., *Stasi-Gefängnis Bautzen II*, pp. 188–91, 203 (abridged)
7. V. Lengsfeld in Knabe, *Gefangen in Hohenschönhausen*, pp. 318–19, 324 (abridged)
8. Ibid, pp. 334–46 (abridged)
9. Hattig et al., *Stasi-Gefängnis Bautzen II*, p. 94
10. See on www.youtube.com under 'Tausche Ostagent gegen Westagent (2/2) Endstation Glienicker Brücke'
11. Article in *Berliner Zeitung*, 1 September 2008
12. *Die Frau vom Checkpoint Charlie*, director M. Alexandre, Arte-TV, 8 October 2007
13. Alexander Latotsky wrote a book about his experiences entitled *Kindheit hinter Stacheldraht* (*A Childhood behind Barbed Wire*), Leipzig, Forum. An English-language summary may be found at http://alex.latotsky.de/Emystory.htm

6

THE NEW CLASS ENEMY

Class warfare was a basic strategy of all the communist governments, conducted against the bourgeoisie, landowners, businessmen and -women, intellectuals and even peasants who worked hard and cultivated more ground than others. In 1981 the MfS created a new class enemy to add to the list: teenagers and young adults, both single and married. This was done quite officially at its annual strategy meeting. Because they had only themselves to look after, young GDR citizens were beginning to take liberties and resented their confinement in less than half a country run by grey men wearing grey suits – and a few grey women – with equally grey minds. Having learned something of the freedom available to their coevals in the Bundesrepublik, they wanted some of it for themselves.

There had, naturally, been some students and other young persons who fell foul of the NKVD immediately after the war and of the Stasi after its creation. Particularly at risk were the informal groups of young friends who, after the building of the Berlin Wall, dug tunnels under it and invented other ways of smuggling friends out of the GDR. Hiding a girlfriend in the boot of a sympathetic foreigner's car and hoping to get her past the guards and sniffer dogs at one of the few remaining checkpoints was a method that failed on more than one occasion, resulting in long years of imprisonment for all concerned. Considering that 'flight from the republic' was a statutory crime under the perverted justice system imposed by the SED,[1] it is amazing that some young people with many different motivations still took similar risks in the knowledge that they would be sentenced to several years' imprisonment, if caught.

A different case – even more innocent – is that of Miriam Weber, dug up by Australian writer Anna Funder when researching her book *Stasiland*.[2] Miriam was 16 during the Prague Spring and thought it wrong that the Stasi broke up peaceful demonstrations with fire hoses, beating and arresting people. She and a friend determined to protest. Knowing that all typewriters were identifiable to the Stasi, they bought a child's printing set of loose letters to be inserted into a frame and then pressed on an inked pad, with which they made leaflets to distribute around Leipzig one night, carefully wearing gloves to ensure they left no fingerprints. A full-scale investigation was launched, with extensive questioning of hundreds of young people until a search of Miriam's home revealed a few of the letters they had missed when throwing the 'evidence' away. Arrested and placed separately in solitary confinement for a month, the girls were broken by each being told the other had confessed. They were released pending a full trial – and every child's printing set was withdrawn from sale all over the GDR!

Determined not to go back to jail, Miriam took a train to Berlin and scouted the crossing points before concluding they were too dangerous. On the way home she noticed a stretch of the line running parallel to a West German line, with just the boundary fence in between. She got off the train and walked through some allotments up to the fence. With a ladder taken from an allotment shed she climbed up to see the barrier better: a wire mesh fence topped with barbed wire, a patrol strip, a 20m asphalted roadway for the patrol vehicles and a pathway for the foot patrols.

With the boldness of youth, she climbed the fence, lacerating her hands badly and getting caught for some time until breaking free. Crossing the roadway she saw a wire about one metre from the ground and supposed it was an alarm. On hands and knees, she crawled under it – to find that it had an Alsatian guard dog chained to it, free to run along its length. Crouching on the ground, she did not move. After a while the dog went away, probably because it was trained to chase a running person, or possibly it lost her scent when an ancient locomotive chugged past, drenching them both with steam. With only a low fence between her and freedom, she hit a trip wire – and that was the end of her escape.

The Stasi interrogator Major Fleischer did not believe that a girl of 16, alone, could have so nearly crossed the GDR's 'anti-fascist protective measure'. Each night Miriam had two hours' sleep before questioning from 10 p.m. to 4 a.m., with no sleeping allowed during the daytime. Realising they wanted to know her accomplices, she invented them and a meeting in a beer cellar – only to get into more trouble for wasting Stasi time when they staked out the beer cellar fruitlessly on several consecutive nights. Her sentence was eighteen months in the women's prison at Hoheneck. On entry, she was ordered to undress and half-drowned several times in a bath of cold water by two wardresses before becoming Juvenile Prisoner No. 725 and having no other name for a year and a half. Apart from basic food, everything in the prison had to be bought or bartered for, including sanitary towels. The political prisoners were controlled by hardened criminals. When she was released, she was, in her words, 'not really human any more'.

The reader might think that Miriam's story could get no worse, but it did.[3]

Once the war on youth began, *all* young people constituted a target group, to be perpetually under surveillance – using especially IMs, who included their teachers, classmates, flatmates, youth workers and sometimes their parents and siblings. Fortunately Gabriele Schnell, a Potsdam resident, compiled a record of detainees' experiences in the Potsdam interrogation prisons,[4] where more than 60 per cent of inmates were younger than 30, and also made a special study of youthful victims of the Stasi.[5]

Like many young people, 20-year-old Potsdam swimming instructor Jens Baumann yearned to travel abroad, partly because he had relatives living in several European countries. For ordinary GDR citizens below retirement age, the only possible foreign destinations were other Warsaw Pact countries. In August 1982 Jens travelled to Bulgaria on holiday with the intention of walking across the south-eastern border into Turkey through wild country – until he found out that more young East Germans had been shot there by border guards than all along the inner German frontier. They were swiftly buried in unmarked graves in what is now the Grandzhda National Park – then dubbed the Death Triangle – still dotted with concrete bunkers to be used in the event of a Turkish invasion.[6] Instead, Jens returned home and, filled with the lust for travel, filed a formal request to leave the GDR two days later. Innocently, he quoted Article 13 of the United Nations Charter of Human Rights:

> Everyone has the right to leave any country, including his own, and to return to it.

He also quoted Article 15:

> Nobody shall be arbitrarily deprived of his nationality, nor be denied the right to change his nationality.

Because the GDR had signed the Charter, of which he had found a copy in the Potsdam library, he thought this was safe. In an effort to speed up treatment of his application, he also requested support three days later in a letter to the IGM in Frankfurt, having heard about the organisation on a West German television programme. The IGM being on the list of 'enemy organisations' held by the Stasi's mail censors, it was stamped *Not to be forwarded* and sent instead to the MfS district office in Potsdam, whose staff had, within the week, conducted a preliminary investigation of Baumann. Although an IM also working in the swimming pool knew nothing against him, his name did figure on a Stasi list of persons who had attended a pop concert – which the MfS termed 'a negative-decadent youth rally' – in the previous year. This and the fact that he had written to the IGM were enough to make his application to leave the GDR technically 'unlawful'.

As though this was a military operation, on 1 September 1982 the Stasi district office drew up a five-page plan of operations, which was put into action the following day, the charge being that Baumann had attempted to contact 'a state-hostile organisation', for which the penalty was one to five years in prison. The full might of the Stasi and Volkspolizei were now brought into play, plus two IMs, who made enquiries of his colleagues and neighbours. Their report revealed nothing; on the contrary, it noted that the swimming instructor was 'friendly, helpful and decently dressed', and that his family put flags in their window on socialist holidays. Furthermore, far from making a secret of it, his divorced mother had openly told neighbours that he was applying to leave the GDR.

On 7 September he was summoned to the MfS office in the town hall, where he learned that his application had been turned down. Although disappointed, he still had no idea what lay ahead. Two days later, during a staff meeting at the swimming pool, Jens was arrested in front of his colleagues and driven away by two Stasi men. Although a medium-size town of less than 140,000 inhabitants, Potsdam had at least three interrogation prisons, to cope with the numbers of people arrested and interrogated. Forced to hand over his clothing and other property, Jens was given a grey tracksuit and locked in a cell without the right to inform his mother or anyone else. By chance a friend of his had witnessed the arrest and hurried to tell her, which gave her time to remove a letter and the Charter of Human Rights from his room just before a Stasi search team arrived to give it a thorough going-over.

Interrogations began the next day, the first lasting eight hours without interruption. The interrogators noted that their prisoner did not seem frightened, but he had no way of knowing that his father, who worked as a conductor on trains travelling between the GDR and the Bundesrepublik, had volunteered several years before to act as a Stasi IM with the code name 'Schorsch', reporting principally on passengers' suspicious behaviour aboard the trains. On 10 September, 'Schorsch' reported to his case officer that he had had little contact with his son since divorcing his wife the previous year and only learned about the exit visa application from a neighbour on 2 September. Further, he reported that a friend of his son had also made an application, the two young men intending to stay with the friend's father in West Berlin.

The paranoia intensified. On 23 September, with Baumann Junior still under interrogation, his father was ordered to report to a safe house, where he made a statement, confirmed in a written report, that he had distanced himself from his son since the divorce, and declared that his ex-wife was wholly to blame for the deviant behaviour. The mood of 'Schorsch' at the meeting was noted by his case officer as 'disturbed'. A further meeting between the two men took place in October, at which 'Schorsch' furnished further information. His son was then still undergoing interrogation. The trial opened on 12 November after two months' solitary confinement. The defending lawyer had never met his client before arriving in court, had no knowledge of the 'case' against him and was not allowed to see the record of interrogation. After an adjournment of two days, the presiding judge sentenced 'the accused for traitorous activity to imprisonment for one year and eight months'. As a concession, which was not always granted in the GDR, the time spent under interrogation was to count towards the sentence. Conditions in the hard-regime long-term prison at Cottbus, where Jens was to serve his time, were extremely unpleasant, but this did not deter him from writing to the MfS district office in Potsdam to reinstate his exit visa application. As reason, he cited his total lack of prospects in the GDR after this imprisonment.

In the spring of 1983 a young man, just released from Cottbus prison, knocked on Frau Baumann's door with a letter from her son, from which she learned that Jens intended doing everything in his power to leave the GDR and settle in the Bundesrepublik after his release. Not knowing that her ex-husband was an informer, she passed this news on to him, which enabled 'Schorsch' to update his case officer and give a full description of the young man who had brought the illicit letter.

With a father like that, young Baumann needed no enemies. Fortunately his name was included in a list of detainees bought by the Bundesrepublik and transferred there on 24 August 1983, to begin life anew as a swimming instructor in Berlin-Tempelhof with a start-up award of DM 2,000 from the West Berlin Senate. His father continued to report what he learned of his son through his ex-wife, making a total of eight clandestine meetings with his case officer that year and twenty-two other reports. He was, however, about to get his comeuppance. With a son now living in West Berlin, 'Schorsch' was forbidden to work on railway trains that crossed the frontier and visits to his own elderly father in Heidelberg were also forbidden. Yet as late as 15 November 1989 – six days after the flood of people just walking through the Wall checkpoints in Berlin, IM 'Schorsch' met a new case officer and declared his willingness to continue spying for the Stasi.[7]

In 1983 Markus Riemann was twenty-two years old. As the son of a pastor, he and his four sisters had grown up in a loving and intellectually stimulating home, the only oddity being that Church policy required Pastor Riemann to move to a new parish every few years. Because of the discrimination against religious households, Markus was not able to attend university and had to earn a living as a gardener in Havelstadt, a suburb of Potsdam. Sharing a run-down flat in Potsdam with his girlfriend, he decided to form a circle of similarly environmentally conscious friends, who were worried at the nationwide pollution and damage to the environment caused by the GDR's mining and burning of lignite.

The British tradition of using fir trees as Christmas decoration is due to Prince Albert importing the idea when married to Queen Victoria. In Germany, it was normal for every church to have a fir tree on display at Christmas. One of Markus's friends suggested that a way of making other people aware of the damage to the GDR's forests from acid rain would be to collect some conifers from near the Czech border, where whole swathes of forest had been poisoned by industrial pollution. Five of the group set off to collect some dead spruces from there after arranging to spend the night in the house of a local pastor in the region. The pastor's telephone line was routinely tapped by the Stasi, with the result that, when they stepped off the train in Potsdam on their return, each holding a brown fir tree 1.5m high, they were arrested and interrogated all night long on the grounds that exposing environmental damage was 'hostile to government policy'.

The whole impressive might of the MfS swung into action, including search warrants and house searches. In Markus's flat, important evidence was seized: his record collection, an empty loose-leaf binder, an address list, photographs, letters and even empty envelopes and his copy of the New Testament. Meanwhile several pastors went together to the Town Hall to protest against the arrest of the five youngsters, informing the official in charge of 'Church affairs' there that at the Midnight Mass the congregations would be told, not just the familiar Christmas story, but also about the arrests. The Potsdam Five were then released, but the dead spruces were confiscated as 'evidence'. The story did not end there, however, because fines were imposed on Markus and two of the other boys totalling 2,000 Marks for 'failing to respect public order in that on 17 December with intent to disturb people they conspired to bring five environmentally damaged trees [to Potsdam] and display them with refuse in Potsdam churches'.[8]

Also in Potsdam, the technical college for training nurses and social workers was kept under particularly close scrutiny although the students were not rebellious intellectuals but ordinary kids seeking low-level professional qualifications. In September 1985 Carola Dessow began her studies there after failing an academic course at the Humboldt University in Berlin. Her divorced mother worked as a nurse in Leipzig, and this may have influenced her choice of back-up studies. Carola already had some black marks in her Stasi file, having voiced her opinions in Berlin about peace and disarmament, and frequented performances by young folk singers whose compositions touched on these issues. Unknown to the students at the technical college, the deputy principal and Carola's class teacher were both IMs, who reported that she continued voicing opinions that did not conform with official policy.

Among her crimes they reported were failing to read the SED newspaper, *Neues Deutschland*, refusing to learn to shoot an air gun in sport lessons and alleging that the GDR was not a democracy. A heavyweight Stasi operation was mounted to trap this student nurse, who was considered to be infecting the student mass. This included co-opting another girl student to report on her circle of friends. On 29 March 1986 when all the students were in the classrooms a fire brigade survey of the student accommodation was conducted, the 'firemen' being Department XX Stasi officers in borrowed uniforms. The building was closed to the public, including students, and a janitor who was an IM opened the door of Carola's room with a pass key. Photographs were made of handwritten and typewritten papers found among her possessions, including a draft 'letter to the government of the GDR'.

At that time when mechanical typewriters were used, the Stasi had an entire department that held specimens of text produced by every typewriter in the GDR, each of which had minor irregularities, such as a particular letter microscopically higher or lower than the others. Thus, any typewritten dissident leaflets could swiftly be traced to their author. Such a person was immediately liable to a prison sentence of not less than two years under sections 219 and 220 of 'the GDR law book'. It was not enough to arrest and imprison Carola, because the MfS wanted to catch all her 'fellow conspirators'. An additional IM was therefore found among the student nurses to join her circle of friends and report from the inside. It was easier said than done because Carola was wary of anyone trying to do this. The Stasi captain in Dept XX who was in charge of the operation noted in his 'Appreciation of the Working Plan' in August 1986 that the several IMs watching Carola had been unsuccessful in 'penetrating her circle'. Checks were run on all Carola's friends in Leipzig, Potsdam and elsewhere, in case any of them had requested an exit visa.

At the start of the autumn term of Carola's second year, a theatre group was formed in the technical college and a new IM was drafted in for this high-priority operation from the Potsdam film school, in the hope of getting close to her. In January another clandestine search was made of Carola's room. The incriminating papers were still in her locker with new ones on the subject of Chernobyl. The deputy principal of the school was 'informed of this by a student' and a four-page plan of operation drawn up. At 7.30 a.m. on 22 January the student IM telephoned the Stasi district office to confirm that Carola was in class. The janitor and an MfS senior lieutenant entered her room and checked that the incriminating papers were still there.

 Twenty minutes later the deputy principal took Carola from the class-room and accompanied her to her room, where the papers were 'discovered' and notification was immediately sent to the Ministry for Health Education, the SED district office in Potsdam and the college administration. Carola was taken in for questioning and, on the following day, a report on her case marked *Urgent* was sent by teleprinter to the head office of Department XX. But this was accompanied by the appalling news that the student body and the majority of the teaching personnel did not agree Carola should be suspended from the college, nor arrested. Rather, she should 'voluntarily' end her studies. And that, in short, is what happened. On 19 March 1987 she packed her remaining belongings and left the college.[9]

 Hers was the good fortune to be found out late in the Stasi years, and thus avoid serving several years in prison, which would earlier have been the case. Her punishment was therefore to be denied *any* further education.

 It is a measurement of SED paranoia that the Campaign for Nuclear Disarmament had been organising public demonstrations against government policy in Great Britain *for forty years* when the campaign against Carola Dessow caused much midnight oil to be burned in Stasi offices and many hundreds of man-hours to be wasted on this one futile 'operation', typical of tens of thousands of similar operations in the GDR, most of which ended more tragically for the Stasi's targets, young and old. Among the victims were the punk rockers and their male and female fans in the GDR, who boldly but ill-advisedly displayed their dyed hair, shaven heads and body-piercing to the public gaze, making themselves natural targets for random round-ups by the Volkspolizei, the Stasi and even the Kriminalpolizei. Their very existence was taken as unlawful criticism of the regime and, when they exacerbated this by flying paper aeroplanes bearing punk slogans or setting up an improvised pirate radio transmitter with very limited range to broadcast their music on a beach, for example, the full force of the GDR law was brought to bear on them. The GDR was governed by miserable old men and nowhere was this made more plain than in the Stasi's war on youth.

Notes

1. Ironically, the author was imprisoned for the crime of *illegale Eintritt* – illegal entry into the GDR
2. A. Funder, *Stasiland*, London, Granta 2004
3. Ibid, pp. 15–32
4. G. Schnell, *'Das Lindenhotel' Berichte aus dem Potsdamer Geheimdienstgefängnis*, Berlin, Links Verlag 2007
5. G. Schnell, *Jugend im Vizier der Stasi*, Potsdam, Brandenburgische Landeszentrale, 2001

6. K. Kassabova, *Street without a Name*, London, Portobello Books 2008, pp. 258–9
7. Schnell, *Jugend*, pp. 40–6
8. Ibid, pp. 47–50
9. Ibid, pp. 51–7

7

LIES, SPIES AND MORE SPIES

By the beginning of 1945 a large proportion of Hitler's millions of men in uniform were not ethnic Germans. They included Orthodox Russians and Ukrainians, Catholic Poles and Croats, Bosnian Muslims, Hindus and Sikhs from India, Belgians, Frenchmen, Scandinavians and even Central Asian tribesmen who could speak no European language. Although multi-ethnic recruitment into the Waffen-SS made the numbers look good on paper, it was obvious to all Hitler's senior officers that they could not win the war because it was impossible to replace the constantly escalating losses of men and materiel. The Nazi state imploded with its cities and factories flattened by ever-larger formations of bombers causing death and destruction by day and night, and its armed forces were trapped between the Soviet armies advancing inexorably on the eastern front and Allied ground forces driving in from the West. While the Western leaders were concentrating on winning the war against the Axis powers, Soviet supreme Josef Stalin was busily planning his strategy for the post-war world.

Many German servicemen of all ranks were convinced that the Western Allies would swiftly rearm them to fight 'the Ivans', who were patently not going to stay allied with the Western democracies for long after the German surrender removed the only reason for their brief alliance with Stalin. They reasoned that, because the USSR was almost certain to revert to Lenin's and Stalin's policy of international sabotage and subversion of the period 1917–39, the best time for the democracies to stamp out Soviet Communism – which they had failed to do with the interventionist forces 1917–22 – was to attack the USSR while it was still weakened by the loss of 30 million military and civilian casualties suffered in the war and the colossal destruction of infrastructure caused by Operation Barbarossa.

The flaw in this reasoning was all too apparent to Stalin. The democratically elected governments of the Western Allies did not have the autocratic powers necessary to declare war on anyone after Hitler's demise because their conscripted servicemen expected to be sent back to their homes and families as soon as the last shots were fired in Germany. They had, after all, been called up – or were given to believe they were in uniform – for 'the duration of hostilities' only. By that was meant hostilities against the Axis forces. Few of them would have welcomed the launching of a new war against the USSR, and millions of discontented soldiers, sailors and airmen voting in the next elections against the governments that were keeping them in uniform was something that no democratic government could contemplate. One of the most notable victims of this was Britain's Winston Churchill, who was described by Clement Atlee, his victorious opponent in the July 1945 general election, as 'the great leader in war of a united nation' yet was deeply dismayed to be voted out of office in that election, a scant few weeks after leading his country to victory.

Patently, other means had to be found to fight the new Cold War. Conveniently established at Pullach, south-west of Munich in the zone occupied by US forces, was a key department of Hitler's military intelligence, the Abwehr. Promoted to the rank of major-general, Reinhard Gehlen had headed the division Fremde Heere Ost (FHO) – Foreign Armies, East – since 1942, and survived the downfall of his boss, the anti-Nazi Admiral Canaris.[1] The admiral's fall from grace was due to telling Hitler in early 1944 that the war was already lost. His execution on 9 April 1945, when he was hanged naked on a gallows at Flossenburg concentration camp, was for alleged complicity in the plot to assassinate Hitler on 20 July of the previous year. However, Gehlen managed to avoid the savage retribution that fell on hundreds of other associates of the conspirators, and also rode out the uneasy reorganisation as the Abwehr was taken over by SS-Brigadeführer Walter Schellenberg and absorbed into the Reichssicherheitshauptamt (RHSA) – or Chief Administration of Reich Security.

Foreseeing the eventual German defeat as clearly as had his executed master Canaris, Gehlen diverted a part of FHO's staff to preparing for life after the war. Shortly before the surrender, he went to ground with his closest staff members after burying fifty-plus separate caches of microfilmed files and other documents relating to the Soviet armies and espionage activities inside waterproof canisters in the Bavarian and Austrian Alps, with which to buy favourable treatment from the Americans, by whom he intended to be captured. The files also included details of a network of pro-German stay-behind agents in the areas of Germany, Poland and Czechoslovakia occupied by the Red Army. According to Stasi sources, there were 600 such trained and equipped agents of Gehlen's organisation in the Soviet zone of occupied Germany alone.

On 22 May 1945 Gehlen voluntarily surrendered to, and was temporarily arrested by, an officer of the US Counter-Intelligence Corps (CIC) in Bavaria. The deal he proposed to his captor would have been outrageous if made to any other agency. It was quite simply to dig up the cached material and place it and his network of agents in Soviet-occupied territory in American hands, in exchange for his release and that of several close collaborators. Gehlen's name was removed from the list of POWs, so that he ceased officially to exist, thus blocking any attempt by the Soviets to demand rendition of this key figure in the struggles of the eastern front. Four months later, after Gehlen's proposed deal had been tossed back and forth between General Eisenhower's chief of staff, General Walter Bedell Smith, 'Wild Bill' Donovan, the former head of the Office of Strategic Services (OSS), and Allen Dulles of the OSS office in Berne, Switzerland. Gehlen knew he had worked out all his moves correctly. In late September, he and three senior staff officers were flown to the US, not as prisoners, but as valued collaborators in preparation for the Cold War. As a small bonus and token of the accuracy of his information, he broke the cover of several OSS officers who were undercover members of the US Communist Party.

Gehlen next surfaced in July 1946, back in Germany under the protection of G-2, the US Army intelligence branch. By the end of the year he had obtained the release of many former Abwehr officers, who became the nucleus of a reborn FHO in Pullach, where control was nominally in the hands of the Central Intelligence Agency (CIA) after it was set up in 1947. Gehlen's staff and network, initially known to its American supervisors as 'the Gehlen Organisation', grew to number nearly 400 officers and several thousand sources. Initially there was an embargo on recruiting former SS personnel. Whether this was on moral grounds or because such men might be susceptible to blackmail by the NKVD or others who knew about an embarrassing incident in their past is unclear. If the latter, it was with good reason – as the affair of Heinz Felfe was to show.[2]

After the inauguration of the Bundesrepublik in February 1949, West German pressure to control its own counter-espionage service resulted in it being officially handed over to the government of Chancellor Konrad Adenauer in 1956, when the official title was changed to Bundesnachrichtendienst (BND) or Federal Intelligence Service. Gehlen was the BND's first president, and held that position until 1968, when he was forced to resign after some spectacular breaches of BND security, including penetration by Soviet and East German agents. Of these, Heinz Felfe was the most embarrassing.

A former SS-Obersturmführer, he worked for British intelligence for some years post-war until being sacked due to doubts about his loyalty. Despite his dismissal, Felfe joined the BND in 1951 and rose rapidly due his ability to uncover low-level Soviet spies, sacrificed by Moscow to conceal his own activities. This record saw him promoted to take over the BND's entire 'Gegenspionage Sowjetunion', or anti-Soviet counter-espionage department. In this sphere, his department had the unrivalled advantage of being able to insist on interrogating every German POW returning from incarceration in the Soviet Union, which provided a constant stream of updates on the recovery of Soviet industry, political conditions, the rise and fall of prominent politicians and military figures – right down to the names of individual officials with whom the POWs had had dealings.

Like his mistrustful MI6 handlers in the British zone of occupation, the CIA liaison officers with the BND also had doubts about Felfe, who openly expressed anger at the 1945 American bombing of Dresden, his home town. He also did not conceal his disgust at what he regarded as the decadent softness of democratic society. In addition, he lived in a style far above what could have been afforded by his BND salary, buying a weekend home on the Austrian border, from where it was easy to slip across the frontier for clandestine meetings with Soviet couriers. His fall came not because routine surveillance revealed suspicious behaviour – since he knew personally all the BND's 'watchers', they could not be used in his case – but through indications from a Soviet defector in 1961. Günther Maennel was a captain in the counter-espionage branch of the MfS who had been paid $20,000 by the Gehlen Organisation as an incentive to stay in place. In debriefing he produced proof of many spies of the Hauptverwaltung Aufklärung (HVA) – or Chief Administration Intelligence – in high positions in the Bundesrepublik and, although he did not know Felfe's name, his description of him made it easy to identify the leak at the top of Gehlen's hierarchy.[3]

In the game of betrayals Maennel v. Felfe, it was discovered that Felfe had betrayed to the KGB more than 100 German agents in the USSR and satellite countries, and sent to Moscow, during the ten years he was spying inside Gehlen's organisation, copies of some 16,000 top secret BND documents in the form of microdots. These contained not only everything about his own department's anti-Soviet activities but also much confidential information about other departments of the BND, the customarily watertight internal security having frequently been waived for him because colleagues considered him a protégé of Gehlen himself.

The main target of Gehlen's organisation came to be the Stasi itself. Although little leaked out to the general public, there was a no-holds-barred war between the two services. In April 1953 former Wehrmacht officer Werner Haase was brought to Pullach by some old comrades and taken on, charged with heading station 120A in West Berlin. His work was to place reliable agents in the GDR. On an autumn evening less than six months after he was posted to Berlin, he was crouching with a colleague beside the Landwehrkanal, a waterway that divided the US sector from East Berlin. The two men were apparently playing with a toy motor boat. It was in fact towing a thin cord across to the other side, where one of Haase's agents was waiting. Catching the boat, he pulled on the cord, which was towing a telephone cable, the aim being to splice this into priority lines in the east, to snoop on MfS traffic. The team was being watched by a Stasi kidnap team, which overwhelmed Haase before the operation was ended and drove him rapidly through a crossing-point into East Berlin. At a show trial before the Supreme Court of the GDR, Haase was sentenced to life imprisonment, but was swapped for a captured Stasi agent after serving just three years.[4]

A stranger adventure played out across the frontier between the two Germanies was that of Otto John. A lawyer by training, he managed not to be caught up in the arrests after the failed assassination attempt on Hitler's life in July 1944 – for which his brother Hans was executed – by travelling to Portugal in the service of Lufthansa. From there, he was spirited away to Britain on a flying boat just before he was to be forcibly returned to Berlin. In an internment camp for German personnel, he met a Berlin-born British journalist named Sefton Delmer, who recruited him to work in black propaganda over Soldatensender Calais – a transmitter beaming morale-lowering and often specious news items to German forces in Europe, interspersed with popular music. A typical 'news item' to worry the men at the fronts was that foreign workers in the Reich were having sex with their wives whilst they were away. After the cessation of hostilities John assisted in screening senior German POWs in the endeavour to repatriate first those who had been anti-Nazi and could contribute to the political reconstruction of Western Germany.

In October 1954 John was invited by Theodore Heuss, first president of the Federal Republic, to become director of the newly established BfV. This was the new West German internal security organisation, still suffering from the backlash of what was known as 'the Vulkan affair', in which forty-four people had been accused of spying for Eastern Germany, but were released because of insufficient evidence. Other candidates for the post of director had been rejected by one or other of the three Allied High Commissioners, who did approve John. He, however, found many high-level enemies among fellow-countrymen who regarded him as a traitor for having worked for the British. On a visit to Berlin, John was drugged by an acquaintance named Dr Wohlgemuth, an agent of Soviet Intelligence, and recovered consciousness to find himself in a safe house used by the newly established KGB in the Karlshorst suburb of East Berlin. The director of West German counter-intelligence was a considerable catch for the

Soviets, who not only pressed John for insider information about the work of the BfV but also wanted him to 'work for a new Germany with them'.

When the news of John's presence in East Berlin reached the media, there was uproar – the more so when he broadcast what seemed like his motives for defecting. He was whisked away into the USSR for a long period of kid-gloves interrogations. Returned to East Berlin under constant surveillance, he began working out a way of escaping back to the West, and eventually managed to evade his watchers when driven across a checkpoint in disguise by Danish journalist Henrik Bonde-Henriksen. Not surprisingly, John was arrested by his former colleagues in the BfV and, nine months later in August 1956, placed on trial for betraying state secrets. It was never proven that he had betrayed any secrets, nor that he had gone voluntarily to East Berlin, but the no-appeal trial by judges trained under the Nazi regime dragged on until mid-December. John was finally sentenced, not to the two years' imprisonment demanded by the prosecution, but to four years in prison. He served thirty-two months of this before being released in the normal way with one-third remission for good behaviour.[5]

Another high-profile spy trial was that of Günter Laudahn, who managed to leave the GDR illegally in 1962 and was spotted by the CIA while in the refugee reception camp at Berlin-Marienfelde. Each side in the Cold War was obsessed with acquiring one of the other's cutting-edge fighter aircraft. After giving a clear account of his escape and much other information about life in the GDR, Laudahn seemed an ideal recruit and was eventually employed as a courier, the most dangerous link in any espionage network. This was in April 1966, when he was tasked with the theft of a MIG-21 fighter of the GDR's Luftstreitkräfte (LSK). The operation was both delicate and highly complicated, not least by the need for the pilot to fly through a forbidden zone near the border, where any LSK aircraft was likely to be intercepted and shot down by faster Soviet fighters. So, there was a provision for the MIG to be escorted by USAF jets once over that zone. Where this might have led is anyone's guess, but fortunately the LSK pilot got cold feet and betrayed the plot. When Laudahn returned to the GDR with false papers, which were spotted at the checkpoint, he was followed night and day until his arrest. In the Supreme Court of the GDR, he was sentenced to life imprisonment.[6] After spending several years in solitary confinement at Bautzen, he too was swapped at the Glienicke Bridge.

As a footnote, there was a rumour circulating at RAF Gatow when the author was stationed there that one Soviet or East German MIG fighter had actually landed on the runway, which was identical to that at the pilot's true base in the GDR because both had been constructed in the 1930s as Luftwaffe airfields. Whether he was talked down by false ground control instructions from West Berlin is unknown. Once on the ground, and realising from the absence of the other aircraft of his squadron that he had made a navigational error, the pilot managed to take off again before the runway could be blocked. But that was just a rumour ...

Notes

1. He had been involved in two unsuccessful pre-war attempts to depose or kill Hitler
2. See N.J.W. Goda, 'CIA Files Relating to Heinz Felfe, SS Officer and KGB Spy', https://www.fas.org/sgp/eprint/goda.pdf, for the 'desensitised' CIA account
3. Dobson and Payne, *Dictionary of Espionage*, pp. 210–11
4. Kierstein, *Heisse Schlachten*, p. 35
5. O. John, *Twice through the Lines*, New York, Harper & Row 1972, pp. 178–316
6. Kierstein, *Heisse Schlachten*, pp. 75–6

8

WAR ON THE WEST

As historian Kristie Macrakis comments in the introduction to her mammoth history of the Stasi,[1] most authors have concentrated on the organisation's internal repression of the population of the GDR. It was, however, from the day it was established, intended by Moscow to exercise the dual roles of internal repression and external espionage which the KGB outstation in East Berlin had been carrying out since 1945.[2] Four months after the foundation of the GDR, in February 1950 the MfS assumed both functions. There was, however, a third role to be filled. On 20 July 1951 Wilhelm Pieck noted in his diary:

> 8 p.m. Visit at home from Grauer and Slawin – Discuss creation of a counter-intelligence service, its head to have ministerial rank.

The two KGB officers he met that day were charged by Stalin with setting up under the umbrella of the MfS an espionage agency, which became the HVA. Its functions were:

> (a) to steal from the West – particularly the Bundesrepublik – political, military, economic and technological intelligence;
> (b) to disseminate disinformation in West Berlin and the Bundesrepublik;
> (c) counter-espionage in the GDR, including infiltration of agents into Western intelligence networks.[3]

As head of MfS, Erich Mielke laid down in a top secret paper that 'It is the aim of the Ministry for State Security to acquire ever-increasing quantities of scientific and technical intelligence from West Germany and other capitalist countries.'[4] This task was allotted to a most unlikely master-spy.

White-haired and unassuming, Heinrich Weiberg rode to work at the huge Normannenstrasse HQ of MfS on a bicycle. Instead of lunching with other high-ranking colleagues in their luxury dining room, he ate a hot dog at the snack bar outside the building. Notwithstanding his modest habits, Weiberg held the rank of major-general and both founded and headed the impressively named Sektor für Wissenschaft und Technik (SWT), whose exclusive function was stealing technical secrets from the West. Its work was given high priority by the SED leadership because it was seen as imperative if the appalling state of factories and research facilities in the GDR were to improve to anywhere near the level of technical development in the West. His top agent was Hans Rehder, code-named 'Gorbatschow',[5] a West German physicist employed by Telefunken and AEG, whose wife, Martha, acted as courier to pass on to HVA much invaluable military, IT and semiconductor research over a 28-year period without the husband-and-wife team ever being detected.

Although most HVA activity targeted sources in the Bundesrepublik, pressure from the KGB also imposed a high priority for anti-American operations. In Russian, the USA was known as *glavny vrag* meaning 'the main enemy' and HVA adopted an almost literal translation: *Hauptgegner* or 'principal adversary'.

During the Cold War many Turkish immigrants came to work in the Bundesrepublik. A garage mechanic named Hussein Yildrim was employed on a US base in West Berlin, where his casual chats with servicemen whose cars he was servicing enabled him to weigh up those who were finding it hard to live on their pay and were desperate for supplementary income. The first important 'find' he passed on to the Stasi was Specialist James Hall, stationed at the National Security Agency (NSA) base on the Teufelsberg, where 1,300 highly trained technicians and analysts listened in to top-level telephone and radio communications in the GDR. These included SED party bigwigs' telephone chats, the GDR and Soviet air force's VHF transmissions and the daily economic and intelligence briefings of the SED Central Committee – none of which was shared with West German agencies for fear of a leak. Known as America's 'Big Ear', the Teufelsberg was an artificial hill 400ft high, made when millions of tons of rubble from the carpet-bombing of Berlin were dumped on a bomb-proof Nazi bunker that could not be demolished. This highest point in the Allied sectors was called 'the devil's mountain' because it was composed of the ruin of so many homes. Aerials concealed within radomes atop the hill enabled US personnel to intercept and direction-find military transmissions over a wide spread of Warsaw Pact countries, the elevation giving a significant advantage over the much lower British intercept aerials at RAF Gatow.

Specialist Hall fed the HVA – who forwarded it to Moscow – just about everything secret that passed across his desk for five years, receiving a total of $100,000 in return. In 1985 Hall was rotated back to the US for advanced training and returned to Germany assigned to a military intelligence battalion based near Frankfurt. There, he rented an apartment off the base where Yildrim would photograph confidential documents at night, for Hall to return on arrival at the base the following morning. One single document was worth its weight in gold to the HVA. *The National Sigint Requirements List* was 4,000 pages long and listed the weak points and gaps in US electronic intelligence operations, enabling the Warsaw Pact high commands to exploit these weaknesses and take counter-measures. Hall also passed across details of President Reagan's Star Wars programme. Unfortunately, when his posting ended and he wished to continue selling confidential material to the Soviets back in the US, his greed got the better of him. He and Yildrim were caught in a sting operation when an FBI agent posed as a Soviet intelligence officer at a hotel in Savannah, Georgia, resulting in a forty-year prison sentence.

An even more ambitious plan was hatched when a US agency in West Berlin worked out how to cause a power cut that would stop transmissions from the control tower at the Soviet airport of Eberswalde, eighteen miles northeast of Berlin. A native Russian-speaker was then immediately to take over the frequency and talk down a Soviet pilot to land on a military airfield in West Berlin, where the runway would immediately be blocked to prevent his MIG taking off again. However, the intricate plan was betrayed by 19-year-old Sergeant Jeffrey, or James, Carney, a trained German linguist working in the USAF 6912th Electronic Security Group at Berlin-Marienfelde. There, analysis was done on intercepts obtained for NSA and US Air Force intelligence at the Teufelsberg listening station in the British sector.

Carney's NVA career began one night when he got drunk in a gay bar and presented himself at a Volkspolizei checkpoint on the sector border, offering in perfect German to spy for the GDR. Proving his bona fides by identifying the voices of several East German pilots that were played back to him, he was immediately recruited by HVA. Perhaps because his case officer Ralph Dieter Lehmann[6] realised that this shy American walk-in with a floppy handshake was an unstable and immature personality, Carney was given the codename 'Kid'. His motivation was neither ideological nor mercenary, but a huge chip on his shoulder from the belief that his undoubted skill at his intercept job was not better appreciated by his superiors. His high security clearance allowed him to copy and supply to HVA 1,983 documents classified 'secret' or above, of which the most important was a 47-page report on Operation Canopy Wing, the code name for an extremely sophisticated American electronic warfare operation to block the command and control communications of Warsaw Pact powers in the event of the Cold War turning hot. It was estimated that handing this to HVA cost the US military the equivalent of $13.5 billion.[7]

Some of Carney's documents were simply dropped at dead-letter boxes in the western sectors, to be picked up by HVA couriers; on other occasions, he took them personally into the eastern sector, for which he was paid 300DM or $175 per trip. He continued spying in this way until he was posted back to Goodfellow Air Base in Texas. This was in the era of the US armed forces 'Don't Ask, Don't Tell' policy on sexual orientation. Scared of being 'outed' as gay during a routine psychological test, Carney fled to Mexico City and requested political asylum at the GDR embassy. So important were the documents he had passed over to HVA that this was immediately granted and he was smuggled out with some sacks of laundry and put on a plane to Cuba. Once in the GDR, he had a nervous breakdown, was given accommodation in the home of two IMs and a well-paid job with the HVA, translating and transcribing intercepted US forces communications – including those of his old unit 6912 ESG. His identity was changed to Jens Karney, and an apartment that was luxury by GDR standards was made available for him, where he was kept under heavy surveillance with his phone tapped, all mail opened and examined – and no passport with which to leave the GDR. Although he lived with a male lover, which shocked the prim and proper HVA case officers, no action was taken over this.

In addition to 'Kid', the HVA had the luck of two other walk-ins from the electronic espionage complex of 6912 ESG. One was code-named 'Paul' and ended up like 'Kid', serving a long term in the high-security military prison designated the United States Disciplinary Barracks at Fort Leavenworth in Kansas. The identity of the other, code-named 'Optik', has never been revealed.[8]

Rainer Rupp was a 22-year-old high-IQ student of economics in Düsseldorf when recruited by the HVA and steered into a job at NATO HQ in Brussels. Working under the code-name 'Topaz', he passed via a courier everything that came his way. After marrying an English wife, who – in the words of HVA spymaster Markus Wolf – 'did not seem to take on board the significance of the fact that they spent their honeymoon in East Berlin', Rupp soon had her helping with the photocopying of documents. It was a small step from that to her getting a job in NICSMA – the NATO Integrated Systems Management Agency – and passing over all its classified material. Rupp's high IQ earned him rapid promotion in NATO, and he was eventually able to pass over *eyes-only* documents including details of Western plans for first-strike nuclear targeting. Worried about her two children, his wife eventually stopped working for the HVA, but Rupp continued all the way until 1989. Betrayed to German counter-intelligence not by Wolf but another former HVA officer, he was sentenced to twelve years imprisonment in 1994 and fined 300,000 Deutschmarks.[9] In recounting the story, Markus Wolf asked the philosophical–legal question:

> How can it be that after the peaceful unification of two states recognized under international law, the spies of one state go unpunished, whereas those who worked for the other state are sentenced to long prison terms and hefty fines?[10]

It is a fair point. There was, in fact, a bill presented to the Bonn parliament giving amnesty to employees of MfS, but it was never passed into law.[11] It wasn't only inter-German spying that continued to be punished after the reunification of Germany. With the demise of the HVA, Carney was trained and given employment as a train driver on the Berlin U-Bahn. He was eventually tracked down after his new identity was betrayed by Lehmann, his former Stasi case officer, to the BfV. When Carney's identity was confirmed by the tattoos on his arms that he thought made him appear more macho, the combined resources of BfV and USAF Office of Special Investigations (OSI) saw him literally kidnapped at gunpoint and flown back to the USA on a military aircraft. This illegal act provoked a formal protest from the German government, and should have prevented any action against Carney in a US court. He was nevertheless sentenced to thirty-eight years in Fort Leavenworth military prison, but released after serving twelve years. Attempting to return to Germany, he was informed that he was not welcome there and moved instead back to his home state of Ohio, where he lived with an adopted son by cutting lawns and doing other menial jobs.[12]

Carney's case has great resonance with the more recent one of Chelsea Elisabeth Manning, who, under her male name and US Army rank of Specialist E4 Bradley Manning, leaked a quarter-million classified files to Wikileaks in 2010 as a protest against the US involvement in Iraq. At Manning's trial in June to July 2013, she was sentenced to thirty-five years' imprisonment with a possibility of parole after eight years. An uninvolved observer of both cases cannot help asking why the US armed forces' appallingly poor security allowed two such low-ranking service personnel to gain access to so many highly classified documents. In addition, Carney was known to frequent gay bars and Manning had openly demanded gender reassignment and sent a photograph of herself dressed as a woman with wig and make-up to her supervising NCO in Baghdad, accompanied by a note reading, *This is my problem*. Half a century after the introduction of positive vetting procedures in NATO armed forces, their sexual conduct made both Carney and Manning security risks for the work they were doing.

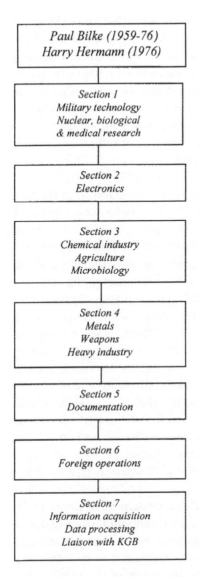

Organisation chart of Dept V Evaluation Unit 1959–76 (after Macrakis).

All the information they betrayed was evaluated by the HVA's Zentrale Auswertungs und Informationsgruppe (ZAIG) – of central evaluation group, where officers with specialist knowledge in many fields evaluated every item of incoming intelligence on a scale from 1 to 5. So important was this activity that the personnel jumped from thirty-five officers at the start to 500 or more twenty years later.[13]

The department was headed from 1959 by Paul Bilke, a serious and highly qualified engineer, but his deputy, a former biology teacher named Walter Thrane, who joined the department two years later, was a maverick.

Despite the daily use of lies, blackmail, sexual seduction and kidnapping in their work, HVA officers were expected to lead blamelessly moral private lives. Yet, after Thrane's marriage broke down – ironically because his wife complained of his very long working days – he began frequenting dance halls and picking up girls. Inevitably, this was reported to Normannenstrasse HQ, where he was *ordered* to sort out his marriage and refrain from such behaviour. As a warning shot, he was also demoted – as a result of which, on 11 August 1962, 34-year-old Thrane and his 20-year-old girlfriend used his authority as an HVA officer to get on a U-Bahn train at the Friedrichstrasse station and get off two stops later in West Berlin.

Strangely, Thrane did not immediately seek protection from the CIA or West German intelligence, which would certainly have been granted. Instead, he visited one of his own undercover agents, by whom his arrival on the 'wrong' side of the sector boundary was immediately reported to Stasi Centre. The HVA had, of course, a plan already prepared to kidnap any officer defecting to the West and bring him back for questioning before he could reveal SWT's secrets to Western intelligence agencies. Within hours, Thrane and the girl were back in East Berlin. Although it rapidly became clear that he had betrayed no secrets while in the West, he was condemned to death without any formal trial and his girlfriend was sentenced to four years' imprisonment for 'flight from the Republic'. Thrane's sentence was commuted to fourteen years in prison, over ten of which he was to serve in solitary confinement, for reasons of security. This case triggered a high-level damage-limitation exercise in HVA, which saw the evaluation team brought inside the structure of SWT. On release, Thrane worked as a bus driver in the grim industrial town of Eisenhüttenstadt, refusing even after German reunification to discuss his work for SWT with any representative of Western intelligence.[14]

Probably, SWT's best agent was Hans Rehder, nearly all of whose material received the highest evaluation. Category 1 translated to an estimated value of DM 150,000 per document, worked out in terms of research and development rendered unnecessary. It was estimated in 1971 that this highly specialised espionage saved a total of 26 million Ostmarks in the fields of chemistry, electronics and machine tools.[15] About one-third of Rehder's material was immediately passed on by SWT to KGB liaison officers in Karlshorst.

One aspect of this industrial espionage that is often overlooked is that some of the documentation could have legitimately been sold to the GDR. Thus Herr and Frau Rehder cost the companies that employed him a considerable loss over the years of their spying. They were not, however, among the 253 agents working in West Germany who were prosecuted for espionage after the German reunification, having died in 1985 at the age of 73.[16]

Probably the highest-paid Stasi agent in the Bundesrepublik was Peter Köhler, head of microchip research at Texas Instruments. During a business trip to the GDR, he found a new girlfriend in Erfurt and was persuaded by an HVA officer pretending to be a businessman to start feeding technical information on TI's development of semi-conductors and the 1MB microchip. It was calculated after the fall of the Wall that Köhler had received DM 500,000 in the course of eleven years' spying for the HVA.

Other top-level spies worked in companies like IBM, Siemens and AEG but many agents were able to access only low-level material and some even packaged publicly available titbits to keep up the appearance of working for the MfS. Others read the writing on the wall as the ultimate collapse of the GDR approached and quietly withdrew from intelligence activity – or did so when promotion in the 'day job' came their way and made the risks no longer acceptable. Borrowed from the KGB, a favourite ploy of HVA case officers working for Markus Wolf was to pick out lonely, and no longer young, single women working for bosses in sensitive situations such as the Bundesrepublik parliament or defence contractors like Messerschmidt-Bölkow-Blohm and Lorenz. A personable and sexually skilled 'Romeo' agent was despatched to seduce them, use pillow talk to compromise them and then oblige the victims to continue feeding information that came their way. One of these secretaries supplied her lover/handler with several hundred items of Category 1 aeronautics and space technology.

There is in espionage no rule which says one cannot mix techniques. In one case a 'Romeo' seduction was also a false flag operation. It would be unrealistic to expect a spymaster to tell the truth, the whole truth and nothing but the truth, but one instance in Markus Wolf's often misleading autobiography is the case of a super-Romeo identified only as Roland G. An accomplished actor and theatre director, he was given voice lessons to acquire a Scandinavian lilt enabling him to pose as a Danish journalist, frustrated because his country was treated as second class inside NATO. Seducing a strongly Catholic secretary named Margarete who was employed at SHAPE HQ, then at Fontainebleau in France, he procured a steady stream of useful information from her – until the day when she announced she could continue neither her espionage for him, nor their sexual relationship without first being confessed by a priest and then getting married to Roland. He managed to convince her that a reliable Danish priest could be found – which he duly was, in the Stasi local office at Karl-Marx-Stadt. After voice coaching to convert his strong Saxon accent into something like a Danish one and learning a limited number of Danish words to impress Margarete, the 'priest' confessed her in a remote country church, after which she continued to feed classified documents to her 'fiancé' until he was recalled from West Germany for security reasons.[17]

Since the emotions aroused in these seductions were real on one side of the relationship, it was never possible to predict the eventual outcome. Another operation recounted by Wolf, which may be true, features a highly intelligent West German postgraduate student named Gabriele Gast, who was allotted the code-name 'Gaby'. She had a 'rough trade' affair with a Stasi officer while researching her doctoral thesis on the political role of women in the GDR. Gaby's high potential had also been spotted by a BND recruiter, through whom she was taken on as a political analyst at the HQ of BND in Pullach. On one of her trips to meet her lover in the GDR, and to undergo espionage training, a form of marriage was arranged. It eventually became apparent to Wolf that the main attractions of her affair were its totally illicit nature and the thrill of working at extremely high level for both the BND and the HVA. Few West German agents actually met any HVA officer above their own case officer, but Gaby was accorded the unusual honour of meeting Wolf himself no fewer than seven times, if his account can be believed. At one of these meetings she surprised him by predicting the spate of anti-Soviet protest movements in the satellite states. Although Gaby was assured early in 1990 that all HVA files relating to her would be destroyed on reunification, she was eventually blown by a Stasi officer who bought himself immunity by giving enough information about her activities and personal details for German counter-espionage officers to arrest her.[18]

Notes

1. K. Macrakis, *Die Stasi-Geheimnisse*, Munich, Herbig 2008
2. Ibid, pp. 13, 15
3. Kierstein, *Heisse Schlachten*, p. 25
4. Macrakis, *Die Stasi-Geheimnisse*, p. 24
5. German spelling of the Russian name Gorbatchev
6. Some sources name him as Hans-Dieter Lehmann
7. *BBC News Magazine*, 19 September 2013. How this was calculated is unclear. It was possibly the cost of setting up Canopy Wing, which had to be replaced by another programme
8. Kierstein, *Heisse Schlachten*, pp. 70–1
9. M. Wolf, *Memoirs of a Spymaster*, London, Pimlico 1998, pp. 299–300
10. Ibid, p. 301
11. Ibid, p. 326
12. Kierstein, *Heisse Schlachten*, pp. 76–7.
13. Some sources say staff peaked at 1,000
14. Macrakis, *Die Stasi-Geheimnisse*, pp. 44–7
15. Ibid, pp. 48, 62
16. Ibid, pp. 32–6
17. Wolf, *Memoirs of a Spymaster*, pp. 137–8
18. Ibid, pp. 142–8

9

WAR IN THE AIR

On 16 August 1951 HVA was given the cover name Institut für wirtschaftliche Forschung (IWF), meaning Institute for Scientific Research. The first head of this new enterprise was Anton Ackermann, another of the returnees who had spent the war in Moscow and returned early to have a career in GDR politics that ended after he unwisely disagreed with SED policy. His Soviet 'adviser' Andreij Grauer was so dictatorial, ruthless and unpopular that his own staff nicknamed him 'Little Beria'. He got on so badly with Ackermann that he was withdrawn by Moscow in the following year.[1] In September 1953 Markus Wolf – perhaps the most famous spymaster of the Cold War – took command of HVA. Known as 'the man without a face' because he was only identified – and that by chance – in 1978, Wolf had also spent the war years in the USSR – in his case, working in the Comintern before returning to Germany posing as a journalist covering the Nuremburg trials.

From 1945 until the building of the Wall in 1961 a steady stream of refugees crossed into West Berlin and the Bundesrepublik. Although low-level security checks were run on them while in the reception camps, it was impossible to catch every HVA-trained agent, who travelled in the stream to take up life as a sleeper or active spy, mainly in Western Germany and the USA. If ever an intelligence service had an easy way of infiltrating spies and sleepers, this was it.[2]

One such agent was Harald Gottfried. Code-named 'Gärtner', and trained in the use of invisible inks, mini-cameras, codes and radio transmitters, he was inserted in the stream of refugees as a 'future agent' in 1956, but produced no results until 1968 because his target area was nuclear research and establishing his bona fides as a loyal West German took several years.

The sheer numbers of Stasi agents in the flood of refugees had, perversely, an inbuilt problem. For obvious reasons, there are no statistics, but there was always a risk when sending agents and sleepers into the West that they would come to like the much more comfortable life, to enjoy the political and physical freedom and, of course, to enter relationships and beget children who would hardly want to return to the greyness and perpetual fear of 'socialist' Eastern Europe. In the course of writing this book, the author has interviewed one false refugee from Poland and one Czech who decided never to 'go back'. Although knowing that there would be no prosecution now for admitting their past, they are still so buttoned-up after decades of clandestine life that they gave little detail as to how and why they came to the West during the Cold War. Secrecy gets to be a habit, as it did for some British friends of the author who were employed on secret work during the Second World War and yet never told their spouses about it during sixty subsequent years of happily married life.

The most successful agent to arrive in the Bundesrepublik as a refugee was without doubt Günter Guillaume. Despite the French surname, he was picked up by the Stasi and approved by the KGB while working as a labourer, living in East Berlin, but employed in West Berlin. Marcus Wolf personally groomed Guillaume, who had the correct anti-Western political views, for his mission. He also had a war-wounded father reputed to have tended the wounds of Federal Chancellor Willy Brandt during the war. In 1956, Günter and his wife, Christel, emigrated to West Germany as pretended refugees. Whether or not the story is true that his father wrote to Brandt asking him to assist his son's career, Günter rose steadily through the hierarchy of the Social Democratic Party of Germany, to become a personal assistant to the West German chancellor. From then on, his slavish devotion to work on Brandt's staff earned him access to everything that passed through the Chancellor's office – all of which he passed to East Berlin.

In 1974 the devoted PA was outed by the BfV, triggering a scandal that could not be hushed up and caused Brandt to resign the chancellorship. Guillaume was sentenced to thirteen years in prison for espionage; for acting as his courier, Christel received a sentence of eight years, but the couple was released in a spy swap in 1981. Sources in the Stasi said that Brandt's political ruin was not intended, but collateral damage – he had advocated rapprochement with the GDR and would have been more useful in office than in disgrace.

When 32-year-old Werner Stiller, the highest-ranking HVA officer to defect, came over to West Germany on 18 January 1979 his SED credentials were impeccable. Active in the Freie Deutsche Jugend (FDJ) – the Communist successor to the Hitler Youth – since the age of 14, he was a physics graduate trained to seek out nuclear research secrets. His final exam paper was on the subject of electron spin resonance spectroscopy research into the behaviour of free radicals. Together with his Hungarian wife, Erzsebet, he settled in East Berlin, supplementing his salary from a day job as a physicist with nightly training by Stasi officers in techniques like surveillance avoidance and the use of dead letter boxes. In 1972 he was given the rank of full-time MfS *Oberleutnant* in the Sektor Wissenschaft und Technik, with glowing reports from his instructors as a politically active and ideologically sound young man who got on well with colleagues. The only black mark against him was his impulsive nature. With his academic background, it was inevitable that he would be used in the acquisition of nuclear research.

His work was more than a desk job, involving contacts in cafes and safe houses, using money and ideological motivation to run three HVA agents, three West German sources in the Bundesrepublik and thirty IMs in the GDR, particularly targeting the nuclear research facility in Karlsruhe and the data processing programs of IBM in Stuttgart and Siemens in West Berlin that had military implications for the East German Nazionale Volksarmee (NVA). He also travelled to meet his West German agents in Prague, Budapest and other cities where they could go without exciting suspicion. The Stasi actually had a permanent office at Lake Balaton in Hungary because it was a tourist resort that could be visited by people from both the satellite countries and the West. In Vienna Stiller set up a network with connections to Silicon Valley that was able to acquire commercially some strategic items that were embargoed for sale to the GDR. Stiller's high security clearance was obvious in one or two trips he also made under false identity into the Bundesrepublik itself – normally a no-go area for any officer knowing all the secrets he did.

In January 1978 Stiller was on the way to meet an agent on the inner-German border, and stopped for a nightcap at a hotel in the winter sport resort of Oberhof, where he chatted up the pretty waitress named Helga, who made no secret of what she felt after being refused a visa to attend her brother's wedding in the West. Was she genuine or a Stasi *provocatrice*? Stiller had to know, so he visited the district Stasi office and found she was genuine. After waiting a few weeks, he paid her another visit and showed her his Stasi ID, to which the universal reaction was fear and loathing. Helga took one look and told him to get out, so he confessed that he was looking for someone to help him make contact with a Western agency. One week later, she telephoned to say she would help. They were both taking a colossal risk, not least because, as Stiller well knew, the West German agencies had many double agents and moles planted by the Stasi and KGB, who might betray their approach. The relationship was complicated by them both falling in love after he explained to her that her known political attitude gave her no future in the GDR, so she ought to flee with him.

He did not tell Helga that he was married, but his domestic life was also complicated, with his wife giving birth to their second child. On the ride back from the hospital with mother and child, Stiller told her that he was leaving her for another woman. She knew enough about the Stasi's moral code to threaten to tell his boss he was having an affair. Things got even worse for Stiller when his immediate superior Horst Vogel saw Stiller and Helga together in Oberhof and called him into the office, to ask who was his lady friend. Four weeks went by and Stiller was given an explicit warning to sort out his marriage, or else. Although his boss knew instinctively that the liaison with Helga was serious, Stiller still was not sure.

At this point – it was now the end of April – Helga's brother Herbert paid a visit from the West, with his new wife, and Stiller gave him a briefcase with a secret compartment containing a letter offering to work for the BND. Herbert, however, misunderstood and handed the briefcase and letter to the West German frontier post on his return journey. The letter apparently reached its destination because Herbert was twice visited by a BND officer who said his name was Ritter, in the hope of clarifying whether Stiller's offer was genuine. Deciding that it was, he sent an oral message to Stiller via Helga on Herbert's next visit to his sister, when Stiller was on holiday in Hungary with his wife and children.

He must have given Helga some form of code to use on the telephone, since all calls into or from the GDR were monitored. After learning that she had received a message from the BND, Stiller went with her to a dead letter drop under a pile of leaves in a Berlin park. Hidden in a false log, they found everything necessary for their flight across the border, including a letter of welcome from his BND case officer. In Stiller's safe house, where he had been hiding files and microfilms in a hole in the ceiling since February, they broke open the log and used the list of frequencies to listen to a coded message that evening, decoding this with the key supplied.

A busy exchange of information began in July 1978, with Helga encoding the replies and sending them, written in invisible ink, and some of the microfilms in envelopes directed to cover addresses in the Bundesrepublik. In these letters were the damning betrayals of Stiller's agents in the West, which he had to give to prove that he was not a Stasi plant. But in betraying his agents, Stiller was taking the greatest risk so far. If the BND had them arrested, the Stasi would arrest him. In fact, on 28 August its mail interception department forwarded a suspicious letter, whose return address did not exist, to the operational-technical section. The coded message of blocks of five digits, written in invisible ink, was swiftly revealed with chemicals and an intensive hunt was launched to track down the spy concerned.

By then, both Stiller and Helga were taking more and more risks. On 7 December she secreted a despatch of material for the BND in a toilet aboard an inter-zonal train, which she left while it was still in the GDR. Her coded telegram informing the BND where to find it was intercepted by the Stasi, whose searchers spent the following forty-eight hours taking eleven coaches apart and checking out the twenty-two toilet compartments without finding anything.

BND 'Agent 688' – i.e. Stiller – had received 1,841 five-digit code blocks in the last six months.

For the BND, the microfilms were the most important proof that Stiller was genuine. The first escape plan in mid-December foundered because Stiller's false passport supplied by BND described his eyes as blue instead of brown. At the same time, Helga made a serious error in despatching her collection of crystal glass to her brother in Coburg, showing her real address in case it went astray. The handwriting on the parcel was recognised by a graphologist in the postal department as being that of the person who had sent the incriminating telegrams. An IM was sent to Oberhof to check Helga's identity but he failed to find her. After learning only that she had a boyfriend in Berlin, he travelled back there. It was the most amazing piece of luck for the two spies, and gave them much-needed breathing space. The new escape plan was for Stiller to travel on an inter-zonal train to Hannover using another false passport, while Helga and her son were to go to Warsaw, where a BND courier would bring them their new identity papers.

By this stage, the Stasi's postal department had checked 462,500 letters and filmed everyone who posted a letter in East Berlin. Their colleagues in the radio intercept department were also busy recording fifteen transmissions totalling 1,841 five-figure groups that BND had sent to 'Agent 688'. Stiller at this point had a crisis of conscience and wrote his wife a farewell letter, enclosing 10,000 Ostmarks, to tide her over what was obviously going to be severe punishment for his betrayal:

> When you read this, the worst lies behind me. Since we first met I have been working for the other side. At the beginning of last year I made the mistake of telling you about Helga. Then Vogel saw us together in Oberhof ... It would make no sense to take you with me because you have lived too long in [the GDR]. The children will be safe here. There are so many things I cannot understand.[3]

That evening – it was 19 January 1979 – after most of the staff had left the HQ on the Normannenstrasse, Stiller collected all the material he could lay hands on. He failed to force open Vogel's safe, but did succeed in finding in the secretary's safe the pass which he and his colleagues used at the Friedrichstrasse U-Bahn station when they wanted to leave messages for agents in West Berlin. Some instinct made him wary of the BND's plan, so he decided on the spur of the moment to use the pass and make his own way independently across the sector boundary. There was, however, one flaw in this plan: the secretary would normally have added a date stamp to the pass. This being missing, Stiller had an uneasy moment at the pass gate in the Friedrichstrasse station before the duty officer accepted his argument that his mission was urgent and let him through anyway. On the platform, waiting for the next train into West Berlin he spent what he called 'the longest six minutes of my life'[4] while doing his best to avoid the closed-circuit cameras in case he was identified by some eagle-eyed colleague watching the screens.

Leaving the train at the first possibility, he took a taxi to Tegel airport in the French sector and there identified himself to an immigration officer. How right he had been to make his own way across was discovered long afterwards in the Stasi's files at the BStU: a flurry of activity at the BND had been picked up by Stasi agents in the West and triggered a special watch on the train he should have taken, which would probably have ended his adventure before he ever reached the West – after which he would have been sentenced to life in jail or shot. First on the scene at Tegel airport was an officer of the Service de Documentation Extérieure et de Contre-Espionage (SDECE), which was then France's most important intelligence service. As the office filled with representatives of West German and other intelligence agencies, Stiller handed the French officer the file on a Stasi agent working undercover in France, and placed on the table a 4in high pile of microfilms – and about DM 14,000 in cash, explaining that he had brought it with him in case he was not paid enough for his betrayal, because he needed capital to start a business!

By the skin of his teeth, Stiller had pulled off his escape, having timed it carefully to fall in the winter holiday season, so that it was not immediately obvious which member of staff had broken into the secretary's safe and taken the pass.[5] That same evening, orders were given to search Helga's apartment and intensify the monitoring of her telephone calls. The following morning, *Neues Deutschland* published her photograph as a person wanted by the Stasi. She and her son were, however, safely in Poland, while Stiller was giving his debriefing officers information on the Stasi agents to be arrested. From there he was taken to Cologne, making the headlines across the Atlantic, where his escape was hailed as an intelligence triumph in the *New York Times*. Broadcasting the news, West German television added the spurious detail that a woman and a child had travelled with him – this to protect Helga, who was still in Poland.

The news was the worst present for HVA spymaster Marcus Wolf, whose birthday it was. He was furious, but his reaction paled into insignificance when compared with Mielke's. When Wolf called, to give the news, Mielke screamed, 'You load of shit! You might as well invite the enemy [sic] to our meetings and be done with it. You all make me sick!'[6]

At the Normannenstrasse HQ a vast damage limitation operation was immediately launched, with agents recalled from the West and a list compiled of compromising material that was missing. Officers visited Stiller's wife, and when told the news, she fainted with the baby in her arms and a doctor was called. When she came to, Erzsebet told them all she knew – about Stiller's increasing drinking, nervousness and irritability that led to bitter arguments and also about his sexual preferences and the time he came home with scratches from Helga's nails on his back. As to his letter for her with the 10,000 Ostmarks, it was intercepted before being delivered. All she did get was an order to change her address and her job – and never again to speak of her husband or what had happened. Next, all Stiller's IMs were hauled in for questioning, from which a profile was built up of their absent case officer as a man who had been giving warning signs for six months that he was under severe tension.

Stiller was by this juncture in an ultra-secure BND safe house in Munich, Bavaria, guarded by twenty men round the clock. When Helga arrived the following day, the reunion was, to put it mildly, a great disappointment for her as he announced that the affair was all over and she was now just a friend to him. His debriefing, which covered not just his own work, but every aspect of the HVA, was interrupted at weekends, when he went climbing in the Bavarian Alps accompanied by armed BND bodyguards. He identified photographs of, among other, Markus Wolf – who was no longer 'the man without a face' when it was published in a March 1979 edition of Der Spiegel. Stiller's debriefing also resulted in 100 trials of Stasi agents and fifteen others were expelled from the Bundesrepublik. More to the point, his debriefing let the BfV know that the MfS main targets for espionage in Western Germany were industrial and scientific intelligence – and also just how widely these key areas in the Bundesrepublik were infiltrated by Stasi agents.

For all this information, he was awarded DM 400,000. Mielke's rage at Stiller's escape did not subside. After having him condemned to death in absentia, he gave orders that the turncoat should be tracked down and brought back 'dead or alive'. His actual words were, 'I want him brought back and, if that can't be done, rendered harmless'.[7] Several agents trained to carry out Smersh-type assassinations were placed on standby, but the security screen around Stiller was apparently impenetrable, despite a number of Stasi deep-penetration agents inside the BND and BfV. The claustrophobic high security around Stiller made Helga feel as though she was in prison. When Stiller was allowed to go windsurfing on Lake Garda under guard, to give him a break, she was not included in the party. While there, he picked up a pretty Italian girl for a brief affair, telling her his true identity before the BND bodyguards could haul him back to Munich.

This made his continued presence in Europe insecure, so he was shipped off to the USA for another three-month interrogation by the CIA, followed by a term in a secure language school to improve his English. To set him up in his new identity as Hans-Peter Fischer, he was also given a social security number, credit cards and a quarter-million dollars – which he proceeded to lose in its entirety by gambling on the Stock Exchange, whose workings fascinated him. Perhaps because of this he either chose, or was advised by his handlers, to take a master's course in business studies. St Louis in the state of Missouri was selected because it was in an area thought not to be covered by any Stasi agents or sleepers. There, he developed an amazing talent for understanding the money markets. His athletic lifestyle and blond good looks impressed younger female students, so he enjoyed every minute of his new life.

Life in what James Jesus Angleton, sometime head of CIA counter-espionage, called 'the wilderness of mirrors' is never straightforward. There are indications that the BND courier who serviced Stiller before his flight was a double agent but, for reasons unknown, did not betray Stiller. When this became known in the Normannenstrasse, he was trapped and sentenced to imprisonment for life, but released after four years, presumably in return for cooperating during his debriefing.

Peter Fischer finished his retraining at the age of 34 and was employed by the subsequently infamous investment bank of Goldman Sachs in New York; he also married a much younger American woman said to have connections with the Mafia without telling her that he already had a wife and two children in the GDR. When this came out, she was horrified – and would have been more so had she known that Erzsebet ended up cleaning toilets for a living because her husband was a traitor. After moving to Goldman Sachs' London office, Fischer specialised in advising the firm's German clients, living a life of luxury in a fashionable loft apartment with a holiday house on the Côte d'Azur. Of this time, he said, 'There is great similarity between spying and banking. In each, you work with personal contacts. [In New York and London], I influenced my clients and they ... wanted to betray me.'

After the reunification of Germany, he moved to the Lehman Brothers branch in Frankfurt, where his luck eventually ran out. After a series of bad investments, he 'was let go', which did not stop him talking his way into setting up a real estate business in Leipzig and continuing his high-life existence and multiple love affairs – and taking part in a film about his double life,[8] as well as writing a book about it[9] and being featured in three articles in the mass-circulation news magazine *Der Spiegel* in 1992.

He might have done better to keep a lower profile. As in many divorces accorded in New York State, he was taken for a fortune by his American wife and also received many death threats from former Stasi colleagues who understandably resented his riches while they lived in poverty after the fall of the Wall. Even his wives, who had every reason to hate him, agreed that he had a golden tongue, which enabled Fischer to talk his way back into a job at Goldman Sachs in Frankfurt, where he was again fired – this time for sexual harassment, which he denied, and for the undesirable publicity he attracted. After marrying another younger woman, a Hungarian, his last known address was in a high-rise apartment in the suburbs of Budapest, where he may also have a real estate firm.[10]

When Kristie Macrakis interviewed Horst Vogel, who had been Stiller's section leader at the time of his defection – and whose career must have suffered severely on that account – he turned, in her words, 'red with rage'. After he had calmed down, he told her, 'People love [the idea of] betrayal, but no one loves a traitor.' Markus Wolf, when he was interviewed by Macrakis, confined himself to saying of Stiller/Fischer, 'He's no friend of mine.'[11]

The motivations of traitors vary from ideological persuasion to hatred of a father-figure to lust for a better lifestyle – the dream of a house in California or Florida with two cars and a private swimming pool incited many KGB and other East European intelligence officers to defect at great risk to their lives. In the case of Stiller/Fischer, the most important factor in his defection was his compulsive womanising, which was unacceptable in the paradoxically puritan MfS, and in the GDR generally, obliging him to seek a society where promiscuity was condoned behaviour in a successful man.

As a sad footnote to the whole affair, there is a book entitled *Verratene Kinder*[12] – *The Children they Betrayed* – written jointly by Edina Stiller, the daughter Stiller left behind in the GDR in 1979, and Nicole Glocke, a daughter of one of Stiller's agents in the Bundesrepublik, whom he betrayed to the BfV after his defection. The title says it all. If things do not work out for defectors, they have only themselves to blame, but very often their families are also punished – in their case, for something they have not done.

Nicole Glocke's father, Karl-Heinz, was 44 at the time of Stiller's defection, employed as chief economist in the strategically important Rheinisch-Westfälischen Elektrizitätswerken company. Aged 9 at the time, Nicole was at least able to console herself later with the thought that her father had spied through genuine ideological motivation and been betrayed by a traitor. An attractive brunette living in Berlin, she grew up to be a successful journalist and scientific rapporteur for the German Parliament. Edina Stiller, aged only 7 at the time of her father's defection, grew up in uncomfortable accommodation with her underpaid mother in an ugly industrial town, to which they had been forcibly reallocated as punishment and where they were shunned by all previous friends. She had to swallow an additional bitter pill when she later learned that her father had betrayed his country for the basest of all motives – sex and money. Worse, he had chosen to abandon his wife and two children, leaving with them the reflected stigma of treachery as their sole emotional legacy. It is not surprising that she was unable to trust any man or keep any relationship for long. She grew up to be rather haunted-looking, employed as telephone and telex operator for the Nazionale Volksarmee, dropped by her friends when she became an alcoholic, hiding the empty bottles and other evidence from her mother, with whom she still lived.

She did not see her father for two decades after the awful morning when his colleagues knocked on the door in Berlin with the awful news. Having tracked him down, living in some luxury in Budapest with yet another young partner, she found him devoid of any apparent guilt, but he did help her to make contact with Nicole Glocke, who had already traced him during a visit he made to Berlin. Possibly for reasons of journalistic curiosity, Nicole wrote to Edina in April 2002, saying that she would like to discuss the effect on her life of Stiller's defection. Edina was amazed that the daughter of one of her father's victims should apparently feel no hatred for the man who had put her own father in prison and ruined his career. Having got to know each other, the two young women collaborated on the book, which proved a useful therapy for Edina. After the end of the GDR she retrained as a lawyer and notary in the reunited Germany.

Notes

1. Kierstein, *Heisse Schlachten*, p. 25
2. C. Andrew and V. Mitrokhin, *The Sword and the Shield, the Mitrokhin Archive*, New York, Basic Books 1999, p. 437
3. Macrakis, *Die Stasi-Geheimnisse*, p. 92 (abridged)
4. Ibid, p. 93
5. Wolf, *Memoirs of a Spymaster*, p. 177
6. Macrakis, *Die Stasi-Geheimnisse*, p. 95
7. Article by C. Fuchs, in *Der Spiegel*, 5 February 2013
8. *Der Agent*, ARTE-TV, 2 February 2013
9. *Im Zentrum der Spionage*, Minden, Hase u. Koehler Verlag 1986 and 1994.
10. Article by C. Fuchs
11. Macrakis, *Die Stasi-Geheimnisse*, p. 102
12. N. Glocke and E. Stiller, *Verratene Kinder*, Berlin, Links Verlag 2010

10

HVA VERSUS MI5

The old German Communist Party KPD had a safe base in London before the Second World War, when a number of its leading lights moved there to keep out of the Gestapo's clutches. They included Jürgen Kucyzinski, employed for a while at the London School of Economics, considered by many at the time and afterwards as a second Lenin School. Kucyzinski's daughter, code-named 'Sonja', repaid the political asylum granted her parents and herself by transmitting to GRU Centre in Moscow the despatches of the notorious Soviet spy Klaus Fuchs, who betrayed British nuclear secrets to the USSR, was imprisoned and then sought asylum in the GDR on his release. There were many other future members of SED and other East German bodies who spent the war safely in Britain before re-emigrating after 1945 to work against their wartime host country. Before and after the inception of the GDR it became difficult to infiltrate East Germans into Britain, but there was an easy alternative: they were first allowed to 'escape' to the Bundesrepublik and afterwards came to Britain with no visa requirement after obtaining West German identity documents.

In 1959 the GDR Foreign Ministry was allowed to set up a trade mission in London, ostensibly to promote business between British companies and potential clients in the GDR. Incorporated under the name KfA Ltd, the mission afforded cover to military intelligence and other HVA officers, its last head becoming the first ambassador to the Court of St James when Edward Heath's government finally granted diplomatic recognition to the GDR in February 1973, just a few months after joining the European Community. From then until the reunification of Germany in 1990 the accredited 'diplomats' in the GDR embassy – in premises at 34 Belgrave Square, an address selected deliberately to be confusingly near to the Bundesrepublik embassy – were for the most part Stasi officers using their diplomatic status as a cloak for spying and subversion. The embassy was, for them, Residentur 201. Presumably the staff in the British embassy in East Berlin were also spying – and being spied on themselves. Who won that game of mirrors will never be known by the common public.

After the expulsion of ninety Soviet 'diplomats' and the declaration as *personae non gratae* of fifteen others who were out of the country in September 1971, the GDR embassy staff arriving seventeen months later were, in a sense, replacements for the missing KGB men. So it is not surprising that at least 50 per cent of their work was directly for Moscow. Like the KGB and GRU (Soviet military intelligence), they increased their effectiveness by using many left-wing Britons to help in the theft of intellectual property and the subversion of British political parties and trade unions. These included members of the CPGB, who were prepared to do favours for the 'socialist' countries and ignore the KGB's and Stasi's appalling human rights record. Many other fellow-travellers, as they were called, later professed surprise that contacts which they considered part of a fight against fascism were actually assisting the espionage service of a state which considered itself – or was considered by Mielke – to be at war with Britain, the country which was referred to in internal documents as *der Feind* – the enemy.

In the same way that satellite state intelligence officers were routinely warned off direct contacts with CPGB members, which 'belonged' to the KGB, so certain party members were ordered not to have any direct contact with Iron Curtain intelligence services or travel to Eastern Europe for the subsidised holidays and medical treatment they could have enjoyed there. Barbara Einhorn, a sociologist at Sussex University, was one academic who had many contacts with members of the GDR embassy, almost certainly knowing that some of them were intelligence officers. Her husband, Canon Paul Oestreicher of Coventry Cathedral, formerly active in Amnesty International, was also involved. Einhorn, who held a New Zealand passport although having German parents, was arrested and interrogated for five days at Hohenschönhausen prison after being picked up for contacting GDR dissidents Ulkike Poppe and Barbel Bohley. She shrugged this off as an unfortunate mistake although would presumably have been enraged to be locked up for several days in Britain simply because she had been talking to someone.

Yorkshirewoman Fiona Houlding (code name 'Diana') was recruited while teaching English in Leipzig in a 'Romeo' seduction by HVA officer Ralf-Jürgen Böhme.[1] Dr Robin Pearson, a student from Belfast at Hull University (code name 'Armin'), collected information for his HVA contacts there and in Edinburgh, Leeds, London and York.[2] He also travelled to Leipzig University, where everyone he met had to report their conversations to the Stasi. Other British collaborators may have had different motives to make contact with the HVA spies. John Sandford of Reading University claimed to believe that repeated meetings with men he must have known worked for East German intelligence were a way of building bridges which might influence the Stasi to moderate its persecution of dissidents inside the GDR. Perhaps an academic could be so unworldly, but it is hard to believe that a reasonably well-informed person like the Labour and Lib-Dem MP Lord Roper, then director of studies at the Chatham House think-tank – officially designated the Royal Institute of Foreign Affairs and frequented by senior government figures – could employ a highly productive HVA officer, code-named 'Eckart', as a research assistant there. He later claimed this was a Foreign Office-approved exercise in bridge-building. Lambeth councillor Bill Bowring; journalists Derek Furse and Dick Clements, editor of the *Tribune*; Bruce Kent and Professor Vic Allen of the Campaign for Nuclear Disarmament; Professor Emeritus David Childs of Nottingham University and a host of other MPs and academics also talked freely to the GDR 'diplomats'.[3]

As historian Anthony Glees points out, in making these connections they were breaking no law and may have betrayed no *classified* state secrets if they had none to betray, but all was grist to the Stasi mill. British informers and agents of influence retailing details of power struggles inside the political parties and hints on strategic policy must have been aware that any GDR citizen behaving similarly with Western intelligence officers would have seen the inside of a Stasi interrogation cell, with all the humiliation, pain and anguish that entailed[4] – and which lasted far longer for a GDR citizen than for Ms Einhorn. Yet Glees has been attacked on more than one occasion for 'outing' the HVA's contacts in Britain – perhaps by well-meaning liberals who believed the GDR Justizministerium's allegation that there were no political prisoners in the GDR.

At least one of the staff of Residentur 201 was an expert in weaponry and explosives. This was during the bloodshed in Northern Ireland. The HVA had links with the IRA, which used the Czech plastic explosive Semtex. Like the Hungarian intelligence officers in London, the GDR diplomats were also suspected of affording facilities to Middle Eastern terrorist organisations. In 1983 Heinz Knobbe, described as the 'deputy ambassador', was expelled from Britain for activities incompatible with his diplomatic status.[5]

On 19 July 1985 the British Secret Intelligence Service 'lifted' double agent KGB Colonel Oleg Gordievskii by spiriting him across the Soviet–Finnish border in a split-second operation that could only work once. Gordievskii having been the *rezident* in the Soviet embassy in London, it is likely there was a connection between his arrival in the West and the apprehension one month later of a 'typically suburban' couple using the names Reinhard and

Sonja Schulze, although some sources aver that the tip-off came from the BND. Whichever is true, they were arrested at their rented home, 249 Waye Avenue in Cranford, near London Airport. The husband was a talented kitchen designer, highly valued by his employer and liked by his clients; his wife worked as a technical translator. Reinhard had come to Britain with a West German passport in 1980, concealing the fact that he also held papers in the name of Bryan Strunze, the British-born son of a German father and English mother, who disappeared on a visit to the GDR. The false Schulze rented an apartment for a few months, but then disappeared to follow a correspondence course in interior design. Although without visible means of income, he seemed to have plenty of cash. After leaving the country briefly, he returned with Sonja, posing as his fiancé, whom he said he had met while on holiday in Ireland. They married in Hounslow Registry Office, where he gave his age as 32; she stated hers as 29 and gave her maiden name as Ilona Hammer.

After renting the house in Cranfield, they were an unremarkable couple to the neighbours and a pair of grey ghosts to monitors in Government Communications Headqaurters (GCHQ). The British government had intercepted messages from a short-wave transmitter somewhere near Berlin giving the newly-weds their instructions, but were unable to decipher the Morse code blocks of five-figure groups. When the house in Waye Avenue was raided by Special Branch officers, a large collection of detailed maps was found, especially focusing on flight paths into Heathrow and other important British airports, together with many British town plans. Various agencies took the house to pieces, and the most incriminating find was inside a can of aerosol in the garden shed, where partly used one-time pads were concealed. These had served to decipher the incoming Morse transmissions picked up in Cheltenham. Whether they permitted the deciphering of the recorded transmissions by staff at GCHQ was not revealed, but it would have been usual procedure to destroy the used sheets associated with those transmissions. A short-wave receiver and tape recorder were also found, but no transmitter. Well secreted in the lining of a hold-all was what appeared to be an escape kit containing false papers for the couple under different names and a supply of cash.

Although one HVA agent had escaped the net just before arrest in 1984, these were the first satellite country spies to be caught red-handed in Britain since the Lonsdale–Houghton–Kroger network was broken up in 1961. Several of the couple's trips abroad were followed by large cash deposits in their bank accounts. Under routine questioning, Reinhard was tripped up by his ignorance of the British family of the real Reinhard Schulze, after which, although refusing to talk about their real activities, they admitted using false papers on entry into Britain.

According to a BBC newsflash dated 28 August 1985, the couple appeared before Horseferry Road magistrates court in London, did not request bail and were remanded in custody. Identified as GDR citizens, they were duly charged under the Official Secrets Act with 'possessing documents detrimental to the public interest'. Both then and during their subsequent nine-day trial at the Old Bailey, they refused to answer any questions about what they had been doing in Britain and the investigating officers were said to be so baffled by the trail of false identities that they had no idea who the couple really were. Yet Schulze requested that the GDR embassy be informed of their arrest and, after they were each sentenced to ten years' imprisonment for preparing an espionage operation for an unidentified foreign power, the Third Secretary at the embassy visited them every week in jail. Under a swap agreement, of which the details were not disclosed, they were released and deported from Britain in 1991.

Notes

1. A. Glees, *The Stasi Files*, London, Simon and Schuster 2004, pp 365–9
2. Ibid, pp. 6–7, 14
3. Ibid, pp. 7–9
4. Ibid, p. 9
5. Ibid, p. 89

II

DEATH OF THE STASI

On 15 February 1989 the last defeated Soviet troops left Afghanistan, invalidating the Brezhnev Doctrine that the Soviet government would support with all necessary armed force any pro-Soviet government that was under threat. Leonid Shebarshin, head of the KGB's First Chief Directorate, controlled all KGB staff in the satellite countries and had taken soundings among them even before the final troops marched out of Afghanistan across the so-called Friendship Bridge into Uzbekistan. In July all the *rezidenty* from Eastern Europe met in Moscow and reported, for the first time more or less honestly, what was going on in their several countries. The news was universally grim, leaving Shebarshin to wonder what could be done about it. The Soviet economy was in such disastrous condition that it could neither bribe the satellite states with aid grants, nor bully them with military force. Some consolation was taken at the conference that the German Democratic Republic seemed still to be 'steering a socialist course'.

Throughout the summer of 1989, as the rifts between the satellite states and Moscow grew wider in one country after another, Soviet publications with any mention of *glasnost* were banned in the GDR. But even the universal terror generated by the Stasi – by far the most powerful secret police force of the Warsaw Pact bloc – could not stop informal groups of people, whose numbers grew increasingly large, from getting together in churches and bars at Leipzig, Dresden and East Berlin to criticise their government's Stalinist rigidity. Many were arrested in the early weeks for expressing the heretical view that they should be allowed to travel abroad or even emigrate. So many people secretly watched the forbidden transmissions of West German television that they had no illusions how far their standard of living had lagged behind that of their compatriots on the other side of the inner German border, who, for example, did not have to 'qualify' and then wait for three years in a queue to acquire a Trabant, Europe's worst-performing and most-polluting car.

By August 1989 so many thousands of GDR citizens had escaped by travelling to Hungary and walking across the open frontier that Honecker banned travel to Hungary when it lifted all travel restrictions on 10 September.[1] The result? His people – or the more enterprising of them – went 'for a holiday' to Prague, where the West German embassy was besieged by hundreds, then thousands, of asylum seekers. There were still over 400,000 Soviet troops stationed in the GDR, but Gorbachev refused to use them to bolster the authority of Honecker's failing regime.

Honecker deplored the break-up of socialist unity because that concept was implicit in the party's name of Sozialistische Einheitspartei, meaning 'socialist unity'. One by one, his supporters crumbled until a cabal of Politburo members including Günther Schabowski forced him to resign 'for health reasons' on 18 October. The cabal included even Stasi boss Erich Mielke, who placed guards around the room where the Politburo was meeting. In the words of Patrick Brogan, who chronicled these events, he was:

> followed into oblivion by a succession of other septuagenarian and octogenarian Stalinists who had governed the country undisturbed for 30 years and were now witness to the complete collapse of their life's work.[2]

On 25 October 1989, during a visit to Helsinki, Gorbachev spoke of 'Finlandisation' as the way for Eastern Europe. Soviet Foreign Minister Eduard Shevardnadze had said two days previously that Russia at last recognized the right of the other Warsaw Pact governments to choose their own way to socialism, and Foreign Ministry spokesman Gennadi Gerasimov appeared on the US television programme *Good Morning America*. Asked to comment on this, Gerasimov explained that the Brezhnev Doctrine had been replaced by the Sinatra Doctrine. 'You know the Frank Sinatra song "I did it my way"?' he asked. 'Hungary and Poland are doing it their way.'[3]

Once used in the grim corridors of power in the Kremlin, the expression spread like a virus. Poland had elected its first non-communist government; Hungary had opened its border with Austria and refused demands from East Berlin to bar egress to GDR citizens who managed to reach Hungarian territory.

It had been sufficiently oppressive for GDR citizens to be forbidden to travel to the West. Now that they were not allowed to travel to most other Warsaw Pact states either, the effect was that of a pressure cooker without a safety valve. Between 30 October and 4 November 1.4 million protesters marched through the streets in 210 separate anti-government demonstrations, demanding not just the freedom to travel, but even free multi-party elections. When demonstrations are reported, there is usually a discrepancy between the organisers' inflated figures and those of the forces of law and order trying to minimise the events, but the above figures come from the Stasi's own records.

Honecker's replacement, Egon Krenz, promised an easing of travel restrictions after pleading with Gorbachev for help on 1 November and being told that under the Sinatra Doctrine, *'Eto vashe dyelo!'* – That's your problem.

The border with Czechoslovakia was reopened and an amnesty announced for all who had left. Confusing announcements were made – that the travel restrictions would be either eased or abolished by Christmas. These caused public unrest to escalate. On 9 November Günther Schabowski was asked at a televised press conference when the travel restrictions would be finally withdrawn. He answered, 'Immediately.'[4] This was not the Politburo's decision. The official explanation of Schabowski's lapse is that he had not been adequately briefed on the details of the new policy; it is equally possible that, as a lifetime Communist and dedicated party functionary, his brain could not absorb the details of the new heresy, so he panicked in front of the cameras and reporters, and said the first word that came into his head.

Whatever the reason, that one word released a media storm. Within minutes, GDR citizens were streaming towards the Wall, expecting the barriers to be open. The border guards had heard over the radio or seen on television Schabowski's press conference. Lacking any contrary instructions, they allowed the first trickle to pass through. With West Berlin television coverage being seen in East Berlin, tens of thousands more rushed to the Wall and walked freely into the West.

Nine years later, when the author was collecting his Stasi file from the BStU in Berlin, he asked Frau Ehrlich, the woman handing over the file, whether she had lived *im Westen oder im Osten* before the reunification. She replied that she lived in East Berlin, where her husband had lost his job after being blacklisted by the Stasi for reasons never divulged to him. On the fateful night, she had not seen the televised press conference and knew nothing of Schabowski's *faux pas*, but received a telephone call from her mother-in-law, whose apartment overlooked a checkpoint, saying, 'You must come here right away.'

Incredulous, the two women watched out of the window as the crowds streamed through into West Berlin. Expecting some violent reaction from the border guards or Volkspolizei riot police, they were too frightened to go down and join them. When the author asked her what she had felt then, Frau Ehrlich's face lit up with remembered joy. 'It was,' she said, 'the most wonderful night of my life.'

It was probably the worst night of Erich Mielke's life, who spent it in the bedroom adjoining his office at the Normannenstrasse HQ. On 7 November he resigned. On 13 November he addressed the Volkskammer, or parliament, as *Genossen*, meaning 'comrades', and was shouted down by a chorus of 'We are not your comrades'. Reduced to stammering, '*Ich liebe doch alle Menschen!*' – but I love everybody – the man who had screamed at his subordinates to club and beat the demonstrators in the streets was baffled to be greeted with laughter and catcalls. The only acceptable SED leader with any popular support, Hans Modrow, was elected prime minister of a country that had a budget deficit equivalent to US $70 billion and an inflation rate well into double figures.

When ordinary people could at last visit the secret and formerly guarded town of Wandlitz, to the north of Berlin, where the party fat cats had lived, their anger reached new levels. While they had suffered all the privations of the failing SED-planned economy, the Honeckers, Mielke and twenty other political leaders had enjoyed sybaritic luxury in Western-style villas with swimming pools, no rationing and large domestic staffs. The trade union leader had even arrogated to himself a 5,000-acre hunting reserve in Mecklenberg and a 200-acre farm to breed 'wild' boars for the hunt.[5] Modrow, just as out of touch with reality as the other SED leaders, planned to restore the Stasi. When the news leaked out, popular anger was such that crowds stormed the local offices and the HQ in Berlin, pushing their way in and hurling entire filing cabinets out of the windows so that nearby streets had a snowstorm of paperwork floating through the air.

In October 1993 86-year-old Mielke was put on trial, not for the deaths caused by the Stasi during his long tenure but for the murders of two Berlin police officers in 1931. Captains Paul Anlauf and Franz Lenck were shot with a revolver by Mielke in front of witnesses during, or just after, a street battle with Nazi supporters. In 1947 two ex-police officers recognised Mielke at a public function and requested that the investigation be reopened. The original records, which had survived all the war damage, were passed to the Kammergericht for action, which was blocked by the Soviet representatives on the Allied Control Commission. They confiscated the papers and handed them to Mielke. For whatever reason, instead of destroying them, he kept them in his personal safe, where they were discovered when his house was searched in 1990. Sentenced to six years' imprisonment for the two murders, Mielke served less than two before being released on the grounds of senile dementia.

As to what happened to the thousands of Stasi officers between the fall of the Berlin Wall and the formal reunification of the two German states, CIA officers in West and East Berlin were ordered to recruit as many as possible in the hunt for details of agents who had penetrated US security. Their first panicking technique was to consult a personnel list supplied for cash by one reliable source, and then use the telephone directory to cold-call one officer named on the chart after another. This met with almost universal failure, apparently because the professionally paranoid Stasi men thought the phone calls were entrapment by their own colleagues. Knocking on doors and proving CIA identity met with better results, as some of those contacted in this way robbed the Stasi Centre registry and offered the loot for money. An odd sideshow of this episode was when the BfV, reluctant to get directly involved in the GDR, asked the CIA office in Munich to handle a Stasi officer with something special to sell. A junior CIA officer rendezvoused with the contact: two men with two cars parked on a lonely country road. In the boot of the Stasi car was a card index whose 17,000 cards detailed transcripts of wire taps and records of telephone numbers – a gold mine for Bundesrepublik counter-intelligence. After sifting the material in the hunt for American references, the CIA turned it over to the BfV.[6]

As for the most critical Stasi files – including those listing real name and cover name, address and activity of spies implanted in the West – intelligence insiders believe that a small group of MfS officers kept their heads when all around them was falling to pieces immediately after the breaching of the Wall and transported these files in microfilm form to the East Berlin airport at Schönefeld, whence they were immediately flown out to Moscow and safe keeping with the KGB. The problem with intelligence stories is to know what is genuine and what is disinformation. That story continues with the CIA buying the files back in Moscow from a crooked KGB officer through a middleman for $1 million. An alternative version has the files being literally carried into a US embassy 'somewhere in Europe' and offered at the more modest price of $75,000. Conveniently, all the players in these scenarios died shortly afterwards.

There was also some private enterprise afoot, with at least one officer raiding his own office safe in the Centre and carting the contents to his allotment out in the suburbs, where he burned everything, to the amusement of the other allotment holders.

Whatever the truth, without in any way condoning the Stasi or its personnel's ruthless sense of duty, one has to acknowledge the sheer professionalism of the officers who flew the main archives to safety when all around them the state they had served was disintegrating and there was a risk that the uncontrolled anger of their hundreds of thousands of erstwhile victims might cost their lives. It contrasts tellingly with the dereliction of duty shown by the CIA officers at Saigon in 1975 who ran away to save their own skins without destroying the lists of their informers. As a result, thousands of men and women the CIA had used against their own people were swept up by the incoming NVA *can-bo* commissars and consigned to the firing squads or the living hell of 're-education camps'.

Despite all the secrecy of the previous four and a half decades, some physical evidence of the Stasi's activities was clearly visible in bricks and mortar. It owned 2,655 separate premises of various kinds and 18,000 apartments including safe houses for clandestine meetings. The vehicles in its garages included 12,000 cars and 5,456 'equipped vehicles' used for surveillance, filming and photographing its targets, which explains how everyone posting a letter in East Berlin on a particular day could be recorded on film. Of its 85,000 personnel, 2,171 were employed steaming open and reading mail; 1,486 were intercepting telephone calls; 2,244 were interrogating suspects and/or recording interrogations; 12,000 were employed on the frontiers; 8,426 were on electronic intercept duty; and nearly 5,000 were bodyguards or on guard duty at various state premises.

Less visible but equally eloquent was the cash salted away in Zurich by the Stasi through an Austrian company called Novum and the Austrian Communist Party, for purposes unknown. This is thought by some informed sources to add up to the staggering sum of DM 50 billion. Even if a lower figure of DM 26 billion – of which only DM 2 billion have been recovered[7] – is accurate, that is still a large amount for an intelligence service to have in ready cash. Who has it now?

Notes

1. Brogan, *Eastern Europe*, p. 14
2. Ibid, p. 39
3. Ibid
4. M. Bearden and J. Risen, *The Main Enemy*, London, Century 2003, pp. 395–6
5. Brogan, *Eastern Europe*, p. 41
6. Bearden and Risen, *Main Enemy*, pp. 435–8
7. Glees, *The Stasi Files*, p. 118

Part 3

State Terror in Central Europe

12

THE POLISH UB

CRUSHING A SUFFERING NATION

After carving up the homeland of the Poles on paper under the Nazi–Soviet Non-Aggression Treaty in 1939, Hitler's first large-scale Blitzkrieg was launched against Poland on 1 September 1939. The Poles resisted heroically but the impossibility of their situation was epitomised by the image of Polish horse cavalry pitted against German tanks. To complete the destruction of the Polish state, on 17 September Soviet armies poured in from the east. As combat ended, Stalin proceeded to install a reign of terror in 'his' half of Poland. An estimated 1.5 million of the 13.7 million inhabitants were tortured, imprisoned, murdered or deported to the Gulag with the aim of terrifying the survivors into submission to their new Russian overlords. This enormous total included many thousands of Poles in uniform, who should have been protected by the rules of war.

After the frontier adjustments following the Second World War, Poland is now 95 per cent Catholic and Polish-speaking. In 1939, however, one-third of the population was Russian, Ukrainian, Ruthenian, Byelorussian, Lithuanian, German or Jewish. This dramatic change is due in part because the country suffered more than any other in the Second World War, losing one-fifth of its population to German and Russian bullets, the gas chambers, malnutrition and exposure in Siberia and starvation at home. On the German side of the new internal border, which divided the country roughly in half, the initial targets were Jews – and children. A little-known horror within all the statistics is the kidnapping of blond, blue-eyed children, who were brought up in special SS-run orphanages, where they were forbidden to speak Polish, so they would become German-speaking cannon fodder and breeding stock. The 'rejects' from these establishments were starved to death in so-called Auslandkinder Pflegestätten or shipped to one of the death camps for disposal.[1] The murderous carve-up between the two dictators came undone when Hitler launched Operation Barbarossa in June 1941, driving out the grotesquely ill-prepared Soviet occupation forces[2] and installing his programme of ethnic cleansing nationwide.

Scrabbling for any allies who might divert some German forces away from Russia, Stalin subsequently did a deal with General Władisław Sikorski, prime minister of the Polish government-in-exile in London. Under a spurious amnesty – for they had committed no crime – he released tens of thousands of Polish POWs held in Soviet prison camps. Knowing that his brother officer General Władysław Anders was a prisoner undergoing interrogation with torture in the NKVD's infamous Lubyanka prison, Sikorski named him commander-in-chief of the new Polish force. When he was released, Anders took command on 22 August of several thousand men whose physical condition was understandably poor after being used as disposable slave labour in the camps. By the end of the year, he had 1,000 officers and 24,000 other ranks organised into three infantry divisions. Early in 1942, this small army was transported to Tashkent in Soviet Turkestan, with the addition of another division. If that all sounds straightforward, it was not, for Anders and his staff had constantly to circumvent every kind of administrative and logistical obstacle placed in their way by Soviet military and civil officials.

For complex reasons, the most important of which was Stalin's determination that these Poles should not complicate his planned occupation of their homeland later in the war – as they had every reason to do – he directed them to British-occupied Iran, designated Polish 2nd Army Corps. At this stage, the corps totalled about 40,000 military personnel and had with it twice that number of civilian dependents, who were permitted to leave with them because the USSR was already short of food. The uncertainty over their exact numbers is because although some were shipped across the Caspian Sea, other released Poles had to find their own way to the Turkestan–Iran border on foot, and many died of malnutrition, hypothermia and disease on the way. The toughest men survived to see service against the Germans in North Africa and the Italian campaign, where their heroism under dire conditions at Monte Cassino is legendary – at the cost to Anders' army of 7,000 lives in that one battle alone.

Long before then, Winston Churchill had put in writing to Foreign Secretary Anthony Eden that a permanent Soviet occupation of eastern Poland would be contrary to the principles of the Atlantic Charter agreed between Britain and the USA in August 1941, and which had subsequently been endorsed by the United Nations, including the USSR. It also ran

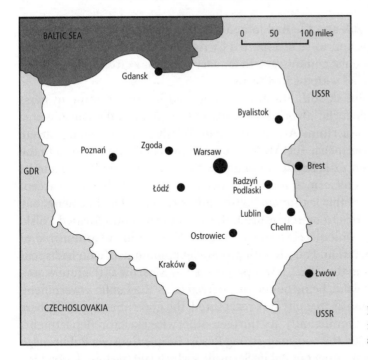

Poland after 1945 frontier adjustment.

contrary to the restoration of national integrity enunciated in US President Wilson's 'Fourteen Points' at the Paris Peace Conference of 1919. However, the US president at that time, Franklin D. Roosevelt, was so much under Stalin's influence that Churchill was unable to obtain from him any support for the restoration of Polish national sovereignty after the war. It was this that drove him to tell General Anders in Italy that Britain could no longer defend the territorial integrity of the country for which it had theoretically declared war on Germany. Anders retorted that the Big Three's carving up of his country was a calamity.

Churchill, presumably ridden by guilt, replied angrily, 'We have enough troops today. We do not need your help. You can take away your divisions. We shall do without them.'[3]

A Polish friend of the author, when asked how he and his comrades in Italy reacted when they heard this, said, 'We thought, what the hell are we doing here, fighting in British uniforms? They don't care about our country, so why should we fight their war? But we carried on because, that way, we were at least killing one lot of enemies.'[4]

In 1943, thanks in part to supplies of materiel shipped in from the West at considerable cost in lives and shipping losses,[5] Stalin's armies launched the massive offensive that would eventually take them as far as Berlin. Included in the Soviet forces was a 75,000-man Polish Communist army commanded by General Zygmunt Berling, formed under Soviet command.

The Polish rank and file had joined as a way of escaping harsh-regime prison camps and were disciplined by rigidly indoctrinated Soviet and Polish Communist commissars. In January 1944, they crossed the pre-war border of Poland with the Red Army.

Once on Polish soil, Stalin recommenced his programme of mass murder and deportation of intellectuals and survivors of the Polish Armia Krajowa (AK) or Home Army – the main Polish armed resistance group fighting the Germans. The AK had 300,000 men and women, loyal to the government-in-exile based in London, which anticipated returning to its homeland when German forces had been driven out. Refusing to accept the existence of this legitimate Polish authority, on 22 July in Chełm, one of the first cities to be recaptured, the Soviet leadership formed Polski Komitet Wyzwolenia Narodowego (PKWN) or Polish Committee of National Liberation. Packed with pro-Soviet communists who had spent the war so far in the USSR, it was proclaimed by Moscow as the future government of Poland, being popularly referred to as 'the Lublin government' because as soon as that city was recaptured, the government moved there from Chełm. Significantly, its thirteen otherwise skeleton departments already included the 200-man-strong Resort Bezpieczeństwa Publicznego (RBP) – or Department of Public Security – which laid the foundation for a nationwide pro-Moscow Polish secret police force before the Germans had been driven out of even 10 per cent of the country.

Occasionally, RBP personnel came under German fire, but most of their activities were against non-communist partisans who were too busy fighting the occupation forces to protect themselves against this new enemy whom they at first welcomed as allies and who spoke the same language they did. Back in Moscow, in July 1944 Lavrenti Beria reported dutifully to Stalin that he had sent 12,000 NKVD troops into Poland behind the Red Army to drive the Home Army out of the forests and punish the civilian population that had been feeding them or providing accommodation. By the end of the year, more than 5,000 AK partisans had been taken prisoner and an unknown number, who could have been fighting the Germans, had been killed by Russian bullets. And so it went on. In the first quarter of 1945, the NKVD itself claimed to have captured or arrested a quarter-million people of many ethnic groups in Poland; 38,000 of these were Poles deported into the USSR, where at least 5,000 died.[6]

In the German-occupied areas of the country, groups of Armia Krajowa men hid out in the forests. Teenage partisan fighter Bogusław Nowakowski gave the lie to later glorification of the partisan life by recounting how it was extremely harsh, with everyone malnourished, unwashed, stinking and louse-infested. The rare RAF air-drops of weapons to the AK groups brought far too few guns and ammunition, so it was necessary to make raids on German 'soft targets' for weapons and on collaborationist businesses to steal money, food and clothing. Enemies were all around. Not only the Germans, but also communist partisans were trying to eliminate the non-communist partisans. Their victims ran into tens of thousands, and Nowakowski's account is typical.

In mid-April 1944 he and four other AK men were returning from a brief visit to their families near Ostrowiec in south-eastern Poland, an area still occupied by the Germans. The town also hid a clandestine weapons workshop and a resistance printing press. On the way back to their forest hideout they stopped for the night at a small guest house. A group of men from the Communist Armia Ludowa (AL), or People's Army, arrived later under the command of a man whose *nom de guerre* was 'Wasp'. The newcomers, who outnumbered Nowakowski's group five to one, forcibly disarmed them. They also robbed them of the money they had stolen at gunpoint from a German business. Only then did they announce that the AK men were to be put on trial allegedly for attacking another communist group. Since they had never done this, Nowakowski's four companions were not too alarmed until they had their hands tied behind them and were roped together in pairs. Being still a teenager, Nowakowski was not tied to another man, but had his hands tied behind his back.

Their captors included several Russians, probably escapees from German POW camps. After marching their prisoners some way into the forest, 'Wasp' ordered these Russians to kill the five prisoners. The AK men protested they had never attacked any other Poles, but were gunned down with automatic weapons regardless. Blinded by the muzzle flashes and stunned by the noise, Nowakowski fell down in shock, thinking he was dead. As one of the Russians was giving a coup de grâce to the wounded who were groaning, he realised that he was not even hurt. The AK men were stripped and relieved of their boots, to be buried in an unmarked grave. When the rope binding his hands was cut by two of the killers, so that they could remove his coat and jacket, Nowakowski leaped to his feet and ran for his life, barefoot.

Bullets struck trees all around him, but he managed to reach a friendly house a few kilometres from the massacre, where the worst of his cuts and abrasions were cleaned and dressed. The Armia Krajova HQ at Ostrowiec was commanded by a Pole who had parachuted in from Britain. When this man learned what had happened, the young survivor of the massacre was ordered to make a full report identifying the murderers, which could be used as evidence in a post-war trial. There never was a trial. Instead, 'Wasp' rose to political power after the retreat of German forces from the area, and continued to hunt down any AK men who could be traced. To save his life, Nowakowski volunteered to go with the retreating Nazi forces, to work as a labourer in Germany. After returning to Poland under a false name at the cessation of hostilities in 1945, he recorded that for years after the 'liberation' 'Wasp' and his men continued tracking down and arresting former members of AK, who were given show trials ending with sentences ranging from five years' in prison to death by firing squad.[7]

So, although Soviet history books refer to this period as 'the liberation of Poland', it did not feel like that at the time for most Poles. After the withdrawal of the German administration of Bohemia and Moravia, known as the 'Gouvernement General', eventually the whole country was placed under the Lublin government, supported by the several thousand members of Armia Ludowa. While the local Red Army commanders happily accepted the help of Armia Krajowa partisans at places such as Lwów, Vilnius and Nowogródek, once the German forces had been driven out and these areas secured, all AK men were arrested, given summary trials and either sent to Siberia or, as at Lwów, murdered by NKVD troops and buried in mass graves, which the victims were forced to dig themselves. The graves were only reopened and the remains exhumed after the collapse of the USSR in 1989.

On 15 August 1944 the PKWN issued a decree ordering all males in the 'liberated' areas to register for military service in Rokossovsky's Soviet puppet army. About 200,000 men found themselves drafted into labour battalions, some of them for the 'crime' of having relatives living abroad. They were put to work with inadequate safety regulations, or none at all, in quarries, coal and uranium mines. There are no official figures for the many who were seriously crippled or killed in accidents. Nine days later, a second decree explicitly outlawed membership of Armia Krajowa, obliging men who had served in it to join other fugitives in the forests or be immediately arrested as 'enemies of the people' for their record of actively fighting the Germans.

Politically inactive Poles were also arrested and transported in unheated railway trucks to labour camps, including a former German concentration camp at Zgoda run by ex-AL man Salomon Morel, who was appointed in March 1945. With 5,000 prisoners, nearly all German-speaking Volksdeutsche, crammed into seven lice-ridden barracks, 1,855 detainees died at Zgoda between then and November 1945. Of the deaths, 1,600 were due to a typhus epidemic, during which the dying were neither isolated nor given any medical treatment. Subsequently charged with starving prisoners and creating conditions in which typhus was inevitable, as well as practising physical and mental torture on detainees, Morel was removed and punished with three days of house arrest.

Of others deported to the USSR, many died of exposure, hunger and thirst en route. In those camps food was poor and disease rife. At one, 1,000 Poles died in the first three months; their corpses were thrown naked into garbage pits. The fittest in the camps continued working in coal, copper and graphite mines, or on collective farms, replacing Soviet citizens who had died during the war. By the time the Lublin government managed to reclaim the surviving deportees in autumn 1945, more than half had died.

Three transports of 1,000 men travelled from Białystok to Ostashkov, midway between Moscow and Leningrad. These Poles were farmers, designated *kulaki* and therefore 'class enemies', with some self-employed tradesmen, teachers and even secondary school pupils – all of whom were considered 'enemies of democracy'. Weakened by torture and malnutrition during their initial imprisonment, many died during the two-week, 600-mile journey in cattle trucks. The harsh conditions in the camp at Ostashkov caused much further mortality until the survivors were repatriated in January 1945. But Poland's nightmare was not over. In the two following months NKVD troops deported some 20,000 miners from Katowice in Silesia to Kazakhstan in Central Asia. What became of them is unknown. Lists of deportees were clandestinely compiled by neighbours and relatives, but when they later tried to ascertain the fate of their missing friends, fathers, sons and brothers, neither the post-war Polish government nor the Red Cross was able to discover what had happened to them.

The men repatriated in January 1945 were the lucky ones. Some other Polish prisoners were detained for two further years without any contact with their families, who did not know whether they were dead or alive. The war being long over, in desperation some of these men went on hunger strike – which takes some doing when one is already severely malnourished – and refused to work. To outwit the strikers, in June of 1947 the NKVD promised swift repatriation. The prisoners boarded trains for what they thought was the journey home, to find themselves delivered to another camp for an intensive four-month political indoctrination course. Only in the October did they at last get transport to Brest on the Polish border.

They returned to a homeland where the eradication of non-Communist figures of authority was still continuing. The most transparent ploy was the enticement of non-Communist Polish leaders from the provisional government in London to join in the formation of Rząd Tymczasowy Rzeczyoospolitej Polskiej (RTRP) or Provisional Government of Poland. It was at this point that the Ministry of Public Security was renamed Ministerstwo Bezpieczeństwa Publicznego (MBP). This government ministry was eventually to embrace internal security, including nationwide telephone monitoring and mail opening, management of the Milicja Obywatelskaya paramilitary police, also the prison and fire services, the Wojska Ochrony Pogranicza border police and concentration camp guards. After mid-1947 it also took over Polish Military Intelligence, becoming even more powerful within Poland than the KGB was in the USSR.

Arrested by NKVD Major General Ivan Serov, tortured and displayed in the 'Trial of the Sixteen', allegedly for anti-Soviet activities in June 1945, the returnees from London who had worked for or been members of the wartime government-in-exile were not immediately executed, due to US President Truman's personal appeal for leniency to Stalin, but few of them survived long. Their bitterest pill was to learn on 6 July that the Western Allies had withdrawn recognition of the London government-in-exile on the previous day and formally recognised the Soviet puppet government in Warsaw as the legal government of Poland – as a gesture to Stalin.

Outside Soviet-occupied Poland, the existence of the puppet army, eventually renamed Sily Zbrojne Rzeczypospolitej Ludowej – or Armed Forces of the People's Republic – and the many Polish-speaking Soviet officers embedded in the new Polish administration, led to confusion over the real political situation in the country. The reality was that the Soviet organs of state terror had been replaced by nominally Polish bodies, such as Urząd Bezpieczeństwa (UB) or State Security established by PKWN on 21 July 1944 and the several Armia Ludowa security corps, which included many Soviet officials who had changed their Russian and Jewish names to Polish ones. Their victims had no better than a fifty-fifty chance of avoiding a death sentence, executed in public, after a summary trial with no defence permitted.

Among the returnees in summer 1945 was Czesław Kisczak, who had been a slave labourer in Austria. After getting hold of and producing a membership card for the Austrian Communist Party, he was sent to UB training schools in Łódź and Warsaw, after which he was posted to Główny Zarząd Informacji (GZI) – or Chief Intelligence Directorate of the Defence Ministry, meaning Polish military intelligence. His first mission saw him despatched to Britain, to 'persuade' the Polish forces there to return home. Kisczak resurfaced internationally as one of the generals who imposed martial law in 1981 in the attempt to crush Solidarność and other free trade unions.[8] Although the law was rescinded in 1983, many of those arrested stayed in prison for two further years.

Two months after the end of the war in Europe, in July 1945 the Białystok region was selected for a massive clearance by NKVD troops of allegedly anti-communist civilians. Known as the 'Giby operation' after the name of a village that suffered particularly harshly, it covered more than 100 small towns and villages. Several thousand people were arrested and interrogated with force by officers of the MBP under NKVD supervision. While the majority were released after a few weeks, an estimated 1,300 of those arrested did not return home. It was assumed they had been deported to the Soviet Union.

However, none was included in the batches of returnees from then until 1956, when Moscow alleged that all Polish detainees had been released, two years after Stalin's death. Under pressure from families of the missing, the Polish Red Cross in Białystok finally had a confirmed list of 1,136 names. Before this could be taken any further, local pro-Soviet officials terminated the enquiry. With extraordinary courage and persistence, a committee of relatives was formed in August 1987 and appealed for help to both Polish and Soviet governments, to the Catholic Church and the Red Cross. Fifty-six prominent Polish figures signed a formal letter of support addressed to the Sejm, or Polish parliament. All this achieved was to have the committee declared an illegal organisation. Undaunted, the relatives pressed on and submitted detailed reports on 370 of the victims to the Sejm on 19 April 1989, together with a complete list of the missing. This material named specific NKVD and Polish security officers involved in the arrests. It also raised three questions. Why were Soviet troops involved when the war had ended at the time? Had the operation been requested by the Polish authorities? Where are the graves?

The wartime Big Three conferences had accepted Stalin's plan – it was hardly original, since this had been an aim of the tsars before the October Revolution – to widen the buffer zone against another German invasion of Russia.[9] Endorsed by Attlee and Truman at the 1945 Potsdam Conference, Poland's eastern frontier was moved westwards by about 250 miles to the Bug river – roughly along the Curzon Line, which British Foreign Secretary Lord Curzon had proposed as the border after the First World War. The western frontier was also moved westwards to the lines of the Oder and Neisse rivers and Poland was awarded the formerly German province of East Prussia – which roughly compensated them for the territory lost in the east. The Polish city of Lwów became Ukrainian and was renamed Lviv; Brest-Litovsk was inside the expanded Belarus; and Wilno became Vilnius, capital of the Lithuanian SSR.

This redrawing of the map involved a population movement of 1.2 million Polish-speakers expelled from their homes and lands because it was reasoned they could be resettled in the formerly German provinces of the west and north. The new government in Warsaw reciprocated by expelling 482,000 Ukrainians from the province of Galicia.[10] According to the statesmen at the conference, these population exchanges were to be conducted in an orderly and humane manner. The reality was very different: in the Volhynia region of southern Galicia, it was common to find Ukrainian villages with Orthodox churches interspersed with Polish villages with Catholic churches. Armed bands of irregulars from the underground Ukraïnska Povstanska Armiya (UPA) looted and burned down many Polish-speaking villages after raping and murdering the inhabitants; in retaliation, Polish guerrillas did the same in Ukrainian-speaking villages.

In East Prussia, ethnic German inhabitants, blamed for the excesses of the Wehrmacht, the Waffen-SS and the Einsatzgruppen, headed desperately westwards, seeking asylum in what was left of the Reich. Before the Polish government got around to organising their expulsion, in the big cities they were herded into ghettoes, partly for their own protection. In the countryside, after the Red Army moved on, Polish gangs robbed and raped them, using violence to drive more than a quarter-million German-speakers across the Oder in the last two weeks of June 1945.[11]

Tens of thousands of these German refugees had to walk hundreds of miles, transporting some belongings on wheelbarrows or farm carts pulled usually by women – because their menfolk were in Allied or Soviet POW camps – across the vast expanse of war-ravaged territory between their former homes and safety. The railways hardly functioned. People considered themselves lucky if they could find space *outside* a carriage and cling to a door handle; exhausted by malnutrition, many grew tired and fell off to die beside the tracks. Many roads were unusable due to demolition of bridges in the German retreat. Somehow, around 200,000 Ukrainians got left behind in Polish Galicia after Stalin closed the frontier. Stranded on the wrong side, they were eventually dispersed all over Poland in small groups without neighbours who could or would speak to them, in order to destroy any sense of being Ukrainian. With them went 34,000 Łemkos, a separate ethnic group living on the northern slopes of the Carpathians. Since both these peoples used Cyrillic alphabets and attended Orthodox churches, they were effectively being sent into an alien land. They were permitted to take some domestic animals with them in the cattle trucks, and were told they would find completely equipped new homes abandoned by German-speakers. By the time they arrived at their designated destinations, everything had been looted. People mocked their strange accents, and their children were beaten for using Ukrainian words in school and shunned by their new neighbours' children.

Few people kept diaries in this cataclysmic summer when people even in a large town such as Łódź were reduced to stealing the furniture from houses of the now empty ghetto and smashing out door and window fittings in order to have fuel for cooking and winter heating. However, Countess Marion Dönhoff did keep a record. As the Red Army advanced far faster than anticipated, she was one of the first Germans to leave, deciding to abandon her family estate near Preussich Holland (modern Pasłęk) in East Prussia while most of her German neighbours were obediently waiting for an order to do so from Berlin. She ate a last meal, left everything on the table and headed west on her best horse without bothering to lock the doors, having packed only a saddle-bag with 'toiletries, bandage material and my old Spanish crucifix.'[12] Whether they left their homes of their own accord, like the countess, or were brutally driven out by the Polish incomers, all Germans in the new Polish territory, like those in the Sudeten region of Czechoslovakia, departed in such haste that the Polish refugees who arrived first to take over their homes found books on the shelves, linen on the beds and even food in the larders. The regions they now inhabited, however, were not home and so devoid of infrastructure and so lawless that they were referred to as 'the Wild West', where might was right.

Nor was life in the east any easier.

Notes

1. L.H. Nicholas, *Cruel World, the Children of Europe in the Nazi Web*, New York, Knopf/Vintage 2006, p. 249
2. The Soviet retreat from Poland is treated in greater detail in Boyd, *Kremlin*, pp. 139–47.
3. Boyd, *Kremlin*, p. 165
4. Personal communication with the author
5. In addition to all the armaments, trucks, etc., there were thousands of Harley-Davidson motorbikes, on which tommy-gun-toting Red Army infantrymen rode as far as Berlin.
6. Applebaum, *Iron Curtain*, pp. 100, 104, 111
7. A full account may be found on http://felsztyn.tripod.com/id21.html
8. Applebaum, *Iron Curtain*, pp. 76–7
9. See at length in Boyd, *Kremlin*.
10. Lowe, *Savage Continent*, p. 222
11. Ibid, p. 233
12. Applebaum, *Iron Curtain*, pp. 127–8, quoting M. Gräfin Dönhoff, *Namen die keiner mehr nennt: Ostpreussen – Menschen und Geschichte*, Munich, DTV 1964, pp. 16–18

13

BETRAYAL, BEATINGS, ELECTIONS AND EXECUTIONS

The inhabitants of the Kakolewnica Forest near Radzyn Podlaski call their woodland *maly Katyn* – meaning 'little Katyn' – for good reason. After the departure of Rokossovsky's troops, the area was occupied by 2nd Polish People's Army, commanded by General Karol Świerczewski, a hard-line Stalinist alumnus of the Frunze military academy in Moscow, who had commanded an International Brigade in the Spanish Civil War using the *nom de guerre* 'General Walter'. Under him, detachments of Informacja Wojskowa – Polish Military Intelligence – worked in collaboration with NKVD teams. The forest was turned into an unobserved execution ground by the forcible evacuation of many local residents, who were not allowed to take their belongings with them. People living nearby, however, heard much shooting in the forest at night, and the comings and goings of military trucks at all hours.

Under a PKWN decree in October 1944, whose effect was back-dated to August of that year, membership of all non-Communist Polish anti-German forces was made punishable by death. As one example of many, 18-year-old Czesław Pekala had been a courier taking messages between different AK bands. Arrested by the NKVD and thrown into Radzyn Podlaski jail, his jaw was broken, he suffered head injuries from severe kicking and splinters were driven under his finger nails. At one point he spent four days lying unconscious in several centimetres of water in a cellar. Released after two months, he had lost half his body weight of 68kg, and was too terrified of re-arrest to say what had happened until 1998, long after the collapse of the USSR.

In one dossier alone, courts martial of 2nd People's Army sentenced sixty-one people to death; forty-three of these were executed. But no one knows how many were killed and thrown into unmarked forest graves, with or without trial, after these areas were cordoned off by security troops and civilians forbidden to enter. When the 2nd Army moved out in early 1945 the area had been levelled and saplings planted. After a few years, heavy rainfall began washing to the surface bones and other human remains. A memorial was erected in 1980. In March of that year the Radzyn Podlaski district prosecutor ordered an investigation of several identified execution pits. The forensic report concluded:

> The executed men had their hands and legs tied with wire. Some of the victims had sustained injuries in the form of broken and fractured ribs, arms, legs, etc. Some of the skulls showed signs of severe trauma caused by a blunt, heavy object [like a rifle butt]. The examiners confirmed injuries sustained by a single shot [to the head] with the entry wounds located either in the rear, or on the side of the skull.[1]

Given the forensic resources of the time, the exhumation failed to identify any individual victim, but established that they had all been wearing winter clothing. Many Soviet-manufactured bullets and cartridge cases were found in the graves. When trees in the area were later being machined in the sawmills, sparks flew all the time, caused by blades hitting the many ricocheting bullets that had become embedded in the trunks.[2]

After this purging of most Poles who *might* have resisted the Communist takeover of their country, Moscow finally agreed to 'free elections' in January 1947. At the time, the UB had only 228 officers in the provinces, running 8,194 informers, most of whom existed only on paper to justify the officers' claims to have recruited anyone at all. The problem this in turn produced was that any failure of a factory to reach its imposed output norms was ascribed to 'sabotage' and strikes – unthinkable in the satellite states – and had to be immediately and punitively suppressed, which was not possible with the manpower available.[3] One curious photograph of the time shows workers marching through the streets of an unidentified Polish town bearing a banner reading: *State Wine and Juice Factory – We vote for improvement in the lives of workers, peasants and the working intelligentsia.*[4]

At the Potsdam Conference, before he was replaced by Attlee, Churchill protested that, whereas the Soviet members of the Allied Control Commission had complete liberty to travel where they wanted in Italy, in Soviet-occupied areas the Western members of control commissions were harassed and followed everywhere and Western aircraft were deliberately delayed by Soviet air traffic controllers. Bolesław Bierut, Stalin's puppet president, claimed to Churchill that Poland had twenty-three political parties, proving that the country was democratic. At the same time, Stanisław Mikołajczk, formerly prime minister of the London Poles, who had returned to his country in order to become one of two deputy prime ministers, told

Foreign Secretary Eden that Bierut was setting up a one-party system, with Communist stooges infiltrated into all other parties, both to spy on them and to influence voting. He, meanwhile, had led a revival of his pre-war party Polski Stronnictwo Ludowe (PSL), known as 'the peasants' party', which had formerly enjoyed majority support in Poland. According to Mikołajczk, if elections had been held a few weeks previously, the Communists would have got 20 per cent of the votes. 'Now,' he said, 'they are so hated that they would not get more than 1 per cent in a free election.'[5]

Mikołajczk was probably exaggerating a little, but while the UB was still small in numbers at this stage, there were in Poland many thousands of NKVD troops who were particularly active in Poznań, Pomerania and especially Lublin against non-Communists. The Lublin government had other, less obvious advantages too. In his memoirs,[6] Pavel Sudoplatov, who held a number of important positions in the KGB's predecessors from 1939 until he fell from power after the death of Beria, alleges that Colonel František Muravec, intelligence chief of the London Poles, was actually an agent of the NKVD, passing on to Moscow all the confidential deliberations of the government-in-exile.[7]

In the January 1947 elections, many PSL candidates were prevented from campaigning. By the elections in 1948, a total of 32,477 non-Communist political activists had been sentenced by military courts for 'crimes against the state'. Even then, the UB applied additional pressure by forcibly recruiting an alleged 47 per cent of the remainder as unpaid informers. After massaging of the election results by the Interior Ministry, the Poles had a parliament with 394 seats for the Communists and their allies, but only twenty-eight seats for the PSL – the reverse of what the PSL claimed was the true result. Mikołajczk immediately resigned from the government in protest and fled to Britain in order to avoid arrest. When Churchill met him in London, he is reported to have said, 'I am surprised you made it out alive.'

In December 1948 the two main leftist parties merged into the Polska Zjednoczona Partia Robotnicza (PZPR) or Polish United Workers' Party, under which label the Communists ruled Poland until 1989. Throughout these four decades, the powers of the MBP and the national and local offices of the UB to carry through the entire pseudo-judicial process, from arrest to trial and execution of sentence, entirely bypassed the legal system. At the height of its power, before the death of Stalin on 5 March 1953, it was calculated that there was one MBP or UB officer for every 800 citizens. The intensity of surveillance is epitomised in the stationing of a UB officer in every factory employing more than a handful of workers, so that unpaid informers could immediately report the slightest indiscretion by a workmate.

As though placing itself even higher above the law, in 1952 the UB established its ultra-high-security Tenth Department, whose duty was to keep under surveillance all PZPR members – including the leadership, with only two exceptions: Rokossowsky and Bierut, a graduate of the Comintern's Lenin School. Tenth Department also provided any material required for the arrest of a party member or his demotion. To show that no one else was above their reach, in July 1951 Władysław Gomułka, deputy prime minister of the provisional government – who had been particularly active in arresting non-Communists – was himself arrested and imprisoned because he disagreed with the pro-Moscow *apparatchiki* in the government. His offence was formally designated 'right-wing reactionary deviation'. The Catholic Church was another especial target of UB, which dedicated an entire department to it – the only one headed by a woman, Julia Brystygier. Her staff framed, arrested and frequently beat up priests and bishops, sometimes killing them. The most famous case internationally was the torture and execution by the UB of Catholic priest Jerzy Popiełuszko in 1984, but the organisation was also widely suspected of killing at least two more priests: Stefan Niedzielak and Roman Kotlarz, who died after a severe beating during interrogation. Even the Primate of Poland, Cardinal Stefan Wyszyński, was placed under 'house arrest' in a monastery.

But Poland had no friends and no international voices to be raised in its defence. In the London Victory Parade on 8 June 1946, not a single Free Polish serviceman was to be seen, lest it upset Stalin, although those who had fought in the RAF were invited. The shameful ruling tarnished the day. The Poles of the RAF honourably refused the invitation as a gesture of solidarity with their thousands of compatriots who had fought in British uniforms with a shoulder flash reading POLAND. Now no longer prime minister, Churchill tried to atone for his discarding of General Anders by telling Parliament how deeply he regretted the prohibition on the Poles' participation, lamenting the situation in Poland, where the Lublin government dared not have free elections in the presence of international observers.

In January 1947 an allegedly free general election was held after non-Communist candidates and activists of PSL had been subjected to harassment, beatings and a few straightforward murders, to ensure they got the message. In some places, their lists of candidates were declared void. Polling day, 19 January, saw PZPR activists marching long columns of workers to the polling stations to vote for the party. The results were so blatantly falsified that many prominent PSL figures fled the country.[8]

Many of General Anders' men who decided to return home after this last betrayal by Britain were arrested on setting foot in their homeland. Some were eventually released with a black mark against them for life that guaranteed they would have only menial jobs in Bierut's Communist state. Others were murdered after interrogation at Warsaw's Mokotów prison, and their bodies dumped naked in refuse pits or other unmarked graves.

Official records show that approximately 300,000 Poles were arrested in the immediate post-war years – and this in a country that counted fewer than 24 million inhabitants in the 1946 census. Of those arrested, at least 5,000 were female. They included pregnant women and mothers of infant children. Mostly accused of spying for the West or plotting to overthrow the provisional government, they were more vulnerable to physical torture than male prisoners, and were also subjected to threats against their unborn or living children. After the women had been sentenced, their children were sometimes released into the care of relatives but were more often sent to state orphanages as part of the punishment; many were never traced after the mothers' release.

Among the cases documented is that of Władisław Sliwinski, who met his wife, Myra, in Britain while he was serving as a fighter pilot in the RAF and she was in the WAAF. Ignorant of the real conditions there – as were most people in the West – they moved together to Poland in 1947. On 4 June 1948 they and their 6-month-old son, Stefan, were arrested in Warsaw as British spies. Since Myra had British citizenship, Władisław offered to divorce her so that she could return to her homeland but, despite being physically maltreated herself, she refused this in the belief that her presence in Poland might in some way protect him. To prove that it did not, he was executed on 15 June 1951, after which Myra was compelled to give up her 18-month-old son, sent to live with his paternal great-grandmother. When the old lady died, an elderly neighbour gave the child a home.

Emerging from prison in 1956, Myra did not know Stefan, nor he her. After her second marriage failed, she returned to Britain in 1975 and was permitted to return to Poland only once, for her younger son's wedding. She died in Britain in 1991 at the age of 69, one of the UB's few female victims to leave any trace of her suffering in Western media.[9]

In addition to individuals targeted by the UB on the Soviet model, class enemies were still being created. In Autumn 1952 UB squads arrested tens of thousands of peasants who had failed to deliver their required quotas of grain. Some were deported to the USSR; others locked up in overcrowded prisons. Unlike Hungary, Poland had not built new concentration camps, but had all the abandoned German POW camps as well as some Polish ones, of which the first had been established in 1934, at Bereza Kartuska near Brest-Litovsk, to hold Ukrainian nationalists and fascists. During the German occupation, it was used to hold thousands of Communists and other leftists.[10]

Following the Russian system, MBP had its own man in the Polish Politburo. Jakub Berman was also the Stalinist boss of the PZPR. At the beginning of 1945, with the war still continuing against Nazi Germany, the largest department was Department One, headed by General Roman

Romkowski. Despite the impeccably Polish adoptive name, he had been born Natan Grinszpan-Kikiel in Moscow. His staff was responsible for a wide spectrum of activities including counter-espionage, fighting 'political banditry' and running the prisons. The first Soviet 'adviser' to the MBP was NKVD General Ivan Serov, who had been responsible for mass deportations of minorities in the USSR both before and during the war. With tens of thousands of Soviet forces stationed in Poland until 1956, the Polish armed forces and security organisations were heavily infiltrated with KGB officers, forming a political corset to keep Polish policies on the strictest Moscow line. In keeping with this, any leaders with too Polish an attitude had to go, but Bierut did not have Gomułka and Jakub Berman shot, apparently because he regretted all the former comrades who had been executed in Stalin's purges. They were, instead, put on ice for the time being; Gomułka was freed in 1954 and, although not reinstated at the top, allowed to acquire his own following. In many other ways the Polish Party leaders managed to steer a less extreme course than the other satellite governments through the political turbulence of 1956, for example, by representing themselves to Moscow as the best compromise and to the Polish people as the only alternative to Russian tanks in the streets. Even the periodic persecution of dissidents was comparatively low-key and the state control of agriculture was relaxed, permitting the peasants to recover their land from the collective farms in 1956.[11]

Everything was carried out under the strictest secrecy until the defection in December 1953 of Józef Światło, a lieutenant colonel in the MBP, whose job had been snooping on top party members, to provide evidence for their prosecution when required.[12] Sent to Berlin to consult with Erich Mielke, he took the opportunity to leap from an S-Bahn train passing through West Berlin and offered his services to US intelligence. His defection had little to do with ideology and more to do with fear for his own life because 'he knew too much' after the death of Stalin and the arrest of Lavrenti Beria in Moscow. As a close collaborator of Bierut, first secretary of PZPR since the arrest of Gomułka, and of General Serov, Światło had personally participated in the arrests preceding the Trial of Sixteen, the harassment of Cardinal Wyszyński and the arrests and torture of many AK members.

After a lengthy debriefing under conditions of strict secrecy – he lived under a witness protection programme in the United States until his death in 1994 – Światło recorded for Radio Free Europe a whole series of talks exposing the routine torture of prisoners under interrogation by UB officers, politically motivated executions and the internecine struggles for power inside the leadership of PZPR. He had also participated in the falsification of the January 1947 election results and personally arrested Gomułka, using forged documents to incriminate him. Among many other revelations was the news that, in addition to the thousands of former partisan fighters summarily killed or executed after fake trials, no fewer than 50,000 had been deported to the Gulag, and were still there.

In all the socialist countries, the fat cats lived well – like the pigs in Orwell's *Animal Farm*, of which they were the models. Światło recounted how Bierut's entire household staff, including cooks, a butler, drivers and cleaners, were all provided free of charge by the UB. Stanisław Radkiewicz, head of UB 1944–54, had an apartment in Warsaw and a villa in the country that did not cost him a złoty from his salary. Even at Światło's lower level perks included a good apartment with domestic staff, cars and drivers, and free clothing, footwear and bedlinen.[13]

As they became known in Poland, from the transmissions of US-subsidised propaganda stations, Światło's revelations were a severe embarrassment for the government, which gave the security services a facelift. MBP was replaced by Komitet do Spraw Bezpieczeństwa Publicznego (KdSBP), or Committee for Public Security, and Ministerstwo Spraw Wewnętrznych (MSW), or Ministry of Internal Affairs. Staff were reallocated to these new agencies and their numbers reduced, a few being arrested and charged with abuse of power. But what's in a name? KdSBP took over intelligence and counter-espionage, government security and the secret police. MSW was responsible for state and local administration, the Milicja Obywatelska and fire services, the prison system and the paramilitary border guards.

In 1956 KdSBP was in turn merged into the MSW, placing internal security and counter-intelligence under the same roof as Polish intelligence on the model of Beria's recently established KGB. In addition to all the pen-pushers and telephone interceptors, it controlled 41,000 soldiers of the Internal Security Corps, 57,500 members of the citizen militia, 32,000 border troops, 10,000 prison officers and 125,000 members of the Volunteer Reserve Citizen Militia. In 1956 Służba Bezpieczeństwa Ministerstwa Spraw Wewnętrznych (Security Service of the Ministry of Internal Affairs), abbreviated to 'SB' for pretty obvious reasons, was set up with many of the same personnel and officers of the Security Service, who were known colloquially among themselves as 'SB-eki', much as KGB officers were informally called 'Chekisty', from the CHE-KA initials of the first Bolshevik secret police.[14] Never to their faces, the SB officers were also called 'ubek', 'bezpieka' or 'esbek', which became terms of abuse in the mouths of their fellow citizens.

That year brought a number of changes to Polish politics. In June 100,000 workers in Poznań demonstrated under the slogan *Give us bread and freedom* in protest at shortages of food and consumer goods – and the poor housing conditions and bad economic policies that produced inflation unmatched by wage increases. With Soviet pseudo-logic, the government declared that the demonstrators were provocateurs, counter-revolutionaries and agents of Western imperialism. In typical Stalinist style, Rokossovsky, as commander-in-chief of all Polish armed forces and deputy chairman of the Council of Ministers, ordered 10,000 armed security police with 360 tanks to put down the riots. In the process, they killed at least seventy-four demonstrators[15] and injured an unknown number. The courage of the workers resisting this onslaught triggered a belated realisation in the PZPR leadership that the riots were the tip of an iceberg of social unrest. At the risk of mixing metaphors, it was decided to defuse the situation by redesignating the Poznań rioters as 'honest workers with legitimate grievances'. Wages were increased by an amazing 50 per cent and other changes were promised.

Within the Party, a Poland-for-the-Poles movement grew in strength, arguing that far too many Russians still held positions of great power. With pro-Soviet Bierut dead, his successor, Edward Ochab, rehabilitated Gomułka, whose only 'fault' had been his conviction that Polish communism should be Polish first and communist second. Despite looking like a walking skeleton after his years in prison both before and after the war, Gomułka insisted that Rokossovsky be expelled from the Polish Politburo and a programme of reforms be put in place, to avoid a general uprising. Rokossovsky flew to Moscow and tried in vain to convince Nikita Khrushchev to send in the Red Army 'to restore order in Poland'. On 19 October, the leadership of PZPR formally named Gomułka First Secretary of the Party – this with the backing of the defence forces and the Internal Security Corps.

These first overt signs that Poland was regaining control over its own destiny alarmed Moscow so much that intimidatingly large-scale manoeuvres were launched near the Soviet–Polish border. This was the iron fist in the velvet glove of a top-level delegation to Warsaw headed by Khrushchev. With extraordinary courage, Gomułka told them that Polish troops would resist if the 'manoeuvres' encroached on Polish territory, but sweetened the pill by portraying his reforms as internal Polish matters, which did not mean that the country was about to abrogate its treaty relationship with the USSR, abandon socialism or withdraw its armed forces from the Warsaw Pact alliance.[16] As the Soviet delegation flew back to Moscow the following day, more or less satisfied, Gomułka's popularity grew – not only in his own country. When neighbouring Hungary learned of these happenings from US propaganda station Radio Free Europe towards the end of October 1956, student unrest in the country turned into a full-blown anti-Soviet revolution, with secret policemen hacked to death in the streets of Budapest.

On 12 December far-reaching increases in food and other prices were announced; this triggered protests that started in the Lenin shipyard at

Gdańsk and spread along the Baltic coast. UB officers were attacked and local party offices torched, which provoked Soviet-style repression in response, with troops shooting rioters dead. Gomułka, blamed for the crackdown, was sacked again and replaced by Edward Gierek. In January he and Defence Minister Wojciech Jaruzelski actually sat down with the strikers in Szcecin and Gdańsk, arguing for a whole day to persuade them to end their strikes.

The UB reduced the number of its officers in the central HQ by 30 per cent and in the regional and local offices by 40 or 50 per cent, but continued to be responsible for political repression, most notably targeting the Solidarność movement, whose co-founder Lech Wałęsa was under constant surveillance until 1989. But lower numbers did not mean quiescence: as late as March of 1981 Solidarność supporters were attacked and beaten in the major city of Bydogoszcz, precipitating a strike by Solidarność's 9.5 million members and many communist sympathisers, representing three-quarters of the working population. Concessions were promised but not put into effect, causing more strikes until on 12 December 1981 a cabal of generals declared a state of emergency, suspending all civil liberties, arresting Gierek and other party VIPs and approximately 10,000 other people, including all visible Solidarność leaders. Sit-ins by workers were ended by sending tanks to smash their way into factories and shipyards and an estimated 100 workers were killed in confrontations with the security forces.

The situation was a stand-off, with Jaruzelski's strong-arm tactics somehow managing to short-circuit direct intervention by Moscow. In November 1982 Wałęsa and his cohorts were released, but it took the visit of a Polish pope to this still premoninantly Catholic country to effect the final lifting of martial law and an amnesty for the majority of jailed dissidents. Just when things might have settled down, in October 1984 came the murder of 37-year-old Jerzy Popiełuszko, the priest who was an outspoken advocate of Solidarność. They first faked a car accident to kill him on 13 October, which failed. Six days later they kidnapped him in flagrant KGB style, beat and tortured him and dumped his body in a reservoir near Włocławek. So great was the fury at Popiełuszko's brutal murder that more than a quarter-million people attended his funeral on 3 November. News of the political murder caused uproar throughout Poland, and the three killers were tried and jailed, together with the UB colonel who had given the orders.

Many people believed that these men had received their orders from the government itself and Poland continued its rocky path through strikes, concessions, inflation and more concessions. After power-sharing with Solidarność, the Polish Party voted itself out of existence on 28 January 1990.

Notes

1. Extract from http://www.doomedsoldiers.com
2. Deposition of Miroslav Barczynski, historian at Museum of Southern Podlaskie, see above
3. P. Kenney, *Rebuilding Poland*, London, Cornell Paperbacks 2012, p. 39–40
4. Kenney, *Rebuilding Poland*, p. 55
5. G. Dallas, *Poisoned Peace*, London, John Murray 2005, p. 563–4
6. P. Sudoplatov, J.L. Schechter and L.P Schechter, *Special Tasks, the memoirs of an unwanted witness*, London, Little Brown 1994
7. Sudoplatov, *Special Tasks*, p. 223. He refers to him as 'Moravitz'
8. Kenney, *Rebuilding Poland*, pp. 54–5
9. M. Scisłowka, article in *Toronto Star*, 10 January 2008
10. B. Wasserstein, *On the Eve, the Jews of Europe before the Second World War*, London, Profile Books 2013
11. Brogan, *Eastern Europe*, p. 53
12. Born Izaak Fleischfarb, he took the name of his wife, Justyna Światło, to conceal his Jewish origins
13. Applebaum, *Iron Curtain*, p. 414
14. Chrezvychainaya Kommissia, meaning 'the Extraordinary Commission'
15. Some sources say fifty-seven deaths
16. Which had been signed the previous year

The Horizontal Spy

The Poles have a long history of espionage, which is not surprising if one takes a glance at the map of Central and Eastern Europe, where the brothers Methodius and Kyril have a lot to answer for. When sent to proselytise the Slavic tribes in the ninth century, these two Byzantine monks disagreed over the alphabet to give their previously illiterate converts. Kyril gave to the eastern Slavs a Greek-based alphabet, modified by the addition of symbols borrowed from other languages for sounds that did not exist in Greek. Methodius chose the Latin alphabet for the western Slavs, with the addition of various accents for sounds that did not exist in Latin. As a result, the Poles, Czechs and Slovaks enjoyed the Renaissance, while the eastern Slavs with their Cyrillic alphabet did not.

Lying on the boundary between the two linguistic groups, the Polish nation has constantly confronted an aggressive, continually expanding people on their eastern border, with little in the way of natural barriers to deter invasion.[1] As a result, the eastern borderlands have been historically in a state of flux, with the tsars and their Soviet successors constantly nibbling away at Polish territory, except for moments when they took large bites. The other neighbours have also done some nibbling and the Poles at times have also grabbed extra land. It would take a whole book to follow the changes, but the online encyclopaedia Wikipedia[2] does a fair job of reducing the flux into two sentences:

In 1492, the territory of Poland-Lithuania covered 1,115,000 km (431,000 sq mi), making it the largest territory in Europe; by 1793 it had fallen to 215,000 km (83,000 sq mi), the same size as Great Britain, and in 1795 it disappeared completely. The first 20th century incarnation of Poland, the Second Polish Republic, occupied 389,720 km (150,470 sq mi) while since 1945, a more westerly Poland covered 312,677 km (120,725 sq mi).

Living where they do, many Poles have developed gallows humour into an art form. They can make jokes about anything, even the million tragedies in every territorial 'adjustment' decided by statesmen at international conferences. There is even one about this flux: having been informed that the border had been moved to the east after the First World War, a Polish-speaking farmer in the disputed territory that was now legally part of Poland, said, 'Dzięki Bogu. Nie więcej rosyjski zimy!' Thank God. No more Russian winters!

Threatened by land-hungry neighbours to the west, south and east, the rulers of historical Poland under its various titles needed good intelligence about the intentions of those neighbours. While low-grade spying was a blue-collar affair, so that no one wept when a spy with a telescope was caught and shot in the field, high-level spying – like stealing the enemy's order of battle – was an upper-class occupation in those class-conscious times.

Fitting perfectly the image of the 'gentleman spy' was Jerzy Franciszek Kulczucki, born into a Polish–Lithuanian noble family in 1640 near Sambor, now in Western Ukraine. Fluent in German, Hungarian, Polish, Romanian, Turkish and Ukrainian, he joined the Zaporozhian Cossacks in search of adventure – and found it. Captured by Turks, he was sold to some Serbian merchants, in whose service he worked as translator in the Belgrade office of an Austrian trading company. In 1678, about to be arrested by the Turkish overlords of the Balkans, he slipped away to Vienna, where he had managed to stash away considerable savings that enabled him to start up his own trading company. Five years later, Vienna was under siege by the 100,000-strong forces of Grand Vizier Kara Mustafa Pasha. Inside the city were a mere 10,000 Austrian defenders. After the Turks had captured part of the walls, Kulczucki and a trusted servant rode casually through the siege lines dressed in Ottoman style and chatting in Turkish with anyone who tried to stop them.

Reaching the camp of Duke Charles of Lorraine, commander of the Habsburg forces, he imparted the latest information about the siege. Returning to Vienna with the news that relief was on the way, Kulczucki persuaded the garrison not to surrender. With insufficient men to make a frontal attack on Mustafa Pasha's army, the Duke of Lorraine harrassed its lines of communication and managed to get supplies into the city until a Polish Christian army under King Jan III Sobieski arrived and drove the Turks off. Kulczucki was the hero of the hour, generously rewarded by the rich merchants of Vienna. The legend has it that Jan III Sobieski himself also gave the city's saviour several sacks of green coffee beans found in the deserted Turkish camp after the decisive battle of Kahlenberg, a few miles north of the city. From his dealings with Turks, Kulczucki knew what to do with the beans and opened Vienna's first coffee house, near the cathedral. With the flamboyant owner supervising the roasting of the beans and serving the clients dressed in his Turkish costume, this became a roaring success. He died eleven years later and was afterwards memorialised like a patron saint of Viennese coffee houses, with a street baptised with the German spelling of his name – Kolschitsky – and his statue on the corner of Kolschitskygasse and Favoritenstrasse showing him in costume serving coffee in the Turkish manner.

Handsome spies, beautiful mistresses who had access to secret plans and rich rewards for success ... Reality in the period between the two world wars puts James Bond to shame. Jerzy Sosnowski – who used many aliases at various times – was a Polish master spy born in Łwów in 1896. At the time, this was Austro-Hungarian territory administered from Vienna, so he grew up speaking perfect German. Aged 18, he was called up for service in an Austrian infantry regiment, was posted to a cavalry training school and fought against the tsarist forces on what was loosely called 'the eastern front'.[3] Following Russia's withdrawal from the war in 1917, he received flying training, making him an all-round soldier by the standards of the time.

After his country gained independence from Austro-Hungary in 1918, Sosnowski joined the new Polish Army and commanded a squadron of cavalry against Trotsky's Red Army, which was trying to repossess Poland's newly acquired eastern provinces. In 1926 he joined the Dwójka, or *deux-ième bureau* of the Polish General Staff, and set himself up in Weimar Berlin in the guise of an anti-communist baron, using the Austrian title Ritter von Nalesc. A horseman of international standard, he was popular with German officers, whom he cultivated as part of his plan to obtain documents relating to the Wehrmacht's plans for an invasion of Poland. One method he used to build the network code-named In-3 was the discreet lending of money to officers with gambling debts who could be useful, so it was probably an unrepayable loan that brought Lieutenant Colonel Günther Rudloff into the ranks of his sources. Sosnowski's other favourite method was to seduce well-connected women into becoming his accomplices. One of his first conquests was Benita von Falkenhayn, the wife of a retired officer, distantly related to First World War Chief of Staff General Erich von Falkenhayn. By the end of the year, she was actively collaborating with Sosnowski, despite knowing that he was a Polish spy.

His increasing flow of material, passed through the Polish embassy in Berlin, seemed to Sosnowski's masters in Warsaw too good to be true. They suspected him of feeding them German disinformation, especially after he seduced four more women, all of whom had connections with the Reichswehrministerium, or War Ministry, where the most secret war plans were prepared. Showing that he had nothing to learn from later practices of the KGB or CIA, Sosnowski flew a false flag to get one of them into bed. Knowing Irene von Jena hated Poles, he pretended to be a British journalist, revealing his true identity only after she had fallen in love with him. All these women supplied top-grade intelligence. In 1929, after one of them handed him a copy of the invasion plans, Sosnowski demanded a bonus of 40,000 Reichsmarks from his masters in Warsaw for handing these over, despite his network already being the major item in the budget of the Dwójka. By this time, Warsaw trusted neither him nor the plans. In the end, Sosnowski passed the plans to Warsaw without payment, but they were regarded as German disinformation and not acted upon.

In autumn 1933, hell had no fury... Whether the Abwehr started unravelling Sosnowski's network thanks to actress Maria Kruse, another mistress of whom he had grown tired, or whether he was betrayed to it by his jealous predecessor in Berlin, a Polish officer who had had no remotely similar success either in espionage or in bed, is impossible to know. But certainly both were somehow involved. A few days after Sosnowski was arrested, most of his network fell into the net. The notable exception was Rudloff, who managed to talk his way out by claiming that his liaison with Sosnowski enabled him to get useful information about Polish plans. He, however, committed suicide in 1941.

The espionage trials in the Nazi Volksgericht during February 1935 led inevitably to sentences of death for treason for von Falkenhayn and another of the women. Benita's second husband pleaded for clemency for her, although she was at the time desperately trying to divorce her third husband and marry Sosnowski in order to get a Polish passport and thus escape the penalty for the crime of treason committed by a German citizen. The two women were beheaded by axe at Plötzensee prison two days after the verdict. Sosnowski and Irene von Jena were sentenced to life imprisonment.

In April 1936, after fourteen months' total isolation in prison – not even allowed to see his guards – Sosnowski was released in a spy swap for three German agents who had been caught in Poland. He recounted how he had been appalled at the deaths of Benita and Irene, but was himself accused of treason for a second time by his own superiors in the Dwójka. On 17 June 1939, as the world headed into war, he was judged guilty of treason in the service of Germany and sentenced to fifteen years' imprisonment. Was he evacuated eastwards by his captors during the German invasion of September 1939? It would seem logical, but nothing certain is known about the remaining lifetime of Jerzy Sosnowski. He may have been shot by his guards when about to be overtaken by the rapid German advance, although some sources aver that he was handed over to the NKVD and worked for them in the Armia Ludowa in Warsaw until being killed during the uprising of summer 1944. It is somehow fitting that the later life of the great horizontal spy should be shrouded in mystery.

Kazimierz Leski became a respected naval architect in Holland by his mid-twenties, designing two Polish submarines – Orzeł and Sęp – for the Nederlandsche Vereenigde Scheepsbouw Bureaux in the Hague before returning to Poland, where he learned to fly and joined the Polish Air Force just before the German invasion of 1939. Shot down a few days later, he was taken prisoner by Soviet troops, but managed to escape although wounded in the crash and made his way across the new Soviet–German demarcation line to reach Warsaw. After joining the Home Army, he was still unfit for guerrilla warfare in the forests and founded instead an intelligence-gathering network, spying on the German troops and forging links with expatriate Poles in Western Europe, through which he made contact with the Polish government-in-exile in London.

In 1941 Leski made his first, highly risky journey to France, disguised as a Wehrmacht lieutenant. Fluent in several languages including German and still suffering from his wounds, he decided to travel more comfortably in future – in first class accommodation as a major general, using the alias Julius von Halmann to collect intelligence on German operations and fortifications. He also found time to smuggle some detainees out of German prisons such as the infamous Pawiak in Warsaw, where 100,000 Poles were held, 40 per cent of them executed there and the others sent to extermination camps. In the Warsaw uprising of August 1944, Leski fought as an infantry commander, although holding no formal commission. When the survivors of the uprising surrendered, he escaped again and became commander of the clandestine Wolność I Niezawisłość – Freedom and Independence – anti-communist partisans in Gdansk.

His pre-war experience of shipbuilding saw him entrusted with the reconstruction of the shipyard there, which had been extensively demolished by the retreating Germans, and his work was recognised in August 1945 by the provisional government's highest award. Later the same day, Leski was charged by the secret police with attempting to overthrow the regime and sentenced to twelve years' imprisonment. Although this was reduced to six years, in 1951 he was charged with having collaborated with the Germans during the occupation. Placed in solitary confinement, he was brutally tortured. In 1956, with Bierut replaced by Gomułka, Leski was freed, aged 44, but was still under suspicion and, although elected to the Polish Academy of Science and holding patents on several inventions, denied an academic chair for his work in computer analysis. Not until the fall of the Communist regime in 1989 did this incredibly brave and resourceful man publish his memoirs, which deservedly became a best-seller in Poland.

Michal Goleniewski was in every way the equal of his illustrious predecessors. Born in 1922 in an area of eastern Poland that is now in Belarus, he held the rank of lieutenant colonel in the Polish army in 1955. After receiving a doctorate in political science at the University of Warsaw in 1956, he was appointed head of the Technical and Scientific Department of MBP from 1957 to 1960. In this position he was also reporting to the KGB and in 1959 he became a triple agent, feeding both Polish and Soviet material to the CIA under the code-name 'Sniper' without revealing his true identity, using anonymous notes left in dead letter boxes. In April 1959 the CIA informed British counter-espionage agency MI5 that 'Sniper' had revealed the existence of a SB informant in the Royal Navy, with a name that he had overheard just once. It sounded to him like 'Huiton'. 'Sniper' also passed over some documents coming from 'Huiton' which made it possible to narrow down his place of work. In addition, 'Sniper' reported a top-level Soviet penetration of MI6 – which turned out to be the mole George Blake. Fortunately, 'Sniper's rank was so high that he learned just in time when the KGB first heard of a mysterious CIA source inside SB, and was able to make his, obviously well-prepared, escape with his mistress to West Berlin at the end of 1960. Once in the West, they were immediately flown to Ashford Farm in Maryland for debriefing, in which he revealed a number of other SB or KGB sources inside NATO forces and intelligence agencies. After his defection, Goleniewski was sentenced by a Polish court to death in absentia.

'Sniper' brought no documents with him, but had already established his bona fides with the stream of leaks while he was still in place, and also revealed the whereabouts of several caches of photographic and other material for eventual retrieval by CIA agents. Given US citizenship, he was placed in a witness protection programme and could have gently faded away from risk. Unfortunately, like many multiple agents, Goleniewski also lived a fantasy life, claiming that he was really the *tsarevich* Crown Prince Alexei, who had miraculously survived the massacre of Tsar Nicholas II and the rest of the Russian royal family. Eventually, he embarrassed his employers too much with this play-acting and he was put out to grass in 1964.

Against this, it has to be remembered that his information led to the unmasking of two important spies in Britain. In 1951 a former Royal Navy master-at-arms named Harry Houghton was posted as a civilian assistant to the office of the naval attaché in the British embassy in Warsaw. It apparently passed unnoticed by the embassy security staff that Houghton was an alcoholic and was financing an extravagant lifestyle by selling on the black market both Western goods and medical supplies, which made him vulnerable to blackmail by the SB. When Houghton's wife complained to his superiors about domestic abuse, he was posted back to Britain in 1952 and sent to the top secret research facility at the Admiralty Underwater Weapons Establishment in Portland. Warnings by his wife that he had brought restricted documents home for an unknown purpose were treated as the bitter allegations of an abused wife, although it should have been obvious Houghton was again living well beyond his means. After, or maybe before, his divorce in 1956 Houghton seduced a filing clerk at the base named Ethel Gee and used her to access files, photocopies of which were passed by him to Polish agents working for the KGB. At the beginning of each month Houghton travelled to London, handed over his material to a contact and received payment in cash.

Examination by MI5 of the naval documents 'Sniper' had passed revealed that they came from the Underwater Weapons Establishment at Portland. Houghton was an immediate suspect because of his excessive drinking and expensive lifestyle. Placed under surveillance at work and on his trips to London, he enabled his followers to identify contacts afterwards referred to as 'the Portland Spy Ring'. On 7 January 1961 Scotland Yard Special Branch officers arrested Houghton, Gee and a man purporting to be a Canadian businessman with the name Gordon Lonsdale – who was actually a KGB deep-penetration agent named Konon Molody – to whom Houghton was handing material in a brush pass on Waterloo Bridge. At the same time US citizen Morris Cohen and his wife, Leontina, who ran an antiquarian bookselling business, using the names Peter and Helen Kroger, were also arrested. At their modest suburban bungalow in Ruislip, searchers found a burst transmitter whose extremely brief transmissions were difficult to detect, plus much other espionage equipment used to process and send back to Warsaw and Moscow the material from Houghton.

His defence in court was that he had been having an affair with a woman involved in his black market operation during his time in Warsaw. Told by SB officers that she would go to jail if he did not cooperate, he started handing over material, but claimed that he only gave them what was already in the public domain. Unimpressed, on 22 March 1961 the court sentenced both Houghton and Gee to fifteen years in prison. With remission, they were released on 12 May 1970 and married the following year. Also in March 1961 Molody, refusing to reveal his real identity, was sentenced to twenty-five years in jail. However, three years later, on 22 April 1964, he walked across the Glienicke Bridge to Potsdam while British businessman Greville Wynne walked the other way in one of the many spy swaps carried out at the bridge. Leontina Cohen received a sentence of twenty years and her husband, Morris, got twenty-five years. In 1969 they too were released early, in exchange for a British teacher of Russian named Gerald Brooke, who had served four years in a hard-regime labour camp for unwisely smuggling anti-Soviet material into the USSR.

Although the officers of KGB, the Stasi and other communist security organisations were supposed to lead morally blameless lives, sexual black-mail was so common that it had its own jargon: the entrapment of a man in this way by a glamorous woman was called a honey-trap. Irving Scarbeck was a popular 38-year-old clerical officer in the US embassy in Warsaw with an impeccable service record. In 1959 he rented an apartment in which to meet his 22-year-old mistress Urszula Dische, who may, or may not, have been working for SB. A few months later, Scarbeck was confronted with photographs of them in bed and threatened that they would be shown to his wife and children, who were also in Warsaw. To save Urszula from arrest by the SB, he handed over an unknown number of classified documents and also arranged her escape to Western Germany, where he continued to send her money. Arrested by the FBI when on home leave in summer 1961, Scarbeck confessed all and was sentenced to three consecutive terms of six years in jail, which was later softened by making the sentences concurrent. One of the luckier exposed spies, Scarbeck had a wife who forgave his infi-delity. He was paroled in 1966.

An important Polish agent exchanged across the Glienicke Bridge was Marian Zacharski. Between 1977 and 1981 the cover of this Polish agent, who brought his wife and daughter with him to the United States, was his job as president of the Polish–American Machinery Company. A former student of business studies, he revelled in making profitable contracts for the sale of his machines. Although various FBI sources considered that Polish spies were after technical and commercial intelligence, rather than military secrets, Zacharski was caught when buying, allegedly for $200,000 classified documents relating to the Patriot, Phoenix and Hawk missiles; radar installed in the F-15 fighter; stealth radar; US Navy sonar equipment and the M1 Abrams tank – all from a single debt-ridden employee of the Hughes Aircraft company in California.

Zacharski and other Polish spies in the US were 'blown' by diplomat Jerzy Koryciński, defecting from the Polish delegation at the United Nations, as a quid pro quo when he requested political asylum in the US. Probably his most valuable tip-off was of cipher clerk Waldemar Mazurkiewicz. Mazurkiewicz, also working in the delegation, had both family troubles and a real drink problem. Eager to start a new life, he was given a new iden-tity and placed under a witness protection programme after betraying the Polish and other Soviet bloc codes.

Zacharski was entrapped when FBI officers placed a wire on his carefully cultivated source inside Hughes Aircraft, and he received a life sentence on the day after Poland's then-Communist government imposed martial law, which can hardly have helped his case. In 1985 he and three other Eastern-bloc agents were traded for twenty-five low-grade Western spies.[4]

As reward for his services in America, Zacharski was made head of the consumer electronics division of Pewex, a hard-currency chain of stores selling luxury goods to Western diplomats and businessmen – and Poles who had dollars to spend. Although few 'blown' intelligence operatives make a success of subsequent careers, Zacharski was an exception, due – so he said – to his business studies in Poland and learning all the lessons of Big Business during his time in the US. Indeed, after becoming president of Pewex, which was privatised at the end of the Communist regime, he lived like an American tycoon: well groomed, smartly suited, with a chauffeur-driven car and a luxurious office in the Warsaw Marriott Hotel. He did however manage to cause more problems in disclosing that the Cold War links between high Polish officials and intelligence officers and the KGB had survived his country's new identity under President Lech Wałęsa. Threatened with prosecution for having spied for Russia over the previous ten years, Prime Minister Jósef Oleksy in turn accused President Aleksander Kwaśniewski with corruption, but was forced to resign in 1996 after admitting that his habit of passing restricted Polish government documents to Soviet diplomat Georgi Yakimishin and KGB officer Vladimir Alganov was inappropriate, to say the least.[5] Until 1989 this would have been normal; after that date it was effectively treason.

That there was plenty of dirt to dig up was shown by the case of Peter Vogel. Convicted in 1971 for murder, he was sentenced to twenty-five years' imprisonment, but was released in 1983 during the period of martial law in Poland. Given a passport and allowed to leave the country, he turned up in Switzerland with considerable funds at his disposal. In 1987 there was a warrant for his arrest which was not executed while he was in Poland, but after his return to Switzerland. Extradited to Warsaw, he was granted amnesty and later pardoned by President Aleksander Kwaśniewski. Vogel had had dealings with KGB officer Alganov as well as former SB officers who appear to be linked to polo-playing Polish oligarch Marek Dochnal, whose clients have bank accounts operated by Peter Vogel. Deals involved range from a Russian takeover of a refinery in Gdansk to a Polish consortium buying a Siberian coal mine for over $100 million.

Whether Zacharski is involved with them is hard to say. As befits a master spy, he simply disappeared after the scandal that brought down the Oleksy government, first travelling to Switzerland, where he was rumoured to have salted away substantial sums. One certain thing is that he left Poland one step ahead of prosecution for flagrant mismanagement of Pewex, i.e. corruption, and illegal trading in imported motor vehicles. Where are you now, Marian?

It seems that Poland will never know peace for long, simply because of its geographical position. The Russian withdrawal from the country after the implosion of the USSR in 1989 left a number of channels embedded in Polish security organisations and a number of 'illegals', who were not known to the Polish security services. So delicate is Poland's relationship with Russia that a GRU officer lived under deep cover for at least ten years as a salesman dealing in telescopic sights for hunting rifles, and was only identified as Tadeusz J. when he appeared in a court closed to the public in December 2010 after being arrested by Agencja Bezpieczeństwa Wewnętrznego (ABW), the current Polish counter-espionage service. As part of his cover, Tadeusz J. had married a Polish woman. Cryptographic equipment and a cutting-edge communications system – transmitting direct to GRU Centre in Moscow and concealed in professionally adapted, commercially available electronic devices – were found in his home when he was arrested after a struggle in February 2009. His feeble defence that he had bought these ultra-hi-tech devices in a street market was rightly rejected by the court, which sentenced him to three years' imprisonment and a fine equivalent to £10,000. The full extent of his mission was unknown, but it is thought to have had something to do with the now discarded US plans for an eastward-facing missile shield to be built in Poland, over which the Kremlin was hostile.[6]

On 5 June 1989 the Polish people voted by an overwhelming majority to place its government in the hands of Lech Wałęsa's Solidarność party, which took power in the city for which the Warsaw Pact had been named.

Hendryk Bogulak was apparently a humble driver employed at the Polish embassy in Paris, who also had family troubles and was about to be sent home when he drove to the US embassy and turned himself in, disclosing seventy agents of Polish Intelligence working in the West. He also disappeared below the horizon after being granted US citizenship and a new identity.

Western counter-intelligence organisations belatedly came to recognise the danger of giving asylum to immigrants from Eastern Europe. As one example, in 1977 Denmark had a Polish community of some 25,000 people and another 20,000 Poles visiting relatives there each year. How many sleeper agents there were among them is unknown. A Polish diplomat who was also an active officer of the GRU was declared *persona non grata* by Copenhagen after attempting to activate one sleeper whose function was to provide in-country assistance to Polish *spetsnaz* units in the event of the Cold War becoming hot, but that was just the tip of the iceberg. Unactivated sleepers were referred to by Danish counter-espionage organisation Politiets Efterretningsjeneste (PET) as 'the quiet Poles'.[7]

Many of them, like the Warsaw Pact sleepers sent into the USA and Britain, decided that they preferred their new lifestyle, got married to

Danish women and had children. One Polish neighbour of the author who came to France during 'the socialist years' and was allowed to bring his wife and two children with him just smiled and stayed silent when asked by the author how this had been arranged.

It is interesting to see how the vast and formerly powerful state security organisations of the satellite states handled the collapse of communism in 1989. In Poland a foxy-faced, sharp-eyed lawyer, convicted dissident and supporter of Solidarność named Andrzej Milczanowski was appointed to purge the UB. When he asked a head of department to show him all the department's files, he was handed a few sheets of paper. 'Is that your whole archive?' Milczanowski asked in exasperation. 'Yes,' the officer replied said with no apparent embarrassment.[8] It eventually became clear that the whole UB had gone on autopilot at the beginning of the year, when its informers and agents inside Solidarność realised the degree of public support Walesa's movement had gained and therefore initiated a programme of destroying anything that might incriminate the service in the eyes of its future masters.[9]

However, the UB's external espionage was, to Milczanowski's mind, too important to disband, because that would be the equivalent of unilateral disarmament. Instead, he selected UB officer Gromoslav Czempinski – recalled from his American posting in 1976 after a defector gave the FBI names of all the UB officers in the USA – to join a committee that would decide which desk officers and agents to keep and which to fire. Like most compromises, it did not give the hoped-for result: officers with no black marks against them were retained, although were more likely to be just idle than sympathetic to the new regime; conversely, many officers with good track records were fired because they appeared to be hostile to it. In the end 400 out of 1,000 officers were 'let go'.[10]

Notes

1. For a comprehensive exposition of Russian expansionism, see Boyd, *Kremlin*
2. 'Territorial evolution of Poland', *Wikipedia*, http://en.wikipedia.org/wiki/Territorial_evolution_of_Poland
3. See D. Boyd, *The Other First World War*, Stroud, The History Press 2014
4. Article in the *New York Times*, 22 January 1991
5. Article in the *Independent*, 25 January 1996
6. M. Day, 'Poland Discovers Russian Sleeper Agent Living in Country for 10 Years', *Telegraph*, 23 December 2010
7. Section by P.H. Hansen in A.K. Isaacs, ed., *Immigration and Emigration in Historical Perspective*, Pisa, Plus 2007, pp. 145–7
8. Bearden and Risen, *Main Enemy*, p. 423
9. Ibid, p. 390
10. Ibid, p. 424

15

The StB Versus the Czechs and Slovaks

Crossing the German–Czech border today, drivers are not even asked to slow down at the multi-lane checkpoint. There are presumably concealed surveillance cameras logging all the licence plates, but no frontier police to be seen. On either side, verdant meadows and woodland stretch away to the horizon with no sign of the watch-towers and barbed wire that cut this country off from the free world during the Cold War. The visitor is struck by how small Europe is, and how close are its capital cities: the shortest route from the German border to the outskirts of Prague is just 45 miles – half an hour in a fast car. Even for a slower Nazi Panzer tank, that was too close for comfort.

Although in small towns there are signs of the 'socialist era', like a once-subsidised communal dining room with a yellowing and outdated menu still in the window, the uninformed tourist driving into this green and pleasant land with its relaxed, well-dressed and prosperous-looking people would not guess that for four decades they or their parents lived under a ubiquitous secret police force run by the Státní Bezpečnost (StB) – a state security organisation suppressing all internal dissent and whose First Directorate, or První Sprava, was, like that of the KGB, charged with external espionage, targeting the Western democracies. Yet this was the description of his homeland written in 1974 by První Sprava officer Josef Frolik after his defection to the West. It was, he said:

one huge concentration camp, a human cage encircled by barbed wire, guarded against [its inhabitants'] escape by minefields and machine guns, and watched over by an all-powerful secret police ... a state where everything is secret, false and prohibited (unless expressly authorised) and where one sleeps with one eye open, always waiting for that ominous

4 o'clock-in-the-morning ring at the door-bell which indicates the arrival of the secret police.

It was (and still is) a state which has been converted from the one-time 'America of Europe' to one where one cannot obtain razor blades which are sharp, refrigerators that cool, automobiles safe to run; where scores of official lackeys must give their consent before your child can attend a high school or you may go off on a week's vacation.[1]

Whether one comes today to the Czech Republic to drink the best beer in Europe – the generic *pils* got its name originally from the city of Plzeň, where it was first made, and the Budweiser brand was produced originally in Česke Budějovice, whose German name was Budweis – or to gaze at the Baroque, Gothic and Art Nouveau architecture of Prague and be enthralled by Mucha's stained-glass windows in St Vitus' cathedral, today's democratic parliamentary republic has worn many masks in the past. On the street, people's faces here are not Slavic, but European. Their country's problem, as in buying a house, is *location, location, location*. In the First World War, the Czechs were vassals of Austro-Hungary and therefore enemies of the Western Allies. In the 1930s they were allies of the West, but we betrayed them to Hitler in what they refer to as first *zrada Západu*, or Western betrayal. After that war, a second Western betrayal handed this young country – it was only founded in 1918 – to Stalin on a plate, for it to become the oppressive society described by Frolik.

During the First World War, Czech expatriates led by Edvard Beneš in Europe and Tomáš Masaryk in the USA formed the Czechoslovak National Council to gain leverage with the Western Allies for *l'après-guerre* at a time when 1.4 million of their compatriots were obliged to fight in the uniforms of the Central Powers *against* those allies. After the end of hostilities on the eastern fronts, eight months before the armistice on the Western Front, a number of civil wars erupted in the resultant power vacuum and some 100,000 Czech and Slovak volunteers fought Trotsky's Red Army across what had been the Russian Empire, all the way to Vladivostok on the Pacific.[2]

In 1918, when the Austro-Hungarian Empire was dismantled, the Czech and Slovak peoples were allotted a space to share on the map of Central Europe. It was thought they were too few in number to have a country each – although Denmark gets along fine with fewer. But then Denmark is a peninsula open to invasion by land only from the south, whereas the Czechs and Slovaks were *surrounded* by potential enemies. The two peoples had in common a history as former vassals of the Habsburgs, the Czechs owing allegiance to Vienna and the Slovaks to Budapest. Their languages are very similar, but educated Czechs also spoke German while the Slovaks had Hungarian as their second language. Slovakia was predominantly rural,

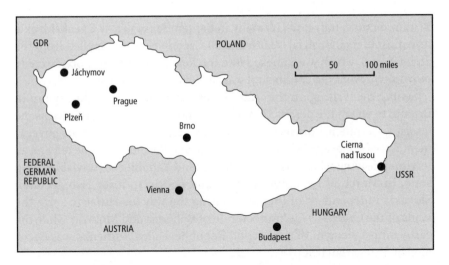

Czechoslovakia after 1945.

whereas the Czech lands in the western half of the new country were culturally in step with Western Europe and contained most of the new republic's industries. On paper, as US President Woodrow Wilson saw it, the two halves of the new-born country were complementary and marrying them fitted in with his belief in 'the right to self-determination of nations' because it gave them independence from the former imperial powers of Europe. However, creating a new state is never as simple as that.

The allotted space on the map was christened Czechoslovakia, and Tomáš Masaryk was declared its first president on 28 October 1918 in Prague, capital of the brand-new country. The Slovaks rallied to the joint state two days later, but the process was not finalised until the Treaty of Trianon in June 1920 carved up the defunct Kingdom of Hungary and left Czechoslovakia with a population of 13.5 million inhabitants and over 70 per cent of the industries of the old Habsburg Empire, largely in the German-speaking Sudetenland. The ethnic minorities in Czechoslovakia were not happy – in addition to the 3 million Germans, there were 500,000 Hungarians, 400,000 Ruthenians and 100,000 Poles in Těšín – but a system of parliamentary democracy like those in Western Europe worked reasonably well; the young republic was the only democracy left in Central and Eastern Europe after 1933. It was also ranked world tenth in industrial output by 1938, which explains why Hitler, proclaiming that all German-speakers were *Ein Volk*, which needed *Ein Reich* and *Ein Führer*, grabbed the industrial heartland of Czechoslovakia on the pretext of rescuing the 3 million Sudetenlanders from oppression – and thus tested the waters for his planned European war. After the Munich Agreement signed by

Britain, France, Italy and Germany in September 1938 saw Czechslovakia lose most of its industrial wealth and all Czech-speakers expelled from the Sudetenland, which was annexed into the Reich, Hitler knew nobody could or would prevent the continental war on which he was intent.

Seeing the writing on the wall, Beneš resigned and sought asylum in Britain, to watch the destruction of his republic from a safe distance as the fascist governments of Germany and Italy then forced the Prague government to cede one-third of Slovakia to Hungary. Poland also annexed Slovak territory, leaving what was called 'the Second Republic' an unviable rump state. In March of 1939 Slovak priest and politician Josef Tiso declared Slovakia independent of Prague, clearing the way for Hitler to seize the lands of the Czechs as his 'protectorate of Bohemia and Moravia' while the easternmost element of the Second Republic, called Ruthenia, was occupied by Hungarian troops.

The dream of the young nation was over, as was the peace.

The London Czechs formed a government-in-exile, recognised hypocritically by the British government in July 1940. During the Second World War, émigré Czechs fought the common enemy in Allied uniforms, but Tiso saw it his priestly duty to declare for the Axis powers. As a result of Hitler's invasion of the USSR and Beneš' compromises with Czech émigré Communists in Britain, Stalin also recognised the London government-in-exile and Beneš made an agreement with him on 8 May 1944, under which all Czechoslovak territory liberated by Soviet forces would be handed over to Czech authority. By that, Beneš meant the government-in-exile after its return to Prague. As usual, what Stalin intended was the confusion of all other parties. A year later, as combat officially ended in Eastern Europe one day later than in the West, the Czech and Slovak capitals, Prague and Bratislava, had been liberated by the Red Army with some assistance from indigenous armed resistance factions, although these numbered far less than in Poland. In apparent compliance with the deal made with Beneš, the Soviet troops withdrew before the end of the year, as did the US Third Army, which had liberated western Czechslovakia under General George Patton. He typically had wanted to continue the drive to Prague, a frustrating 45 miles to the east of his front line, but the White House decreed there must be no clash with Stalin's troops – this in line with President Roosevelt's expressed belief that Stalin was a gentleman, who would play by the rules of the Western democratic game.

At the 1945 Potsdam Conference Stalin held all the cards, with the two new players in the game of Big Three suffering a considerable disadvantage. President Roosevelt's successor, Harry Truman, had never been briefed on anything by Roosevelt, and Attlee was only elected halfway through the conference. Their body language in photographs taken at Potsdam says it all: the Soviet dictator sits rock solid and inscrutable while Truman and Attlee lean awkwardly towards, but try not to look at, the man who is getting everything his own way. Among the decisions taken there was the punitive expulsion of nearly 3 million German-speakers – some of whose families had lived in the Sudetenland for six centuries – in one of the massive deportations that changed the ethnic make-up of Central and Eastern Europe during and after the war. This emigration at gunpoint involved old men, women and children walking very long distances into what remained of the Reich, where there was no provision for them and little food even for those already there. It was achieved by a specially formed paramilitary police that was to be the nub of the pro-Communist irregulars who executed the coup of 1948. All these great events hide a multitude of individual tragedies. The parents and sister of successful U-boat commander Fregattenkapitän Reinhard Suhren, who was in an Allied jail, were so terrified after German forces withdrew westwards from the Sudetenland that the father killed his wife and daughter to prevent them falling into the hands of Czech irregulars, and then killed himself. There are no statistics to tell us how many others did the same.[3]

The first government of the so-called Third Republic, in which both Czechs and Slovaks were reunited, was a coalition consisting of left-wing and 'democratic' parties with some religious representation from Catholic Moravia. In hoping that his newborn country would be a bridge between East and West, Beneš the democrat was being optimistic, but most of his people rightly mistrusted the Western democracies after their betrayal of 1938. Free elections in May 1946 led to another coalition in which the Communist leader Klement Gottwald was named prime minister and Komunistická Strana Československa (KSČ) – the Czechoslovakian Communist Party – gained control of the most important posts, including the interior ministry and defence ministry.

As early as 30 June 1945 a nationwide secret police force was set up: Státní Bezpečnost (StB) or, to give it the correct Slovak title, Štátna Bezpečnost. For convenience, both organisations will be referred to as 'StB'. Under Václav Nosek, Minister of the Interior, its role was to be 'the sword and the shield of the party' – not of the country, or even the government. It was modelled closely on, and 'advised by', the NKVD, whose title changed to Ministerstvo Vnutrennykh Del (MVD) the following year. The professed brief of StB was to hunt down and punish German stay-behinds, Czechs who had collaborated with the German occupation authorities, as well as all dissidents and people guilty of sabotage and espionage. The StB considered these legitimate targets for the state security organisation of a country that had just emerged from a brutal occupation by German forces, but StB also intimidated or put out of circulation political opponents of KSČ, using forged evidence and confessions obtained under torture and by the use of drugs, thus accelerating the Communists' rise to total power. From its inception, StB used telephone intercepts, interception of much domestic and *all* international mail, widespread surveillance and a photo archive of several million secretly taken photographs. The StB's První Sprava, on the model of the KGB's First Chief Directorate, set up in Prague a company manufacturing costume jewellery, which was a traditional Czech export. The company's offices abroad became a cover for illegals.[4]

After getting new orders from Stalin in 1947, Gottwald upped the pressure from the superficially democratic approach, forcing the twelve non-Communist ministers to hand in their resignations in February 1948 – which they did in the hope of provoking a new election, but President Beneš refused to accept them and did not call an election. The KSČ then mounted a coup d'état, presenting him with a new cabinet of its choosing. In very suspicious circumstances, the democratic Foreign Minister Jan Masaryk died in a Moscow-style 'suicide by falling out of a window' in the Foreign Ministry. A contemporary cartoon shows him by the window, hands tied behind his back, in the grip of two KGB thugs with a third asking him to kindly sign a declaration that he is jumping of his own free will.

His country found itself a 'people's democracy', where all dissidence was to be brutally purged as in the other countries of Eastern Europe. The Catholic religion was ousted by the creed of Marxism–Leninism and Czechoslovakia was forbidden by Moscow to join the European Recovery Programme – the Marshall Plan – and obliged instead to become a founder member of Comecon. On the orders of Molotov, Pavel Sudoplatov gave to a former KGB *rezident* in Prague a receipt signed by Beneš' secretary in 1938 for an unrepaid loan of $10,000, to enable the Czech statesman to escape to Britain. He in turn waved it at Beneš as a threat to reveal his former relationship with the Kremlin. Under that pressure, within a month Beneš stepped down and handed power in a bloodless coup to the Kremlin's man, Klement Gottwald. At the time of the coup, Sudoplatov landed at a Soviet military airfield outside Prague with 400 *spetsnaz* troops dressed in civilian clothes but equipped for clandestine operations – just in case.

Today the church of St Bartholomew still stands on Bartolomějská Ulice in Prague, but in 1950 the other religious properties on the street included a convent that housed 1,000 nuns working in the capital's hospitals as nurses and doing charitable work. On one night in 1950, the nuns were forcibly expelled and transported in trucks to a prison camp so that the complex of buildings could become the head offices of StB. Day and night, cars arrived bringing arrested people in for questioning with all the techniques mentioned above. Most of the nuns' cubicles in the convent were turned into holding cells for prisoners and some were used for 'intensive' interrogations.

The neighbouring St Bartholomew's church was converted into a firing range for StB officers.

By 1950, in the climate of growing paranoia, it became important to denounce one's neighbours before they denounced you. Even some students thought it prudent to join the party. In October 2008 the Czech magazine *Respekt* published an article based on research by a young worker at the Institute for Study of Totalitarian Regimes, who had unearthed the police report of a denunciation dated 14 March 1950:

> Today at around 1600 hours a student, Milan Kundera, born 1.4.1929 in Brno, resident at the student hall of residence on George VI Avenue in Prague VII, presented himself at this department and reported that a student, Iva Militka, resident at that residence, had told a student by the name of Dlask, also of that residence, that she had met a certain acquaintance of hers, Miroslav Dvořaček, at Klarov in Prague the same day. The said Dvořaček apparently left one case in her care, saying he would come to fetch it in the afternoon ... Dvořaček had apparently deserted from military service and since the spring of the previous year had possibly been in Germany, where he had gone illegally.

The unfortunate Mr Dvořaček, a conscript in the fledgling Czechoslovakian Air Force, had fled abroad with a comrade during the 1948 coup and returned clandestinely to Czechoslovakia, allegedly as an agent of a Western intelligence agency. He was arrested when returning to Militka's residence to collect his suitcase – and sentenced to hard labour in one of eighteen strict-regime camps around Jáchymov, in the north-west of the country, near the border with the GDR. This was intended as a 'socially useful' death sentence. Under the supervision of Red Army personnel who had mining experience in civilian life, the prisoners laboured in inadequate clothing under grotesquely unsafe conditions in uranium mines, digging out the ore needed for the Soviet nuclear programme. Many died from radiation sickness. Dvořaček survived fourteen years' slavery in the mine.

The preceding paragraph is true, but the name of Kundera, a student representative already known to StB as a dissident, was inserted in the report *when the original was rewritten*; his signature does not appear anywhere, which would have been the case if he had made the denunciation. Deeper digging by the young researcher would have revealed the falsified report to be no more than a delayed-action smear on the name of the famous author which, for whatever reason, was never used. Fortunately, a Czech friend of the author reacted angrily to the original story, saying, 'Kundera would never have done that.' And yet, he recounted how a friend, when a young and healthy student, had been imprisoned for the 'crime' of belonging to a group of intellectuals who imported and listened to Western pop music like the Beatles. Emerging from prison after three years, his left leg was severely damaged but he agreed to act as an informer for the StB, presumably to avoid worse treatment. Perhaps the most evil aspect of the Stalinist terror regimes was the fear induced by the fact that one never knew which friend was an informer, commonly referred to as *fizl* in Czech – a word that seems to be derived from *fies*, a German word meaning 'nasty' and the diminutive *–l*, so 'a nasty little man'.

Another young man labouring in the mines at Jáchymov was Ctirad Mašín, sentenced to two years' slave labour in 1951 for failing to report someone else's plan to flee the country. A teenage son of General Josef Mašín, a Czech tortured and eventually killed by the Germans in the massive reprisals for the death of Reinhard Heydrich, Ctirad was fortunate to be tried on this minor charge, because he and his brother belonged to an anti-communist armed gang, whose members later escaped to West Berlin, some shooting their way to freedom.

Those are personal dramas, unimportant except to the individuals involved. There were more important things for Czechs to worry about in March 1950. After Beneš' resignation, with Gottwald replacing him and Antonín Novotný heading the party, StB proceeded to accuse anti-Soviet politicians of treason for blatant show trials during 1952, most of which ended in death sentences. Nor were rank-and-file party members immune. Stalin deeply mistrusted anyone who had travelled in the West and therefore could compare life in a democracy with the repression and perennial shortages in the centrally planned economies of the socialist bloc. The Czechs have their own sense of humour and joked that their socialist society was locked in a heroic struggle with problems that would not exist under any other system. Those targeted included decorated heroes who had fought on the communist side in the Spanish Civil War, men who had fought in Allied uniform during the war, as well as Jews and Slovaks – the last being accused of 'nationalist deviation'. All these categories were arraigned in show trials and executed or given long prison sentences.

KGB General Alexandr Beshchasnov came to Prague with a support team to 'explain' to the StB officers the motivation that had supposedly led these traitors to commit treason. They transmitted regular reports back to Stalin.[5] It suited his paranoia to have the various treason trials in the satellite states linked because this looked like proof of a Western conspiracy against the entire socialist 'sixth of the world'. The vital link turned out to be Noel Field, an American who had been employed by the State Department pre-war before leaving to manage the Swiss activities of the Unitarian Service Committee, assisting refugees from Nazi Germany. Since these included many communists, he assumed after the war that he was welcome in their countries, but not in his own – not least because there is some evidence that he was an undercover NKVD/MVD agent and did not want to become ensnarled in the Alger Hiss investigations back home. Travelling about Central and Eastern Europe, he was in Prague – some say Budapest – in May 1949, when he mysteriously disappeared. His wife went there to look for him, and also disappeared. A brother and a stepdaughter of Field also vanished in other Communist capitals. Field's government background and mysterious activities in Switzerland enabled the Soviets to portray him as an American agent and, since the USA was now being talked about as *glavny vrag* – the main enemy – it was sufficient to manipulate the suspects' confession obtained in the usual Moscow manner to include admission of contact with him as proof of treason that would be accepted by a rigged court.[6]

After Tito broke away from Soviet domination in June 1949, Stalin's paranoia focussed on the satellite rulers who, in his warped opinion, were putting the needs of their own countries before those of the USSR. This was called 'Trotskyist–Titoist deviation'. For Stalin, Rudolf Slánský, the General Secretary of KSČ, was also guilty of the crime of 'cosmopolitanism' because he was Jewish and had relatives in other countries. Following the 1948 coup d'état, Slánský was the next most powerful person in the country after President Gottwald. When Gottwald accused two of Slánský's associates of betraying the party, Slánský joined in the baying for their blood, unaware that he was only buying a little time for himself by organising a purge that saw thousands of KSČ members arrested and imprisoned, and hundreds executed.[7] Gottwald delayed the arrest of Slánský until he himself was threatened, and then threw Slánský to the wolves, together with thirteen other 'leading lights' of the party – of whom ten were also Jewish. They were arrested and put on trial for high treason after a year-long interrogation under torture, which methods Slánský was later accused of having introduced into Czechoslovakia. Films of the long trial in November 1952 showed the defendants – as in the Moscow show trials of the 1930s – admitting everything and asking to be punished appropriately. The verdicts included eleven death sentences. Five days later Slánský was publicly hanged outside Pankrác prison and his ashes scattered with no grave or marker to show where. The message of the trial was clear: it was one thing to murder Jews and priests, but executing the General Secretary of the party meant that *no one* was safe.[8]

Another of the accused who had been deported from France to Mauthausen during the German occupation was Artur London, a veteran of the Spanish Civil War, who had been appointed Deputy Foreign Minister on his return to Czechoslovakia in 1949. Arrested two years later, he was one of the fourteen accused in the Slánsky trial and convicted on the basis of confessions obtained by torture. Sentenced to imprisonment for life, he was rehabilitated in 1956 and left his homeland in 1963 to settle in France.

The point of the Czech show trials was, as in the USSR, to 'prove' that central planning according to Marxist–Leninist doctrine was infallible; therefore, any failures must be due to spies, Western agents, 'enemies of the people' and saboteurs, who had to be rooted out and made to pay the supreme penalty. To obtain the confessions, the accused were kept standing at all times while teams of interrogators questioned them for up to eighteen hours a day for months on end. During the theoretically permitted six hours of sleep each night, they were awoken every ten minutes, forced to stand and report their identity in the formula 'Detention prisoner XXX reports. Number in cell, one. All in order.'

Former first deputy minister of foreign trade Eugen Loebel, who survived to tell the tale, described his interrogation, which:

> was conducted by three men, each taking his turn and consisted of a never-ending flood of insult, humiliation and threats ... I was not allowed to sit. I even had to eat standing up. You could not even sit on the toilet, because what was provided was a so-called 'Turkish closet' [just a hole in the floor]. Walking [and standing] for sixteen hours a day, however slowly, meant covering 15 or 20 miles – on swollen feet. Such a day seemed endless and the prisoner could scarcely wait for night. Yet lying down caused more pain than anything else. The sudden change in pressure brought such violent pain to my feet that sometimes I had to scream out.[9]

Prolonged sleep deprivation is a torture which destroys the brain's ability to distinguish between real memory and suggested versions of the same events. In addition, mock executions were used to destabilise the detainees, as were drugs. Loebel described the latter as feeling 'as though a hand had thrust itself through my forehead into my brain.'[10] His trial, which opened on 20 November 1952, was, in the words of historian Patrick Brogan, 'pure theatre', in which the accused had learned their parts by rote and knew even at which points the judge or prosecutor would interrupt with specific questions. The verdicts, to which the condemned were instructed to refuse their 'right' to appeal, having been announced, eleven of the defendants were executed, cremated and their ashes scattered on a snow-covered road as grit.

Back to Frolik. Before being called up for military service in 1949, he was a trainee accountant and an obedient member of the KSČ. Discovering that officers of 2nd Infantry Regiment, in which he was serving, had looted millions of crowns worth of art treasures from a monastery, he reported this to military intelligence and had his honesty rewarded with an invitation to join StB – as an accountant. Promoted to other duties after a few months, he realised that the organisation was not the unswervingly honest 'organ of the party' he had assumed it to be, and that false confessions were routinely obtained by torture. Moreover, the Deputy Minister of the Interior, who controlled StB, was Colonel Antonin Prchal, a Czech black-mailed into working for the KGB because of his record of collaboration during the German occupation. It was he who described the honourable president of the People's Republic as 'that drunken paralytic.'[11]

After two years Frolik was moved into counter-espionage and kept his head down. He must have acquired a good service record to be posted to the Czech embassy in London as 'labour attaché', a title that explained his contacts with trade union personalities and Labour MPs. After the Soviet invasion of his country in 1968, he decided to defect and was 'lifted', with his wife and son, in a James Bond-style operation by MI6. Among the disclosures he made during debriefing was that, during his time in London, První Sprava had thirty full-time spies in Britain and 200 informants. Frolik said another První Sprava officer, named Robert Husak, had run an agent code-named 'Lee' who was Labour MP Will Owen, originally recruited by Lieutenant Colonel Jan Paclik, an StB officer accredited as Second Secretary at the embassy. Among themselves, the Czechs code-named Owen 'Greedy Bastard' because he took monthly retainers of £500, expected to be given free holidays in Czechoslovakia and pocketed as many cigars as he could get his hands on when invited to parties at the embassy.[12]

On 15 January 1970 Owen was arrested by Special Branch officers at his home in Carshalton, and charged with the catch-all offence 'communicating information that may be useful to an enemy'. He resigned his seat in the Commons a few days before he was found 'not guilty' after trial at the Old Bailey on 6 May 1970. Although Owen's counsel admitted his client had been paid a total of £2,300 in brown envelopes by the Czechs – Owen claimed it was much less than that, such as £5 or £10 each time – he was acquitted because it could not be proven that he had passed across *classified* material, which seems to make nonsense of the charge in view of the fact that he had sat on the Defence Estimates Committee and a sub-committee dealing with Admiralty matters.[13]

A very different agent working for the Czechs in Britain at the same time was Nicholas Praeger. Born in Prague, where his father worked as a clerk in the British embassy, but also acted as a spy for První Sprava, Nicholas came to Britain with his parents, wife and child in 1949 and was given British citizenship. Volunteering for service in the RAF without disclosing his foreign birth – why did routine vetting not reveal it? – he trained as a radar technician and passed to Robert Husak photocopies of the complete documentation of the radar-evasion system on RAF bombers at the time. Code-named 'Marconi', he left the RAF and worked for the English Electric Company, continuing to pass classified material to Prague until he was caught and tried in 1971. Although sentenced to twelve years' imprisonment, this was reduced to six years when his offences were compared with punishment for similar offences, although his defence that he had been blackmailed by threats against his wife's family in Czechoslovakia was pretty thin in view of his father's espionage experience. Freed in 1977, Praeger was stripped of his British nationality and deported. His wife and child were then living in West Germany, which refused him entry when he tried to go there.

In 1953 a new boss was appointed for StB, who sacked all the KGB-type thugs who used torture. Rudolf Barak was a dark-haired, quick-witted man who introduced more sophisticated methods and made a point of not kowtowing to the KGB 'advisers' who had wielded the real power in the past. A popular chief, he himself fell from grace after allegedly stealing some secret funds, and was sent to prison for fifteen years; he later emerged as a filling station employee. By the time Novotný became president in 1957, he was ruler of a completely purged party. In 1960 he proclaimed the Czechoslovak Socialist Republic (ČSSR).

In Prague, the Jalta hotel on Wenceslaw Square is described with understated Czech humour as 'more decadent and sexier than ever' by the hotel's PR director, and as 'A nice curiosity, a five-star boutique hotel with a bunker.' The Jalta was built 1954–58 as a luxury hotel for Western businessmen, politicians and diplomats, who stayed there unaware that the building was constructed over a Second World War bomb crater. Below the hotel cellars was a bomb- and radiation-proof bunker on three levels with its own power generator, water supply and operating theatre, designed to shelter 150 top government officials for up to two months in the event of nuclear war. In the bunker, to which access was forbidden for hotel staff, was an StB listening post: all the hotel's best rooms and public spaces were bugged by listeners far below their feet, who could also snoop on the staff. When the premises were used as West Germany's embassy in the 1970s, the StB tapped its telephones and many of the rooms. The bunker is now open as a must-see museum of the Cold War.

On 5 January 1968 the Party Central Committee elected Slovak politician Alexander Dubček to replace Novotný as First Secretary of the KSČ. On 22 March 1968 Novotný resigned from the presidency and was succeeded by General Ludvík Svoboda, whose surname ironically means 'freedom'. During what became known as 'the Prague Spring', Dubček oversaw an end to censorship of the media and permitted anti-Soviet articles in the press. Social democrats formed a new political party. Taking the precaution to reaffirm the loyalty to the Soviet camp of the KSČ, Dubček declared his hope that Czechslovakia could improve relations with all countries. His overall aim, he said, was 'to give socialism a human face'.

A short-lived but amazing freedom developed, without equal anywhere in the world. Politicians, students and private individuals dropped in at all hours on the presidential office in the castle overlooking the city of Prague to question Dubček and express their views on what was to be done next. At the time, the author was a BBC assistant television producer working on an international student debate to be recorded in Holland. Waiting at Schiphol airport to welcome the debating team from Czechoslovakia that was due to take part, he was immensely relieved when they emerged from immigration control. Then came the bad news: they announced that they had come to make an appeal for support from the West, but would be catching the next flight back to Prague because 'the situation was changing hourly' and they wanted 'to be present in Dubček's office when certain events happen'. Having been gently persuaded by the programme's producer that the best exposure they could get was by taking part in the planned debate, the Czechs agreed to do this before flying back to Prague. In return, the motion to be debated was changed, with the consent of the sympathetic Dutch debating team, to make a better platform for them.

The changes of policy announced under Dubček rang all the alarm bells in Moscow. The Warsaw Pact called a summit meeting in Dresden, after which Brezhnev, Ulbricht, Kádár and Gomułka brought considerable pressure on Dubček to backtrack on all the liberalisation. Particularly, they were affronted by the press freedom he had introduced. Massive 'manoeuvres' of the Pact armies – excepting Romania, which refused to join in – took place near the Czech borders with the GDR, Poland and Hungary.

On 27 June a journalist named Ludvik Vákulík published a manifesto entitled *Dva tisíce slov* – two thousand words of protest – signed by seventy leading intellectuals pledging their support for Dubček. Ten days later Dubček was summoned to Warsaw to recant. He refused to go, and rejected also an invitation to Moscow, for obvious reasons, so Brezhnev travelled to Čierna nad Tisou, just inside the Czech border with the USSR. There, he 'negotiated' by subjecting the Czech leaders to verbal abuse and threats, but they did not back down.

When the Warsaw Pact forces invaded on the night of 20 August most members of the KSČ Central Committee were surprised that they had not been consulted beforehand. All over the country, in the streets people of all ages – who had studied Russian as a compulsory subject at school – courageously harangued the soldiers pointing loaded guns at them. Radio Prague announced that this invasion was a violation of national sovereignty, but then carried a Soviet announcement that the 400,000 invaders were there to 'help the workers who had been betrayed by their leaders'.

Dubček and his main associates were arrested and forcibly flown to Moscow for more 'negotiations'. They must have been thinking back to the unhappy fate of other political leaders who had dared to question Soviet hegemony and been taken for a ride. The one-sided 'negotiations' strengthened the KSČ and gave it control of the media, limited national sovereignty, banned the Czech Social Democratic Party and saw Dubček and thousands of others stripped of their party membership. He was eventually rusticated to a position in the forestry service of his native Slovakia and would not emerge above the political radar horizon for nineteen years – which was still a lot better than the fate of Slanský and Hungarian Prime Minister Imre Nagy.

More ominously, the new treaty provided for the 'temporary' presence in Czechoslovakia of Soviet troops. Yet Moscow could not crush the Czechs' yearning for freedom. On 6 January 1977 West German newspapers printed a manifesto initially signed by 243 prominent Czechs which had collected 800 signatures by the end of the year. Referred to as Charter 77, it accused the Czech government of failing to respect the basic human rights of its citizens, even those guaranteed by the state's constitution. The StB arrested and interrogated playwright Vaclav Havel and many of the other signatories and mounted a new offensive against the Church. Havel went to prison for five years. But they could not prevent a student named Jan Palach symbolising Czech protest by setting fire to himself in Prague's main square ten days later; he was given a solemn and sad funeral by a huge crowd of mourners.

It was a gesture of despair. From the promise of the Prague Spring, Czechoslovakia had sunk back into a Soviet-style depression where most people just wanted to 'keep their noses clean'. On the first anniversary of the Warsaw Pact invasion, in August 1969, tanks patrolled the streets of Czechoslovakia's main towns and massive protest demos were broken up by riot police with unnecessary violence. With the StB watching Dubček and the other dismissed leaders, they lay low.

Notes

1. J. Frolik, *The Frolik Defection*, London, Leo Cooper 1975, pp. vii–viii
2. See Boyd, *The Other First World War*
3. L. Paterson, *U-Boat War Patrol, the hidden photographic diary of U564*, London, Chatham Publishing 2006, p. 189
4. Sudoplatov, *Special Tasks*, p. 233
5. Applebaum, *Iron Curtain*, p. 303
6. Ibid, pp. 307–9
7. Brogan, *Eastern Europe*, p. 86
8. Applebaum, *Iron Curtain*, p. 304 (author's italics)
9. Quoted in Brogan, *Eastern Europe*, p. 88
10. Ibid
11. Frolik, *Frolik Defection*, p. 11
12. Ibid, p. 97
13. R. Deacon, *Spyclopeadia*, London, Futura 1989, pp. 293–4; Dobson and Payne, *Dictionary of Espionage*, p. 235

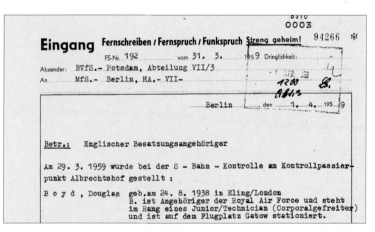

Eingang Fernschreiben / Fernspruch / Funkspruch Streng geheim! 94266 ✳

FS-Nr. 192 vom 31. 3. 1959 Dringlichkeit:

Absender: BVfS.- Potsdam, Abteilung VII/3

An MfS.- Berlin, HA.- VII-

Berlin den 1. 4. 1959

Betr.: Englischer Besatzungsangehöriger

Am 29. 3. 1959 wurde bei der S – Bahn – Kontrolle am Kontrollpassier-
punkt Albrechtshof gestellt :

B o y d , Douglas geb.am 24. 8. 1938 in Eling/London
B. ist Angehöriger der Royal Air Force und steht
im Rang eines Junior/Technician (Corporalgefreiter)
und ist auf dem Flugplatz Gatow stationiert.

The *streng geheim* telex from Potsdam to Stasi Centre announcing the detention of the author (above).

The author in the exercise courtyard (left) indicating the window of the solitary confinement cell he occupied.

Facade of the Lindenstrasse interrogation prison in Potsdam (below), now a memorial to all who suffered there. Only the bars on ground floor windows still hint at the suffering that went on there.

When the Red Army marched into Berlin in 1945, this is what it looked like after months of carpet bombing (above left).

It was a world of the very old, children and women, most of whom had been raped, like these refugees trudging across the Potsdammer Platz (above). All healthy men were in Allied POW camps, so there was no one to protect them.

The Fuhrer of the Third Reich, Adolf Hitler (far left) had committed suicide in the bunker, saying that the German people deserved to be wiped out because they had not been strong enough to beat the Allies in the war.

Sitting safely in the Kremlin was Josef Stalin (left) who planned to use the survivors as pawns in his geopolitical chess game for world domination. During the war, several thousand German Communists had been trained in the USSR to turn the Soviet Zone of Occupation into a prison state.

At Yalta in February 1945 (left) Stalin got everything his own way. US President Roosevelt was convinced Stalin was a gentleman who wanted nothing but victory. Prime Minister Winston Churchill knew Stalin's game but Roosevelt would not listen to him.

At Potsdam in July-August 1945 (left), Roosevelt was dead, replaced by Harry Truman, unprepared to handle US–USSR relations. Churchill was in despair. Before the Conference ended, he was voted out of office and replaced by Clement Atlee. Stalin had won game, set and match.

Despite undertaking at Yalta to allow the populations of the Soviet-occupied states to hold free elections after the end of the war, Stalin had 'educated' thousands of their nationals as Communists in the USSR. Their job was to return home with the Red Army and impose Communist governments and secret police forces modelled on the NKVD in East Germany, Poland, Czechoslovakia, Hungary, Yugoslavia, Romania, Bulgaria and Albania. This gave him a vast buffer zone between the western democracies and the USSR.

In June 1948 Stalin attempted to drive the Western Allies out of their agreed sectors of Berlin by blocking all access by road, rail and canal – and cutting off electricity supplies. To avoid a third world war, the Allies created the airlift, ferrying into the airfields of the three western sectors of the divided city everything from toilet rolls to toffees and children's shoes to coal. Seaplanes even brought cargo to Berlin's lakes. In May 1949, Stalin capitulated and access was restored.

After the Russian Zone of Occupation was re-named 'German Democratic Republic', life there was increasingly regimented with the two Erichs, President Honecker and Stasi boss Mielke (above) congratulating themselves on their rule of iron.

Even the 'spontaneous demonstrations' of the workers on Mayday were joyless manifestations of the cult of personality, with marchers carrying giant posters of Party leaders.

The Stasi Centre
on East Berlin's
Normannenstrasse
epitomised state terror.

Strikes were forbidden,
but on 17 June 1953
workers downed tools all
over the GDR and found
themselves confronting
riot police, the army and
Soviet tanks. Many died.

Extrablatt

BERLINER MORGENPOST

Berlin, 13. Aug

Ost-Berlin ist abgeriegelt

S- und U-Bahn unterbrochen
An allen Sektorengrenzen Stacheldraht – Straßensperren
Volksarmee rund um Berlin

In der letzten Nacht hat Ulbricht die Sowjetzone endgültig zum KZ gemacht. Um 2 Uhr 30 riegelten Volkspolizisten und Volksarmisten, die mit automatischen Waffen ausgerüstet waren, die Grenzen zwischen Ost- und Westberlin ab.

Während an allen Sektorenübergängen Stacheldrahtverhaue gezogen und mit Preßlufthämmern die Straßendecken aufgerissen wurden, gab der kommunistische Rundfunk eine Erklärung der Sowjetzonenregierung bekannt.

Danach hat die Sowjetzone in Übereinstimmung mit den Regierungen der Warschauer Vertragsstaaten beschlossen, an den Grenzen der Zone einschließlich der Grenze zu den Westberliner Sektoren Kontrollen einzuführen, „wie sie an den Grenzen jedes souveränen Staates üblich ist".

Diese Grenze darf nach der Erklärung der Sowjetzonenregierung von Bewohnern Ost-Berlins und der Zone nur noch mit einer besonderen Bescheinigung passiert werden.

In 1961 it was still possible for a GDR citizen to take a train in East Berlin and get off in one of the western sectors. To block this last route to freedom, on 13–14 August the GDR cut rail links and erected barbed wire barriers on the sector boundaries (above left), guarded by sentries ordered to shoot to kill anyone trying to cross (above right). Desperate people living near the boundaries bundled some belongings into sheets and literally ran for their lives into the West before it was too late (left).

Within a few days the barbed wire was replaced by a concrete block wall (above) that snaked through Berlin's streets, cutting off parents from children and workers from their jobs (US satellite photo below).

From this office in Stasi Centre, now a tourist attraction (below), Erich Mielke (left) waged a relentless war on his fellow citizens of the GDR *and* an undercover war targeting the Western democracies, especially the Federal German Republic.

Major General Reinhard Gehlen (POW ID photo left) surrendered to US forces at the end of the war, bringing the Abwehr archives with him. His reward was to be made head of the new West German intelligence service – and Mielke's sworn enemy.

A bridge of spies ... a bridge of sighs, of relief. The Glienicke bridge between West Berlin and Potsdam in the GDR was the scene of many high-security spy swaps during the Cold War. Illicitly taken, the picture above is of a swap in the winter of 1986. Today, the bridge is ... just a bridge.

Nikita Khrushchev called West Berlin 'a swamp of espionage'. Among its denizens were the author and fellow RAF linguists in the Signals Section at RAF Gatow (below) logging in real time VHF transmissions from Soviet and GDR pilots flying aircraft like this MIG 15 (above).

When Josef Frolik (left) spied in London for Czech intelligence, among his informers was an MP nicknamed 'Greedy Bastard.' But Frolik defected to the West and betrayed all his secrets, maybe.

Otto John (below with his wife) defected to the British during the war, and was promoted in 1950 to head the Bundesrepublik's counter-espionage service. In 1954 he vanished, to re-appear in GDR accusing Chancellor Adenauer of being a militarist. In 1955 he 'came home.' Sentenced to four years in jail for betraying secrets, he swore he was innocent.

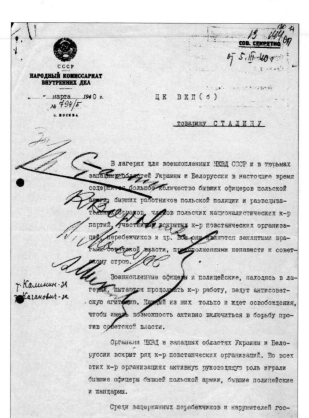

Perhaps the Poles suffered most. The document (left) counter-signed by Stalin, Voroshilov, Molotov and Mikoyan ordered the murder of thousands of Polish POWs in 1940.

Catholic priest Jerzy Popiełuszko was tortured to death by the UB in 1984.

These Home Army men (above) fighting the Germans in the winter of 1944 (below) were all murdered by Stalin's Communist Poles.

This Home Army fighter emerging from a Warsaw sewer in summer 1944 is about to be shot by the Germans dragging him out.

Picasso's 'dove of peace' was the symbol of Soviet-backed unilateral disarmament groups in the West. When the USSR invaded Czechoslovakia in 1968, this dove (above) was behind bars and the slogan read: 'Socialism, yes. Occupation, no!!!'

On 27 June 1968 journalist Ludvik Vákulík (left) defied the StB and Moscow's tanks in the streets, publishing a manifesto entitled *Dva tisíce slov* – two thousand words of protest – signed by seventy leading Czech intellectuals. That took some courage!

16

The ABC of Espionage

Agents, Blackmail, Codes

Every intelligence organisation dreams of a really top-level walk-in. Early in 1956 Colonel Pribyl, military attaché at the Czech embassy in London received an offer which illustrates how much the technology of spying has changed. It arrived in the form of the fifth carbon copy of a typewritten letter, in which the letters were so indistinct that nobody could identify the machine on which it had been written. With the letter were copies of reports sent to his British case officer by a Dr Potoček, director of the First Czechoslovak Insurance Company, from which it appeared Potoček had a network of at least eight agents working for him, enabling him to pass to London the complete specifications of the new Soviet T-54 main battle tank and actual samples of nerve gases made for use by the Warsaw Pact forces in the event of war. Given the code-name 'Light', the author of the near-illegible carbon copy asked that Pribyl pay him £1,000 after verifying this information.

Pribyl, however, was enjoying his comfortable London posting and was afraid that pursuing this lead might get him declared *persona non grata* and expelled from the United Kingdom. He sat on the letter, but mentioned it to a colleague, who immediately sent a coded cable to Prague, which resulted in the arrest of Potoček and his agents. Potoček and one other were sentenced to death; the others, to long terms of imprisonment. Meanwhile an experienced agent handler by the name of Jan Mrazek set up a meeting with the mysterious 'Light' and paid him, not £1,000 but £1,500. At the time, 'Light' refused to reveal his identity, but it later transpired that he was an émigré Czech named Charles Zbytek, who had been in the Free Czech Army during the war and afterwards decided to 'jump ship' and stay in the UK while on tour with a Czech choir performing at a Welsh eisteddfod. He took a job with the anti-Communist Czech Intelligence Office (CIO), one of many revanchist organisations in Britain run by refugees from the satellite countries.

From the sublimely simple – in espionage terms – to the ridiculous. In October 1960 Josef Frolik was transferred to work on the British desk of První Sprava, thanks to his friendship with a slightly insane colleague who had been trying to poison all the staff at Radio Free Europe (RFE) by placing cyanide crystals in the salt cellars of the canteen, and had to be spirited out of Austria after the plot was betrayed by a double agent! From his new office, Frolik looked across the Danube to the British embassy, a building constantly bugged by StB staff employed as household servants, debugged by British technicians flown out for the purpose and rebugged as soon as they had gone home. 'Light' was handed over in 1961 to Frolik, who spoke good English, as his case officer. His colleagues had various theories for why this émigré was betraying CIO agents in-country. It was Frolik's opinion that 'the Czech Philby' did it for the money, but the golden eggs were no longer being laid at the same speed because CIO had lost all credibility with its sources of finance after the betrayals and failures due to the treachery of 'Light'. Yet, for two further years, he continued to betray his colleagues at, as Frolik later said, 'a cost in human life and misery that cannot be calculated'.

By the time that his feed of information dried up completely, he had been paid a total of £40,000 – a comfortable sum at the time, which enabled him to buy a boarding house in Folkestone, send his daughter to a private school and forget about espionage for good.[1]

About this time, Britain's future prime minister Edward Heath[2] was targeted by Czech intelligence. Because he was unmarried and showed little interest in women, the Czechs assumed this meant he was homosexual and set a gay honeytrap, to be sprung on a visit to Czechoslovakia. But how to get him there? One of Heath's passions was playing the organ, so První Sprava arranged for a bisexual Czech organist named Professor Reinburger to give two recitals in London, to which Heath was invited. Naturally, the two organists chatted and the bait was laid. Reinburger offered to arrange a visit to Prague, where Heath could experience the pleasure of playing on the famous organ at St James' church, one of the finest in Europe. Although arrangements appeared to be fixed when the two men parted, Heath was advised by British security that it was not a good idea for an up-and-coming politician to expose himself to possible blackmail in this way, and the visit was cancelled.[3]

In June 2012 BBC reporter Gordon Corera was exploring the declassified archives of StB while investigating the attempted blackmail by Czech agents of former British prime minister Edward Heath. Instead, he uncovered the fact that a junior Conservative minister spied for Prague against payment.

During the Cold War the author attended many receptions in Warsaw Pact embassies, but was never approached as was Raymond Mawby in November 1960. Handing over confidential political information including a sketch plan of No. 10 Downing Street to his StB case officer, who gave him the code-name 'Laval', he was rewarded with monthly instalments of £100, later increasing to £400 – a decent sum at the time.[4]

The undercover war against Britain also used agents of influence. In the early 1960s many British scientists were being enticed to work in the USA for salaries far in excess of what they could earn in their home country. It was called 'the brain drain'. Learning from a pro-Moscow Labour MP that another MP was acting as a recruiter for one large American company, První Sprava asked its man to raise this in Parliament, with the result that the recruiter's bona fides were ruined and there was a wave of anti-American outrage in the British media.[5]

In April 1956, while going through the personal files of Czech expats in the West who might be coerced into spying, the StB found that Alfred Frenzel, a member of the West German parliament who served on the Bundestag's Defence Committee, had access to secret material on West German rearmament. Frenzel had fled his homeland after the 1948 takeover and successfully inserted himself into West German society. An officer of the StB, who had known Frenzel before, visited him in West Germany and recruited him by threatening to have his wife arrested during her current visit to Prague. He also threatened to expose Frenzel's past – which allegedly included some pre-war criminal activities. Since this would have destroyed Frenzel's career in West Germany, he cracked. Travelling to Austria in July, he met Major Molnar, his První Sprava case officer, and was handed an initial payment of DM 1,500, for which he unwisely signed a receipt with his true signature. Given the code-name 'Anna', Frenzel fed highly secret material to Prague for more than four years. The quality of his material, which included many top-secret German documents and details of the latest US aircraft, was evident from the very comfortable house he was given in Czechoslovakia and generous payments into a bank account opened in his name in a Czech bank.

Frenzel passed his disclosures to Molnar using the gamut of 'containers', such as modified toilet articles designed by the StB technical department to auto-destruct if opened without the proper precautions. Molnar, in turn, passed these on to Czech diplomats for forwarding to Prague. However, Molnar's successor, who took over as case officer in September 1959, lived beyond the style possible for someone declaring a small income to the German tax authority. This relatively banal offence was used to justify his arrest by agents of the BfV shortly before he boarded a flight to Prague. His grossest indiscretion, since he had no diplomatic immunity, was to be carrying a tin of talcum powder in his luggage. Opened in a BfV laboratory, it was found to contain a roll of film, which was developed. Among the images of defence installations and documents, just visible in one exterior shot was the number plate of a car owned by Frenzel and carelessly parked in shot. From this lead, other evidence was gathered, earning him a sentence of fifteen years' imprisonment. He was, however, exchanged in a spy swap five years later, recognised as the highest-level 'asset' První Sprava had in the Cold War, and retired from active espionage, to die of natural causes three years later. Nothing was as simple as the officially publicised story, however. In this instance Gehlen's BND had also contributed to Frenzel's arrest by discovering certain secrets he had passed to Prague, and which could only have come from him.[6]

In addition to the 'illegals' working without diplomatic immunity in a target country, there are, of course, all the diplomats in post there who conduct espionage at the risk of nothing worse than expulsion. One such was Ladislav Bittman, accredited as press secretary at the Czech legation in Vienna, who defected in 1968 in a carefully prepared flight to a hideout in Switzerland. He later published two books on Soviet deception operations.[7] One bizarre activity of StB which he reported was the preparation of a vast archive of material for forgery, which involved the sending of numerous Christmas cards to important people in the West, most of whom responded with letters of greeting or cards bearing their signatures and sometimes their official letterheads.[8]

When Josef Frolik was posted to the London embassy in April 1964 as industrial attaché, there were eighteen officers of První Sprava and twelve officers of Czech military intelligence there, all accredited as diplomats subordinate to the ambassador – who was, however, not allowed to know what any of them was doing. Frolik's seventeen colleagues were collecting political information and commercial intelligence, also stealing secrets of industrial processes or smuggling new technology physically back to Prague.[9] The man of whom they were all frightened was a Major Koska[10] whose job was to spy on them all. Frolik described him as 'a heavyweight boxing champion during the Nazi occupation, which was evidenced by his pug nose. He had black wavy hair and a pale oval face, which set off his dark, wary eyes that often reminded me of a snake.'[11] Koska, it transpired, was a double agent, also reporting back to the KGB what Czech intelligence was up to in London.[12] It was, however, he who taught Frolik how to live like a jet-setter while in post, by inventing fictitious 'contacts' who had to be expensively entertained. Since this was an important part of the plot of Graham Greene's novel *Our Man in Havana*, and since Greene had worked for Secret Intelligence Service (SIS) during the Second World War, perhaps this way of augmenting income is widespread in intelligence circles.

One should never place too much credence on spies' accounts of their work but, according to his own published memoirs, Frolik was not very successful during his London posting. One field he did plough assiduously was the cultivation of active trade unionists, many of whom had been CPGB members before the war, and therefore sympathised with the so-called 'workers' states' behind the Iron Curtain. More than once, Frolik was warned that he was 'trespassing on KGB territory' because Moscow regarded trades unions in the West as its preserve and card-carrying members of the CPGB were off-limits to StB. Otherwise, all the techniques of espionage were used by Frolik during his London posting, especially blackmail and the compromising, by making them sign receipts for cash payments, of at least two MPs and others with access to secrets.

His next assignment was very different. In 1960 the Soviet government founded the 'people's friendship university' for intakes of overseas students, which was subsequently named in honour of the late Patrice Lumumba. Since Western counter-espionage organisations kept a fairly close watch on Warsaw Pact diplomats, the students studying there were all evaluated by the KGB for suitability to act as illegals in later life. Czech intelligence followed suit, founding the University of 17 November to provide degree courses for 4,500 African and Asian students. Frolik was recalled to Prague to recruit selected students at this university for later use as 'illegals'. To his surprise, he learned – this was, after all, the 'wilderness of mirrors' – that some of the students were already working for Western agencies and had been sent to Prague to infiltrate the stream of 'graduates' of this spy school.

After the Soviet invasion to repress the Prague Spring in August 1968, Frolik had more and more problems with the increasing KGB influence on První Sprava and decided to defect to the West. His problem was that his new masters mistrusted him to the point of giving notice to terminate his contract – after which he would not be allowed to cross any frontier for five years. So he built up a secret dossier of real and cover names of some 400 Czech legal and illegal agents working in the West, and contacted a carefully chosen CIA officer, who set up an escape plan, which involved a 'holiday' in Bulgaria, from where Frolik was clandestinely transported to a safe haven in Turkey. On arrival in Langley, he paid for his asylum with the list of names.

One name apparently not in Frolik's dossier was that of Karl Koecher, who arrived in the USA in 1965 at the height of the Cold War, accompanied by his wife. On the surface, the Koechers deserved political asylum because his carefully contrived legend showed that he had several times fallen foul of the StB for writing radio comedy scripts that mocked regime policies. In fact he had been an officer of První Sprava since 1962. Once settled into American life, he studied for and was awarded a doctorate of philosophy from Columbia University. Looking every inch the typical moustached, bespectacled, liberal American academic of the time, Koecher was accorded US citizenship in 1971. Mrs Thatcher's comment that she would never trust a man who spoke more than two languages had apparently not been heard in Langley because Koecher was employed some years later as a translator for the CIA due to an apparently impeccable record and his competence in several European languages.

Given the necessary security clearance to monitor intercepted phone conversations of Soviet diplomats and other suspects, he passed warnings back to his První Sprava case officer, who in turn warned the KGB when their agents were under surveillance. He also betrayed double agents working for the CIA – among them a Soviet diplomat posted to Colombia. Now, this is where it gets complicated. Aleksandr Ogorodnik – the surname means 'market gardener' – was a fairly low-level 34-year-old Soviet diplomat working in the Soviet embassy in Bogotá who imprudently got his local mistress pregnant. Blackmailed by Colombian counter-espionage agents, he handed over to them documents of local importance. After being notified that he was to be promoted and transferred to the Foreign Ministry in Moscow, Ogorodnik was passed over to the CIA, for whom he agreed to continue work, once he got there. Given the code name 'Trigon'[13] – apparently by Aldrich Ames, himself later revealed as a KGB double agent – Ogorodnik was given instruction in the use of codes and dead letter drops.

This is where 'the widow spy' comes into the story. Martha Peterson is now a respectable suburban grandmother living 'somewhere in America', whose children were amazed to learn that she and their father had both been CIA officers. When younger, she was an attractive, blonde, just-married 'embassy wife' in Laos, where her first husband, a former Green Beret, was involved in infiltrating CIA-trained Laotian guerrillas to cut the Ho Chi Minh trail during the US war in Vietnam. After he was killed when his helicopter was shot down, the young widow was repatriated in shock. Coming to terms with her loss, she volunteered for an active role with the CIA and was posted to Moscow, where female embassy staff were not trailed everywhere because at the time the KGB did not take women seriously. From 1975 to 1977 Martha worked in the embassy as a low-grade clerk, popular with her colleagues, who had no idea of her CIA work. In secret, she collected Ogorodnik's increasingly important material from dead letter drops, leaving in exchange espionage equipment like preset-focus ultra-miniaturised cameras concealed inside harmless-looking lumps of concrete.[14]

KGB officers arrested Peterson after watching her make one of these dead drops near the Krasnoluzhskii Rail Bridge. Slightly roughed up when she resisted arrest, she was held for three days in the Lubyanka, before being released under her diplomatic immunity. Ogorodnik was already in the prison, but dead. Before being posted back to Moscow, he had insisted on being given a cyanide pill, so that he could end his life on his own terms if caught. This was hidden inside an expensive Montblanc fountain pen. At his first interrogation, he slipped the pen out of his pocket and bit through the specially weakened casing to release the poison. From then on, it became KGB routine not only to handcuff suspects with hands behind their back at the time of arrest, but also to remove any personal possessions immediately.

Koecher was richly rewarded by his KGB masters for uncovering 'the market gardener' double agent. As Martha Peterson later said, case officers under diplomatic cover are at little risk, but their agents have no such protection and pay a high price if all goes wrong – in this case because Koecher was given clearance for material he should never have seen. Or was Ogorodnik betrayed by Ames? In the wilderness of mirrors, everything is possible.

Another highly placed Czech defector in 1968 was General Jan Sejna. As a deputy Minister of Defence who had served on Warsaw Pact committees, he brought with him not just Czech secrets but also information about the networks of 'sleepers' for sabotage if the Cold War should heat up. One operation was to put out of service large parts of the London Underground railway. This plot seemed to his confessors to be rather far-fetched – until Soviet defector Oleg Lyalin, who had worked in the KGB's Fifth Directorate, whose business is sabotage, confirmed in 1971 everything Sejna had said.[15]

No spy can rest on his or her laurels. In 1975 Koecher was called to an interview with KGB boss Oleg Kalugin, who accused him of being a triple agent, ultimately loyal to the CIA. After that, Koecher left the CIA for a safer teaching job, but was recalled after Ronald Reagan was elected to the White House in January 1981. Shortly afterwards, the Koechers were taken in for questioning by the FBI, during which Koecher offered to become a double agent if he was granted immunity from prosecution and allowed to return to Europe.

Somebody rightly had second thoughts about this, so after the couple had sold their apartment and were about to fly to Switzerland, they were arrested – he for espionage and she as a material witness. However, if we are to believe the official story, the whole business was so badly conducted by the FBI that Koecher could not be prosecuted under US law and his wife was able to plead her constitutional right not to testify against her spouse. Although allegedly attacked in federal prison, which Koecher said was an attempt by the FBI to kill him, the couple walked to freedom across the Glienicke Bridge in February 1986.

As a reward for services rendered, Koecher was welcomed home, given a house and a Volvo car – rare in Cold War Czechoslovakia – and a job. He then disappeared into the obscurity proper for a retired spy, except when it was alleged – that word again – he had been involved in procuring for Mohammed Al-Fayed forged documents 'proving' a British Secret Service plot to murder Princess Diana and her friend, Al-Fayed's son, Dodi. The last laugh went to Hana Koecher, who unbelievably was employed as a translator at the British embassy in Prague and only sacked after a Czech journalist informed the embassy staff of her history.

On 5 September 1968 a 23-year-old employee of Radio Brno named Pavel Minařík – code-name 'Ulyxes'[16] – who had just finished a year's training in espionage techniques, 'fled' to the West after being guaranteed that his salary would be paid monthly into a Czech bank account and with 3,000 Czech crowns for expenses in his pocket. He was granted political asylum in Austria, where his broadcasting background saw him given a job in the Vienna office of RFE. He must have been competent, because by the end of the year he was working in the main station at Munich. Each month he delivered, through dead letter drops, a report that was picked up by Czech diplomats, who forwarded it to Prague.

These eventually mounted up to some 21,000 pages of reports covering RFE's management and financing by American agencies, plus compromising gossip of sexual relations among the staff, especially Czech émigrés, and their alcohol, sex and money problems, in addition to confidential internal documents he had copied. He also managed to search colleagues' apartments for compromising material and infiltrated a number of émigré Czechoslovak groups. All this was useful to První Sprava, but its main interest was in RFE's in-country sources who fed up-to-date information designed to show that RFE had a presence inside Czechoslovakia, because these people were vulnerable to instant arrest.

Minařík was young and headstrong. At meetings in Vienna with his case officer, Jaroslav Lis, in April and November 1970, he offered to blow up the RFE station, showing Lis many photographs he had taken inside the building, and he repeated the offer before the 1972 Munich Olympics, but his masters in Prague were not interested. Minařík kept pushing his idea for blowing up RFE but, although RFE's broadcasts were a source of annoyance for all the satellite governments, the station was a magnet for many émigré dissident groups, making it easier to keep an eye on them. In the event, the big news of those Olympics was the murder and hostage-taking of the Israeli team by Black September terrorists.

In January 1976 Minařík was recalled to Prague, to broadcast his insider knowledge of RFE over Radio Prague. It was no surprise to anyone when he disclosed the US influence in RFE, but he also dished the dirt on the management and individual members of the station staff in an attempt to discredit RFE as a reliable news source. He then disappeared from active espionage, but was to get his comeuppance after the one-party state ended in *sametová revoluce* – the 'velvet revolution' in late 1989. In May 1993 he was charged with being a paid member of První Sprava and having planned a terrorist act against RFE in Munich. Found guilty, he appealed and the ding-dong legal battle between the public prosecutor and his defence team lasted more than four years, ending with a final acquittal.

The Munich-based US-funded radio stations were not in themselves a threat to Czechoslovakia but, on the grounds that some émigrés working there *might* be dangerous, a second deep-penetration agent code-named 'Albort' was given a legend and trained in fieldcraft between 1978 and 1982 while ostensibly working as a musician with Czech groups touring in the West. To establish his standing as a dissident, on one such trip he handed some *samizdat* publications over to an anti-Communist émigré living in West Germany. In October 1982, 26-year-old 'Albort' walked away from his colleagues in the Czech National Symphony Orchestra on tour in Italy, jumped on a train and requested political asylum in the Bundesrepublik, after which he settled in Munich and was taken on as a freelance contributor to RFE's Czech service. His job was to pass on to diplomats of the Czechoslovak embassy in Bonn background information used in preparation of broadcasts and also about staff employed there and their contacts with other émigré networks.

But 'Albort' was no Minařík. By September 1988 he was fed up with the precarious life of a spy and voluntarily confessed his espionage role to BfV investigators. Tried in June 1989, he was sentenced to two years' probation on the grounds that he had turned himself in and co-operated fully with his interrogators – and also that his activities had not actually caused any harm to people or property in the Bundesrepublik. Perhaps 'Albort' was fortunate also that the Soviet bloc was already crumbling, with strikes in Poland and the Hungarian government actually dismantling its barbed-wire fences on the borders. It was time to end the madness of the Cold War.

This was a process undertaken differently in each satellite state. In Prague demonstrations on Czech National Day of 1989 had been so feeble that Václav Havel was seriously depressed in case the wave of liberalisation sweeping through the satellite states was going to bypass Czechoslovakia, leaving it an island of tyranny – in the words of CIA officer Milt Bearden, 'a European Cuba'.[17] Thinking that the peaceful demonstration planned for International Students' Day on 17 November would be just another timid gesture, Havel did not go to join it in Wenceslaw Square but the news from Berlin brought 15,000 students, schoolchildren and others into the streets. Because so many had seen on television the changes taking place in the other satellite states, they had the confidence to confront the police in the largest demonstration so far, but were met by units in full riot gear with tear-gas grenades and automatic weapons, who laid into them with staves, beating several demonstrators very badly. This completely over-the-top reaction by the authorities proved to be the spark in the powder barrel. Two days later 200,000 demonstrators marched in protest. This grew to an estimated 500,000 on 20 November. On 24 November the party leadership resigned en masse, followed by a two-hour general strike on 27 November.

In an incredible process of political acceleration, three days later the constitution had been amended to permit other political parties. A few days after that, border guards began removing the barbed wire entanglements from the frontiers with West Germany and Austria, and the streets of Prague were filled each evening with people unafraid at last of StB repression as they marched, jingling their key rings in 'the music of the velvet revolution'. On 10 December President Gustáv Husák endorsed the first multi-party Czechoslovak government since 1948, and tendered his own resignation. But – and it was a big but – the 17,000 officers of StB were still reporting for duty each day. Just before Christmas the six KGB officers 'advising' První Sprava flew off to Moscow and did not return.[18]

Alexander Dubček was elected speaker of the federal parliament on 28 December and Václav Havel made President of Czechoslovakia on 29 December 1989. It was Havel who commented that one of the worst legacies of his country's Communist years – and the industrial pollution was the worst in Europe – was universal hypocrisy, with everybody saying one thing while thinking another. It is an observation that applies to all totalitarian states, including the USSR and its Cold War satellites.

In March 1990 Havel appointed Jiří Křižan to the post of national security adviser with Oldrich Czerny – a long-time Havel supporter – as his deputy. Czerny was an unlikely-looking intelligence man: a small, slightly built, sandy-haired writer and translator who wore tinted glasses and clothing that looked as though it belonged to a much bigger brother. His previous experience of StB had been loss of his job in a publishing house after he refused to spy on fellow dissidents after Charter 77. Having fluent and idiomatic English, Czerny was then approached by První Sprava. After turning down its offer of employment, the only job he could find was badly paid work unloading cargoes from barges moored on Prague's quays. His surprise can be imagined when Křižan ordered him to work with Jan Ruml, another unlikely figure, sporting a ponytail hairstyle, whom Havel had appointed as a deputy minister of the interior, to 'get rid of the intelligence service'.[19]

'We have all these old Communists [in it],' Křižan said, 'and we have to get rid of them. Havel wants you to do it.'

'All right,' Czerny said. 'When do you want me to start?'

'Right now,' Křižan replied. 'We are five minutes late for a meeting with British Intelligence.'

The StB had already been formally disbanded the previous month and replaced by a totally new agency. This re-employed many officers who had been sacked after 1968 for lack of party loyalty. Unfortunately, they had recommenced the jobs for which they had been trained during the Cold War, and started trailing yesterday's enemies, the British and American intelligence officers stationed in the Czech Republic. The new administration therefore decided that the way to handle things was to form a much smaller organisation staffed by former dissidents with no intelligence training. This was something that the new Polish government thought madness, and led to a stormy meeting with Andrzej Milczanowski, who did not mince his words.[20]

The first thing was to decide what to do with the immense archives of StB and První Sprava, which went back forty years. Unlike the situation in Poland, where UB officers had destroyed anything that could be used against them, most of the StB records were still intact, proving that internal intelligence had functioned with 10,000 active informants, like the IMs of the Stasi, infiltrated into every branch of national and local government. To avoid a rash of denunciations and embarrassing trials, Havel's new administration is said to have decided on the destruction of all active files, keeping only closed or historical files.

To train the new boys, Czerny turned to the CIA to set up a new secure communications system and ensure the president's personal safety, as the Secret Service did in the USA. One has to wonder how many Trojan horses came concealed within the American system. The British government supplied SIS officers to train Czech intelligence officers working abroad. Written into the deals was that Prague must deactivate any existing active agents in the West, and recall them and all the sleepers infiltrated in the democracies. The last requirement proved to be a problem: many sleepers refused to 'come home', preferring their new lives and having no intention of causing problems in their adopted countries.[21]

Internal security in the Czech Republic morphed through several titles and forms in the next four years to become BIS, standing for Bezpečnostní Informační Služba, or Security Information Service. Its website reassures any citizen who cares to consult it that BIS – unlike its predecessors of ill repute – is not interested in anyone's politics, personal beliefs or activities, so long as they do not impinge on national security, or involve organised crime or terrorism.

Marx had declared that every society contains the seeds of its own destruction, but seemingly none of the thousands of party fat cats realised that the Soviet-imposed Communist societies on which they had battened were no exception to Karl's creed. As the Western European countries grew more prosperous in the 60s, 70s and 80s, the satellite states, crippled by their planned economies, lagged further and further behind. The Soviet joke *They pretend to pay us and we pretend to work* was not funny, but tragic. One result of their fatal inability to exploit initiative was the massive borrowing from Western banks required to stave off the evil day, as they saw it. But in the space of a few months towards the end of 1989 the nightmare was over and even the Warsaw Pact a phenomenon of the past.

Yet, every now and again echoes of the suffering emerges to ripple the surface of the present. On 23 March 2014 the death was announced in Prague of Miroslav Štěpán, aged 68. The name probably meant nothing to people outside the Czech Republic, but it meant a great deal to Czechs, who remembered him all too well as the KSČ party boss responsible for brutally putting down the first demonstrations in 1988 and 1989. After a student demo in Prague on 17 November 1989, he made a famously ill-timed speech:

In no country, not even a developing country or a capitalist or socialist country, should one see kids of fifteen years old deciding when the president should go or who he should be.

He was speaking in a factory of a state company employing 50,000 workers, who were on strike in sympathy with the demonstrators. Few could hear his words clearly due to constant interruptions by whistling, foot-stamping and chanting of, '*Nejsme děti!*' – We are not children! They also demanded the resignation of this man who commanded the people's militia known as 'the fist of the working class', and sent in riot police to break up the demos – for which he was labelled People's Enemy No. 1. A few days later, Štěpán resigned all his political and public offices.

In 1990 he was the only high party functionary to be put on trial, and was condemned to two and a half years' imprisonment for abuse of power in using water cannons and tear gas against the peaceful demonstrators in October 1988. After one year's confinement he was released and created an extreme-Left party under the banner of Czech Communism, which had no success in elections. To his last days, Štěpán remained convinced that his downfall was the result of a treacherous deal between the Kremlin and the West, and a great mistake.[22]

So, were the StB files all destroyed? Many Czechs think that they still exist but have been closed to the public and may only be consulted by the president or other high government officials investigating candidates for public office. Certainly Putin's aphorism that *chekisty* always stick together is borne out in the Czech Republic, where an *émigrée* friend of the author was trying to gain custody of her teenage daughter, but could get no favourable judgement in a Czech court because the father had been a low-grade StB employee. According to her, his former colleagues still have influence in the right places and will use it for him. At the top of Czech society, Minister of Finance Andrej Babiš – the second-richest man in the country – is believed by many of his fellow-citizens to have collaborated with, or been an officer of, StB under the code name 'Bureš'. In 2013 he sued the Slovakian Memory Institute for publishing this allegation, but neither he nor his witnesses ever came to court. After the elections of 2014, the trial was adjourned *sine die.*

Notes

1. Frolik, *Frolik Defection*, pp. 48–51
2. He was prime minister June 1970–February 1974
3. Frolik, *Frolik Defection*, pp. 41–2
4. *Intel News*, 29 June 2012
5. Frolik, *Frolik Defection*, pp. 58–9
6. Ibid, p. 60
7. L. Bittman, *The Deception Game*, New York NY, Ballantine Publishing 1981; L. Bittman, *The KGB and Soviet Disinformation*, London, Brassey's 1985
8. Deacon, *Spyclopeadia*, p. 271
9. Frolik, *Frolik Defection*, pp. 77–9
10. Or possibly Kleska, according to some sources
11. Frolik, *Frolik Defection*, p. 80
12. Ibid
13. Some sources give the code name as 'Trianon'
14. M.D. Peterson, *Widow Spy*, Wilmington, Red Canary Press, 2012
15. Dobson and Payne, *Dictionary of Espionage*, p. 285
16. Changed to 'Pley' in 1972
17. Bearden and Risen, *Main Enemy*, p. 403
18. Ibid, pp. 408–9
19. Ibid, pp. 402–3
20. Ibid, p. 423
21. Ibid, pp. 424–7
22. Český Rozhlas 7 – Radio Prague, 24 March 2013

17

AVO AND BLOODSHED IN BUDAPEST

Early in November 1944 Soviet forces drove the Germans out of the Hungarian city of Szeged, just twelve miles from the Romanian border. Even at this early stage, Stalin was leaving nothing to chance. Never mind the Red Army's urgent need for every available aircraft for military purposes, three Hungarian NKVD officers were immediately flown in to prepare the ground for a pro-Moscow provisional government. The first act of Mihály Farkas, Ernő Gerő[1] and Imre Nagy, who had been an NKVD agent code-named 'Volodya' for two decades,[2] was to celebrate the anniversary of the Bolshevik Revolution in 1917.

In January 1945, after the liberation of Debrecen, Stalin's forces occupied two out of the three largest Hungarian cities. Into Debrecen flew another Moscow puppet, to set up the first government. Mátyás Rákosi, however, had been ordered by Stalin not to place himself in the government because he was (a) Jewish[3] and (b) widely hated inside the country as a Communist extremist remembered for his involvement in the Red Terror of the 1919 Hungarian Soviet uprising under Béla Kun. The new party was called Magyar Szocialista Munkáspárt (MSzMP) – the Hungarian Socialist Workers' Party – with no mention of the word communism in order to distance it from Béla Kun's Komunisták Magyarországi Párt, of which many older Hungarians had reason to hate the memory. The first Minister of the Interior in the provisional government was, however, an undercover Communist by the name of Ferenc Erdei, who took his orders from Soviet General Fyodor Kuznetsov. The only worry Erdei apparently had about this relationship was that Kuznetsov concentrated on the minutiae of organising the secret police and completely ignored the skyrocketing crime wave in the liberated areas.[4]

After the defeat of the Axis forces, Hungary was occupied under an Allied Control Council, headed by Marshal Kliment Voroshilov, who refused to consult his American and British colleagues on the council as he was officially obliged to do.[5] Hungary also had to pay huge reparations to the USSR. With the currency changes, it is difficult to estimate exactly the cost to the Hungarian people, but it was about 17 per cent of GDP in 1945–46 and 10 per cent higher in 1946–47, dropping to a still punitive 10 per cent thereafter as it became apparent that the Hungarian economy was otherwise heading for complete meltdown. In addition, it had to bear the costs of the Soviet occupation forces, which came to another crippling 10 per cent of GDP.[6]

The NKVD clone which the new regime imposed on the Hungarian people was known as Allamvédelmi Osztálya (AVO), meaning State Security Division. For its HQ the Soviet occupiers selected the same building in Budapest[7] that had been used by the torturers of the Arrow Cross fascists after they deposed the Horthy regime in favour of continuing to fight for the Axis. Although No. 60 Andrassy út was convenient in the sense of having fully equipped torture chambers, it seems likely that the address was chosen because it already terrified people before the AVO moved in.

The brief of the AVO under its NKVD bosses was, as in the other satellite states, to eliminate any resistance to Soviet hegemony. Some 200,000 civilians – including, under USSR State Defence Committee Order 7161, 44,000 Hungarians with German names – were deported and split up among 2,000 Gulag-style work camps as far away as Azerbaijan, the Urals and Siberia, where 400,000 Hungarian POWs already languished in labour camps.[8] Of these, one-third died in captivity from dysentery, exposure and malnutrition; many of the survivors were released years later. But the arrests and deportations did not stop there: 23,000 members of the Arrow Cross fascists, ex-officers with pre-war service and members of Admiral Horthy's *Levente* youth movement were rounded up, as were whole categories of people, such as innkeepers, shopkeepers, tobacconists and hairdressers – people who had large circles of acquaintants – because they had the *possibility* of disseminating hostile propaganda, anti-Soviet gossip or jokes.[9]

The most infamous camps were at Kistarcsa, Recsk, Tiszalök Kazincbarcika and Bernátkúton Sajóbábony. Although the names and whereabouts of the camps were widely known, nobody dared to speak of them openly. The above figures cannot be exactly verified because all records covering the early years were controlled by Soviet personnel, never released to the public and were destroyed in 1956. Yet, even if each detainee left behind only one or two family members unprovided for, the scale of concomitant suffering among women, children and the elderly is impossible to imagine. Adding to the chaos, in February 1945 the Soviet authorities ordered all remaining Germans in Hungary to leave their homes and report for labour service at the front line, which they were unlikely to survive.

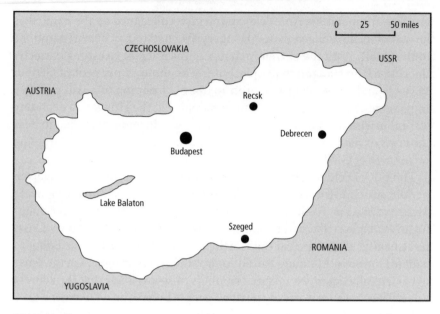

Hungary after 1945.

Farkas admitted later what everyone knew but dared not say at the time: that he and his colleagues used all the classic tortures in their investigations – deprivation of sleep, humiliation, malnourishment, beatings; when these failed, the suspect was handed over to MVD 'friends', who would use more extreme measures to break the prisoner.

Yet, resistance to the Soviet occupation could not be stamped out, as witnessed by the voting in the November 1945 election, when the renamed Magyar Komunista Párt (MKP) – Hungarian Communist Party – received just 17 per cent of votes as against 57 per cent for the agrarian Smallholders' Party, which enabled it to install its leader, Zóltan Tildy, as prime minister. This led to the establishment of a republic in the following year. A part of the reason for the MKP's failure at the polls was that Hungarian primate Cardinal Jószef Mindszenty issued a condemnation of godless communism and called upon Hungarians to revert to traditional values: by supporting the Smallholders' Party they could put the nation back on track after the turmoil of the wartime Axis alliance.

The year 1946 was a nightmare for virtually all Hungarians. Never mind the political situation, the country was suffering galloping inflation, which reached a peak where several billion *pengos* were required to buy a chicken and some vegetables for dinner in a market. In addition to Soviet occupation money, quadrillion-pengo notes were in circulation and sextillion pengo notes were printed but never issued. Wages were effectively so worthless when received that many workers survived on a daily meal in the factory canteen; others were paid not in money but food.[10] On 1 August 1946 a new currency unit was introduced: one *forint* was equivalent to 400,000 *quadrillion* pengoes. That is 4 with twenty-nine zeroes. Contemporary photographs show street cleaners sweeping piles of worthless million-*pengo* notes out of the gutters for burning.

The first appointed director of AVO was Péter Gábor, tasked by his Soviet masters with destroying the Smallholders as a political force. Accusing the party of actively collaborating with the Nazis, he proceeded in typical NKVD/MVD style to use torture to extract confessions from his victims. However, in the August 1947 election, MKP still gained only 24 per cent of votes, despite the authorities having disenfranchised half a million people and a further 300,000 being too afraid to go to the polling stations. In addition, a number of 'voting flying squads' were transported in Hungarian and Soviet military vehicles to cast votes for the MKP in several districts, one after another. A Social Democrat called Sára Karig, who had been very active in the anti-German resistance movements, protested at this blatant abuse – for which she was arrested without trial, tortured and deported to a Gulag camp in the far north of Siberia, whence she returned only after Stalin's death in 1953.[11]

Undeterred by the setback at the polls, Gábor continued the AVO reign of terror. Target groups to be destroyed were the Church, Jews (because of what Stalin called 'their cosmopolitanism'), Freemasons and anyone who had been active in other political parties. In 1948 psychoanalysts too would be declared 'enemies of the people'. As a Jew, Freud was totally discredited anyway, but his theories also conflicted with Marxism–Leninism and practitioners of psychoanalysis were stigmatised as bourgeois reactionaries who yearned for an American lifestyle.[12]

From time to time, news filtered out of the closed countries east of the Iron Curtain. On 16 June 1947 United Press reported from Budapest:

Colonel Istvan Zemes was arrested yesterday after his apartment had been searched and six or seven other members of the Smallholders Party of former Premier Ferenc Nagy [no relation of Imre Nagy] will be expelled from the party tomorrow.

On the third day of the mass trial of 44 alleged conspirators, former Smallholder deputy Paul Yacko admitted today that he had been in contact with 'a secret organisation', but he denied other charges. Yacko said that, as high sheriff of Vas county on the Austrian border, he attempted to establish escape routes for prominent men accused of conspiracy.

A Polish UB officer present as an observer in court noted the presence of a red-haired Russian MVD general, who appeared to be stage-managing the whole trial.[13]

The AVO had drawn up a list of top people now 'revealed' as saboteurs and spies, but whose only crime was to be less than 100 per cent pro-Soviet. It included the name of Interior Minister László Rajk. Tortured for twelve days, he eventually confessed after being promised personally by János Kádár that this would save his family from suffering the same fate. An AAP newsflash dated 25 September 1949 read:

A Budapest court yesterday sentenced Rajk, one of Hungary's leading Communists and a former Foreign Minister, to death for spying on behalf of the United States and Yugoslavia and other acts of alleged high treason.

Despite the promise that Rajk's family would not suffer for his 'crimes', they were all executed shortly after his death. The lesson was not lost on a later Interior Minister named Sandor Zőld, who murdered his whole family before killing himself after falling foul of the party in 1952. In the second purge of the Hungarian Party, approximately 40,000 people were arrested, tortured and executed or given long terms of imprisonment and several hundred thousand people were dispossessed and deprived of their livelihoods.[14] In 1949 even the primate, Cardinal József Mindszenty, was arrested, tortured and forced to make a patently false confession that 'justified' his sentence to life imprisonment for treason, while the party rec-reated the Church under the banner *Pacem in Terris* – or 'peace on Earth' – and appointed obedient puppet priests to its hierarchy.[15]

Dr Istvan Ries served as Minister of Justice for three years from July 1945. Living through the 1917 October Revolution while a POW in Russia, he had fought in the Hungarian Red Army after his return home and had to leave the country for two years before he could return and take up his law practice, specialising in defending labour activists and joining the Social Democrat Party in 1924. He spent most of the Second World War living underground and emerged with the Soviet 'liberation' to take office as min-ister, but when the MKP manoeuvred the non-communists out of power in 1947, he resigned.

In 1950 the AVO changed its title to Allamvédelmi Hatósag (AVH), meaning State Security Authority, but so little else changed that it contin-ued to be referred to by people as 'Avo', and was hated just as much. Ries was clinging to office, assisting in the merger of the Social Democrats and MKP to form Magyar Dolgozók Párt (MDP) – the Hungarian Workers' Party – headed by Mátyás Rákosi. The Russian 'advisers' in Budapest sneered that the leaders of MKP had been practising 'salami communism', slice by slice for the sake of appearances, but the result was the same in the end. Although Ries's legal background was useful in the drafting of a new, Soviet-style constitution of 1949, he was arrested on 7 July 1950, while still in office, and died in Vác prison after excessively violent torture during interrogation. Like many other victims of this stage of Hungarian Communism, he was rehabilitated in 1956.

In 1951 pro-Soviet Hungarian communist Rudolf Garasin returned from what he claimed was a stint working as manager of a printing works in the USSR, although indications are that he was actually employed in some capacity within the Gulag administration. This would explain why he was given the job of creating a directorate for public works, known by the acronym KÖMI, to run extremely low-cost state enterprises employing prison labour in quarries and on construction sites – in other words, a Hungarian Gulag. This was at first under the Justice Ministry, since it used convicted prisoners, but later moved under the aegis of the Interior Ministry, alongside AVH. In less than two years, Garasin was the boss of 27,000 work-capable prisoners confined in a nationwide network of work camps, including chaotic transit camps with little provision for the unfortunates stranded there or passing through.

The most infamous camp at Recsk was modelled on the Nazi *Nacht und Nebel* precedent. This prison had no number and the 1,700 inmates, denied any contact with the outside world, officially did not exist. They included members of the Smallholders' Party, artists, journalists, Hungarians who had lived abroad and were therefore treated as Western spies, former anti-German partisans and many others who had no idea why they had been arrested. The first prisoners were set to building the fences and barracks, living in farm buildings shared with animals and their attendant flies and other parasites. With no mess hall, they ate the inadequate rations standing outside, whatever the weather. The ubiquitous mud prevented them sitting or lying down. An added misery was the excessive number of roll calls. Infraction of any regulation saw prisoners deprived of food and water and locked into a waterlogged cell where they could neither sit nor lie down in the knee-deep mud.

After a bad harvest in 1952, 400,000 peasants were arrested for failing to deliver their grain quotas to the state collection points, as they were in neighbouring Poland. Some went to prison, others to the concentration camps. In addition, as in the other Soviet-occupied states, people were required to report on their colleagues and were in turn reported on themselves. The scale of manpower devoted to any one case is illustrated by husband and wife journalist team Endre and Ilona Marton. They were among the last stringers for Western news agencies in Eastern Europe, he working for Associated Press and she for United Press. They were snooped on at home, had their telephones routinely tapped and were followed night and day. Their AVH dossier totalled 1,600 pages of reports when they were arrested in 1955 as 'Western spies' and interrogated about *everyone* they had met since 1945.[16]

On that fateful night in February 1955, the Martons had been to a reception at the US embassy in Budapest. After their return home, a squad of AVH officers arrested Endre Marton and charged him with espionage and plotting against the 'people's democratic regime' on the grounds that he had betrayed state secrets to the US ambassador. His wife was arrested with some violence in June, when she managed to make arrangements for her two daughters to stay with neighbours whom they hardly knew. Endre was sentenced to seven years in jail; Ilona, to three years. In a sense, they were lucky, as they were released during the rebellion of 1956 and given assistance to leave Hungary with their daughters and settle in the United States.

In the Soviet tradition that saw heads of the NKVD, such as Yezhov, and of the KGB, such as Beria, executed when they 'knew too much' about Stalin, Gábor also was arrested in 1952 and accused of forming 'an Anglo-Zionist conspiracy' with László Raik and Rudolf Slánský to assassinate Stalin. At the time he was heading an organisation of 5,751 full-time officers and thousands of informers – the thirty-three highest-paid full-timers being embedded MVD officers.[17] Surprisingly, after confessing, Gábor was not executed but sentenced to life imprisonment in 1954 and released in 1959, to start a new career as a librarian! Did anyone dare to bring back an overdue book with such a man behind the counter?

Stalin's death in 1953 sent waves throughout the USSR and its satellites. In Hungary Rákosi's authority waned and he was replaced as prime minster by Imre Nagy, but kept in the government. In a palace revolution, Rákosi managed to regain control, but was then forced to resign after Nikita Khrushchev's 'secret speech' at the twentieth congress of the USSR Party on 25 February 1956 denouncing the crimes of his predecessor, Josef Stalin, with the exception of those in which he had participated. When the process of destalinisation led to protests by Polish workers in Poznan at the end of June, suppressed by Soviet armed intervention, news of this stimulated unrest in Hungary, which the government could not control, so Anastas Mikoyan deposed Mátyás Rákosi on 18 July under the pretence that he was ill and urgently needed 'treatment in Moscow'. Before leaving, Rákosi managed to hand the position of party leader to Ernő Gerő, who had also spent two decades in the USSR after the bloody Béla Kun Soviet uprising of 1919, and was doubly unpopular for his recent participation in the collectivisation and industrialisation programmes.

Gerő's previous international 'claim to fame' was from the Spanish Civil War, when he was one of the commissars accused of the murder of Andrés Nin and other leaders of the POUM faction in the International Brigades. Even now, he refused to make concessions to the demonstrators and repeatedly requested Moscow to keep Rákosi in the USSR to avoid his return upsetting the delicate political balance in Hungary. Gerő's short reign, lasting only three months, was characterised by increasing unrest, not only from intellectuals and workers' representatives, but also his own colleagues at the head of the party, who considered him headstrong and deaf to criticism or advice.

On 23 October 1956 peaceful demonstrations and demands for reform were met by Gerő ordering the police to fire on the demonstrators. Like the obedient puppet he was, he also called on Soviet Ambassador Andropov for help. He advised Khrushchev to send in tanks and Soviet troops moved into the city early on 24 October, to find themselves attacked by students. Reports of the crisis in Hungary caused the Soviet politburo to despatch the deputy chairman of the Council of Ministers, Anastas Mikoyan, to Budapest with Mikhail Suslov on 24 October, tasked with assessing the situation. The AVH being unable to control the violence in the streets, Mikoyan and Suslov travelled to meetings in an armoured personnel carrier. They were informed by Gerő that, unsurprisingly, the presence of Soviet troops was viewed unfavourably by the population. Equally unpopular was his own dictatorial broadcast speech taking the nation to task. The Soviets then retired Gerő after a reign of only three months, with the Hungarian Central Committee appointing the relatively liberal János Kádár as party leader and Imre Nagy – who had been deposed as prime minister on Moscow's orders in early 1955 for the crime of being 'too Hungarian' – appointed prime minister because he was considered the only leader capable of handling the rebellion.

Instead of obeying the government's orders, some Hungarian military units mutinied and distributed light weapons to the demonstrators. Prudent party officials lay low. Officers of the AVH secret police who were careless enough to be caught by their erstwhile victims were gunned down in the streets. In the provinces, local councils sprang up, with peasants reoccupying their confiscated fields and political prisoners freed from prisons and labour camps. Anxious to avoid civil war, Nagy pleaded with the demonstrators to go quietly home and let the party sort things out, but it was too late for that.

Unrest continued to grow. On 29 October the embedded Soviet 'advisers' with the AVH wisely assembled their families and followed Mikoyan and Suslov back to the USSR. That they were right to do so was obvious when daylight came and AVH men were found gunned down in the streets, beaten to death and hanged from street lamps. The new government was powerless to calm the unrest. Anarchy ran wild, with red stars hacked off the facades of state and party buildings. Some 8,000 political prisoners were released, among them Cardinal József Mindszenty, the Roman Catholic Primate of Hungary jailed for life in 1949 for resisting the Communist takeover. Cheering crowds escorted him back to the primate's palace in Budapest. Students took over the national radio network.

The Budapest chief of police and Nagy's Minister of Defence Pál Maléter declared for the demonstrators, many of whom had served as conscripts and knew how to handle rifles and anti-tank weapons and make Molotov cocktails – which eventually cost 200 Soviet tanks over four days of conflict. Whether from prudence or sympathy with the Hungarians, some tank crews parked up, opened the hatches and did nothing, but on 25 October when AVH snipers started shooting at them, the tankers replied with machine gun fire and cannon shells in a confrontation that killed around 200 people in and around the parliament building.[18] The disorder was nationwide, with agricultural workers plundering the collective farms and all factories closed by strikes.

John Sadovy, a 31-year-old photographer born in Czechoslovakia who was working for *Life* magazine at the time, compiled the most graphic photoreportage of the Budapest fighting. On 30 October, after the undamaged tanks had been withdrawn from the city, forty-seven AVH officers took positions on the roof of the Central Committee building and fired on the crowds, killing scores of people. Forced to emerge and surrender, they were grabbed by the demonstrators. So densely packed was the crowd that Sadovy had to get very close to the action, using a wide-angle lens on one of his two Leica 35mm cameras to photograph what happened before, during and after their executions. His verbal account included this passage:

> The first to emerge from the building was an officer, alone. The next thing I knew, he was flat on the ground. It didn't dawn on me this man was shot. Six young [secret] policemen came out. Their shoulder tabs were torn off. Quick argument: 'Give us a chance,' they said. Suddenly one began to slouch forward. They must have been close to his ribs when they fired. They all went down like corn that had been cut. Another came out, running. He saw his friends dead, turned, headed into the crowd. The revolutionaries dragged him out. I could see the impact of bullets on clothes. They were shooting so close, the man's body acted as a silencer.[19]

The intensity of the terror under which Hungarians had been living with the AVH was evident from the vicious punishment handed out by ordinary people. At least one officer was strung up from a tree, doused in petrol and burned to death; others were beaten to death with bricks and sticks, to be left lying in the streets. And not only employees of the AVH were set upon. Sadovy's photographs record informers, including women, being attacked in the streets and begging for their lives. At the same time, tens of thousands of political prisoners were being liberated by the rioters, among them prisoners who had been in jail since the end of the war, twelve years before.

The most important liberated prisoner, Cardinal Mindszenty broadcast an appeal on national radio for reconciliation, but nobody was listening.

After forming a coalition government of socialist parties to negotiate the withdrawal of Soviet occupation troops, on 1 November Imre Nagy announced Hungary's secession from the Warsaw Pact, which it had only joined the previous year, and requested the UN to recognise his country's neutral status, hoping this would lead to protection by the Western powers, but timing was against him. France and Britain were embroiled in armed intervention in Egypt to punish the government of President Nasser for nationalising the Suez Canal and Eisenhower was furious that his European allies dared to take such action without his approval. Seeking to legitimise its own armed intervention in Hungary, Moscow canvassed support from neighbouring Romania, Czechoslovakia and Yugoslavia. Knowing what had happened to people who went to Moscow 'for consultations', President Tito refused to leave his holiday island in the Adriatic, obliging Khrushchev and Malenkov to make a nightmare journey to obtain his approval, partly in a light aircraft in bad weather and a small boat in storm-tossed seas.

Nagy had received reassurances from Soviet Ambassador Yuri Andropov that the USSR would not interfere but, with Britain and France involved in the Suez crisis, Khrushchev judged that the US would not risk a global confrontation over Hungary. On 1 November he ordered Soviet occupation troops to take all measures to 'restore order'. A quarter-million Hungarians grabbed the chance to cross the temporarily unguarded western frontiers and 'voted with their feet', abandoning their homes and taking only what they could carry before the Soviets upped their military presence.

On 4 November the five Soviet divisions already stationed in Hungary were reinforced by twelve more Warsaw Pact divisions, and the fate of the Hungarian uprising was a foregone conclusion with Budapest surrounded by 2,500 armoured vehicles plus artillery and multi-barrelled rocket launchers. Eleven years after its 'liberation' by the Red Army, some parts of Budapest were again a battlefield; in others, life seemed normal and even telephones still worked. A BBC Hungarian Service translator calling an aunt in Budapest for an update heard the trams running as usual in the background – followed by bursts of heavy machine gun fire not very far away.

When all was lost, Nagy advised Mindszenty to seek asylum in the US embassy. A Marine corporal and a master sergeant were standing behind the grille at the entrance to the embassy with the Air Attaché, when the cardinal and an English-speaking monsignor arrived and asked to enter the building. The corporal asked the attaché, 'What should I do, sir?' but received no reply. He then asked the master sergeant, who replied, 'Do your duty.' The corporal opened the grille; his act was justified a few minutes later when a telex arrived from Washington instructing the embassy to extend every courtesy, should the cardinal request asylum. Mindszenty was to stay isolated in the safety of the embassy for fifteen years. His 'brother in Christ' Canterbury's Reverend Dean Hewlett Johnson condemned Britain for the Suez invasion, but said that 'politically, the situation is different in Hungary [where] the action of the Soviet Union was to prevent [a return to] fascism.'[20]

Nagy was not so lucky. He took refuge in the Yugoslav embassy, which was swiftly surrounded by Soviet tanks. Minister of Defence Pál Maléter was invited to negotiate with the Soviet command, but was instead taken prisoner. In the early morning of the same day, János Kádár broadcast a speech proclaiming a new pro-Soviet government with himself as prime minister. Retracting Nagy's secession from the Warsaw Pact, he did, however, promise that once the 'counter-revolution' was suppressed and order restored, he would negotiate the withdrawal of the Soviet army of occupation. Some credibility was given to this and his promises of reforms because it was known that he had been imprisoned by the AVH and tortured under the Stalinist regime of Máyás Rákosi. Yet armed confrontations between Hungarians and the Soviet troops continued.

Among the few Hungarian politicians who did well out of the 1956 uprising was János Kádár, who was transported with a skeleton administration to his office in Soviet armoured vehicles while Soviet tanks continued to shell nearby buildings from which sniper fire was coming. To acquire a semblance of democratic reform, Kádár promised free elections, the withdrawal of the Soviet troops and a general amnesty.

Courage and rifles are no match for tanks. Soviet losses totalled 1,250 wounded and more than 650 dead, against 17,500 wounded and 2,500 dead on the Hungarian side by the time the fighting ended in January 1957. The workers used the only other weapon they possessed and proclaimed a general strike. It was several months before daily life reverted to normal. Meantime, Nagy had been tricked out of the Yugoslav embassy by an offer of safe conduct signed by Kádár, but was forcibly abducted to Romania. He, Maléter and their associates endured an ignominious two-year captivity that ended with him being returned to Budapest for a trial in camera, his years of loyal service to Moscow as an agent of the NKVD availing nothing.[21] Nagy, Maléter and the other VIP prisoners were hanged in a prison there on 16 June 1958. Lesser activists were deported to the Soviet Union, never to return.

In the 'free' election following the rebellion, the official result was a 99.6 per cent vote for the Communist-dominated Patriotic People's front. Then the shark showed his teeth: one by one all the slight concessions of the previous three years of destalinisation were cancelled: agriculture was recollectivised and many former AVH employees reappeared, working for the Interior Ministry in a new repression that began early in 1957. By 1960 they and their KGB 'advisers' had brought the country to its knees again and, with the loss of all those who had fled abroad, the economy was in dire straits. In a search for incentives, Kádár's regime introduced an amnesty for political prisoners, lifted the press censorship and allowed foreign travel that gradually saw a million Hungarians visiting the West in a single year.

It is impossible to over-estimate the importance for all the satellite states of the Hungarian government's decision in May 1989 to dismantle the barbed wire, watch-towers and minefields along Hungary's western border with Austria. On 16 June the Hungarian people showed what it felt about the forty-five years of Soviet domination by reinterring, after a televised state funeral, the remains of Imre Nagy and Maléter, the three other men hanged on 16 June 1958 and a sixth coffin symbolising all the other deaths.

Notes

1. He was born Ernő Singer.
2. Sudoplatov, *Special Tasks*, p. 367
3. He was born Mátyás Rosenfeld.
4. Applebaum, *Iron Curtain*, p. 79
5. Ibid, p. 70
6. Ibid, pp. 38–9
7. No. 60 Andrassy Place is now a museum known as The Terror House.
8. Glavnoe Upravlenie NKVD SSSR po delam Voennoplennikh I Internirovannykh (GUPVI)
9. Applebaum, *Iron Curtain*, pp. 118–19
10. Lowe, *Savage Continent*, p. 201
11. Applebaum, *Iron Curtain*, pp. 225–6
12. Ibid, pp. 419–20
13. Ibid, p. 303
14. Brogan, *Eastern Europe*, pp. 121–2
15. Ibid, p. 122
16. Applebaum, *Iron Curtain*, p. 91
17. Ibid, p. 82
18. Brogan, *Eastern Europe*, p. 128
19. Quoted in Brogan, *Eastern Europe*, pp. 129–30 (abridged)
20. L.S. Wittner, *Resisting the Bomb*, Stanford, Stanford University Press 1997, p. 89
21. Sudoplatov, *Special Tasks*, p. 367

MAGYARS ON MISSION ABROAD

In addition to AVO/AVH responsible for internal security there was the Hungarian Intelligence service Belügyminisztérium Állambiztonsági (BA), which was so little respected by the KGB and other Warsaw Pact services that its officers were nicknamed 'the cafe Chekists'. This slur perhaps harked back to the days of the Austro-Hungarian monarchy, when Central European spies could earn a sort of living by sitting on the terraces of pavement cafes eavesdropping on the latest gossip of indiscreet politicians and military men or the ladies who were privy to their secrets. The BA particularly targeted expatriate Hungarian circles, which were hardly a risk to the new regime, since none of them even dreamed of conquering their former homeland. The aim was, it seems, to coerce expats with family inside Hungary to cooperate in various ways, but also to discredit important figures in the Hungarian diaspora. If it seems logical that neighbouring countries like Yugoslavia, Austria and the Bundesrepublik were targeted – as witness many thousands of files now conserved on the extensive shelving in the Hungarian state intelligence archives Állambiztonsági Szolgálatok Történeti Levéltára (ABLT) – so also was the Catholic Church, and particularly the Vatican.

Before the uprising of 1956, the number of AB staff was nearly 6,000. Immediately afterwards it was down to 1,500 and rose to something like the old strength by the mid-1960s. Of these between 200 and 500 were posted abroad at any one time, more to acquire much-needed Western technology than to collect military secrets. It was believed in the intelligence community that BA officers also assisted several anti-Western terrorist organisations on occasions, for example by shipping equipment and some weapons in the diplomatic bag, exempt from customs examination.

When liberal-thinking people imply that everyone claiming refugee status should be given asylum in a democratic country, alarm bells are ringing in the corridors of national counter-espionage services because, in addition to those arriving because their lives are genuinely at risk in the homelands and others coming for the welfare handouts and a generally easier lifestyle, there will be some purported refugees with very hostile motives for entering their target country. The flood of Hungarians leaving their homeland for Western Europe after the uprising of 1956 certainly included some BA officers.

In addition to BA with its specific tasks, there was also Magyar Néphadsereg Vezérkara 2 Csoportfőnöksege (MNVK2), the 2nd Chief Directorate or *deuxième bureau* of Hungarian People's Army General Staff, i.e. Hungarian military intelligence. The most successful MNVK2 agent in the 1956 refugee stream was Zoltan Szabo. After serving in the US army in Vietnam, he held the rank of Sergeant First Class but also happened to be a colonel in MNVK2. How long he might have continued his undercover activities is an open question, but he was uncovered by a double agent working for the CIA. Sometime in 1979 a GRU officer serving in Budapest named Vladimir Vasilyev passed to his CIA controller the alarming news that the USSR had obtained a shattering amount of NATO hot-war plans from a source in Germany. US Army Counter Intelligence Corps (CIC) began investigating all personnel who had access to these plans and narrowed the list down until they were investigating Clyde Lee Conrad. As so often, one of the damning indicators was his standard of living, far in excess of his official income.

Conrad arrived in Germany in 1974 and was posted to 8th Infantry Division, based in Bad Kreuznach, with the rank of Sergeant First Class. His assignment in G3 War Plans Section was to take custody of the ultimate top-secret plans for deployment of the US Army in Europe in the event of the Cold War turning hot. In his archives were also details of the disposition of American nuclear weapons in Europe. He was to take over from Sergeant Zoltan Szabo, who had been passing classified information to Czech and Hungarian military intelligence for several years, but was about to retire from the army. Seeking to recruit a successor, Szabo, who was a cool professional, took his time sizing up Conrad's circumstances before approaching him in 1975. Married to a German woman with two children from a previous marriage and who had one child with him, Conrad was short of cash. But he did have a very high security clearance, access to a vault of top-secret documents, and – unbelievably – the use of a secure photocopier which did not record his usage of it! When Szabo made his pitch, the inducement was simple: money and lots of it for handing over documents from the vault to Szabo's contacts, who would pass them on to Hungarian and Czechoslovakian case officers, who in turn would forward them to Moscow. Under the code-name 'Charlie', Conrad took the bait and began delivering files and other information, for which he received cash payments that allegedly totalled several million dollars, some of which was shared with accomplices whom he recruited over the following ten years, during which time more than 30,000 classified documents were passed over.

Two other known members of Szabo's spy ring were Hungarian-born Swedish citizens, the brothers Imre (code-named 'Viktor') and Sandor (code-named 'Alex') Kerecsik, but so tight was the group's internal security that nobody was ever entirely certain how many others were involved. In 1983 Conrad recruited his assistant, Sergeant Roderick Ramsey (code-name 'Rudolf'), to help copy and pass on classified documents for the following two years. Others known to have been in the ring were Jeffrey Rondeau, Jeffrey Gregory and Sergeant Kelly Theresa Warren. Ramsey would later reveal that there were at least ten others involved, one of whom became an American general, according to him. The ring may have become leaky, with so many people involved. Whether for that reason or simply from Vasilyev's tip-off, payment of Conrad's retirement pension was stopped for several months without him apparently noticing, which indicated that he had other sources of income for his very affluent lifestyle.

Conrad was arrested in 1983 by Federal German counter-espionage officers, neither the American military nor the FBI having jurisdiction because he had retired from the army and settled in Germany. Strangely, his service record indicated that he had not been vetted for seven years, during which time his popularity and reputation for hard work had several times led his superiors to request prolonging his work in the top-secret vault until he retired from the army. Possibly, there was some collusion there too.

Some insiders believed that the decision to arrest Conrad came after an acquaintance of his was observed in Vienna with a known Hungarian agent.[1] Whatever triggered the arrest, one has to ask why it had taken four years from Vasilyev's tip-off to stop Conrad's treasonable activities. Was there perhaps a double game being played, with him unknowingly passing to the Hungarians information from files that had been falsified?

Whatever the truth, he was tried and found guilty by the Koblenz State Appellate Court on 6 June 1990. Judged to be the head of the spy ring, Conrad was sentenced to life imprisonment. Judge Ferdinand Schuth said that Conrad's treachery meant that, if war had broken out between NATO and the Warsaw Pact, NATO HQ would have been forced to choose between capitulation or the use of nuclear weapons on German territory, turning the whole country into a battlefield.

In addition, on 12 February 1999 Jeffrey Rondeau and Jeffrey Gregory were sentenced by a Florida court to 18 years' imprisonment each; Kelly Theresa Warren, to 25 years. Zoltan Szabo received a 10-month suspended sentence in consideration for testifying against the others and identifying documents that had been passed to his masters in Budapest for forwarding to Moscow. The post-Communist Hungarian government was also apparently helpful in providing some evidence.

For once, a life sentence meant until death. For all the $1.2 million he had been paid – and at the trial it was stated that he had a safe deposit box in a Swiss bank stuffed with gold bullion – Clyde Lee Conrad died from a heart attack at the age of 50 in Koblenz prison on 8 January 1998.

The end of Communism in Hungary came more gently than in other Warsaw Pact states because of prior relaxation under the Kádár regime, which is why the dismantling of the frontier wire and other obstacles enabled so many citizens of other states to escape via Hungary to the West before their governments changed. According to ABLT the greater part of the pre-1956 archives were destroyed in the uprising – whether by the protesters or by officers seeking to protect themselves, is unknown. Public debates were held in 1997 and 2003 about access to the ABLT archives. So far, more than a half-million copies of documents have been supplied to 27,000 researchers. The majority were of general interest, but there have also been scandals involving revelations of past activities of politicians, artists and writers. The most shattering was the record of former Prime Minister Pétér Medgyessy, now known to have been an undercover agent of AVH. [2]

Notes

1. J. Rusbridger, *The Intelligence Game*, London, Bodley Head 1989, p. 110
2. For more information see www.targetbrussels.be/article/hungary's-cafe-spies

PART 4

State Terror in Eastern Europe

19

THE KDS

Dimitrov's Lethal Homecoming Present to Bulgaria

As with the other satellite states, the problem for Bulgaria during and after the Second World War was its geographical position, it having common borders with Romania, Serbia, Macedonia, Greece and Turkey and with Soviet Ukraine only 300 miles to the north and the USSR's Black Sea fleet a short voyage to the east. Ruled by a constitutional monarchy under Tsar Boris III, it managed to stay neutral until 1941. On 13 December 1941 Tsar Boris's government was obliged by Berlin to declare war on Britain and the USA, the price of which was the bombing of Sofia and other Bulgarian cities by Allied aircraft. The alliance with the Axis offering the hope of recovering territory in Macedonia and Thrace that had been lost in the First World War, Bulgarian forces occupied areas of Greece and Yugoslavia, fighting partisan forces there in conjunction with German and Italian troops. However, after the launch of Operation Barbarossa the Comintern ordered the Bulgarska Komunisticheska Partia (BKP) to go underground in preparation for anti-Axis guerrilla warfare. To camouflage the lines of command, it merged with other leftist groups and called itself the Fatherland Front.

Although there were some minor actions against vessels of the Soviet Black Sea Fleet, Bulgaria did not formally declare war on the USSR. Summoned to Rastenburg by Hitler in August 1943, Boris refused to hand over the Bulgarian Jews; nor would he agree to send troops to the increasingly hard-pressed eastern front. A few days after returning to Sofia, Boris attended a dinner at the Italian embassy and died the following day, with poisoning suspected. As a result of his refusal to participate in the Final Solution, Bulgaria ended the war with an *increased* Jewish population.[1]

On 23 August Romania reversed its pro-German policy and declared war on Germany, allowing the Red Army to cross its territory and reach the Bulgarian frontier. Stalin declared war against Bulgaria on 5 September, the day on which Agrarian Party Prime Minister Konstantin Muraviev abolished all anti-Semitic laws the Germans had imposed. Three days later, Muraviev declared war on Nazi Germany, but it was too late to qualify as a friend of the USSR because the Red Army was already crossing the border.

In a swift and relatively bloodless coup that deposed Muraviev's seven-day-old government, which was attempting to make peace with the Western Allies, the pro-Soviet Fatherland Front took over the reins of government under Kimon Georgiev. He ordered the Bulgarian armed forces not to resist the Soviet invasion, and signed a treaty of alliance with the USSR on 9 September. All these geopolitical manoeuvres caused considerable strife within Bulgaria, principally between pro- and anti-German factions. Also, the Bulgarian ground troops in Macedonia had to fight their way free from their erstwhile German allies in order to regain their native soil.

After the Red Army's arrival on Bulgarian soil Georgi Dimitrov, Stalin's blue-eyed boy who had controlled all the foreign Communist parties for him in his capacity as boss of the Comintern, arrived to commence his very hands-on style of rule. The Fatherland Front was ostensibly a merger of political parties that would run the country with an appearance of democracy. Yet, its first priority was to purge anyone who had a record of thinking independently. In the usual Soviet way, they were declared to be fascists and imprisoned or executed in two purges: in Dimitrov's own words, 'the wild one' and the judicial one. Figures for the victims arbitrarily killed range as high as 138,000.[2] Dimitrov's Minister of Defence, General Ivan Genaro, later boasted to KGB General Sudoplatov, 'Bulgaria is the only socialist country without dissidents in the West because ... we wiped them out before they were able to escape [abroad].'[3]

That was a euphemism for the massacre of tens of thousands of Bulgarian intellectuals, non-Communist politicians, journalists and academics under a programme supervised by Dimitrov to crush any sense of Bulgarian nationality.[4] A notable exception was made for Tsar Boris's widowed consort and her 8-year-old son, Prince Simeon, who were allowed to take into exile at least some of their personal wealth – which makes one suspect some shady deal behind the scenes.[5]

A very different sort of woman operated the Fatherland Front's network of local search-and-kill committees. She was a violent and ruthless ex-partisan named Tsola Dragoicheva, who had spent several years in a concentration camp. Her technique was to compile random 'black lists' of *possible* opponents for trial in 'people's courts'. As happened to other activists, she herself eventually fell foul of the system in 1949 and was put out to grass, but not imprisoned or executed.[6]

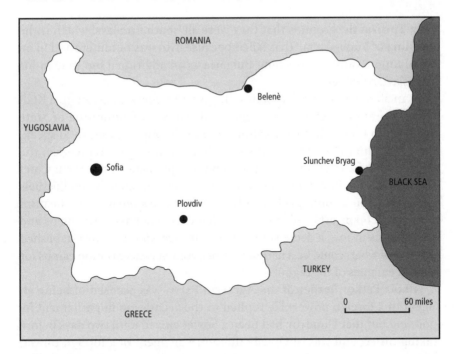

Bulgaria after 1945.

Among the early moves of Dimitrov's regime in Bulgaria was the reform of the Bulgarian Cyrillic alphabet by removing letters that did not exist in the Russian alphabet – itself reformed by Lenin in 1917. The argument was that these letters were bourgeois and elitist, therefore not permissible in the new 'socialist' Bulgaria. This move was pushed through despite strong opposition from surviving writers, educators and others, who resented this distancing of their orthography from Old Slavonic, simply to fall in line with Soviet practice. As from 27 February 1945 only documents written in the modified alphabet had legal effect in Bulgaria. It was a strange priority when nearly half a million Bulgarian soldiers in three armies were still fighting in Yugoslavia to hamper the withdrawal of German forces in Greece. Also in 1945, with Dimitrov's aid, the KGB started mining high-grade uranium ore at Bukovo, only forty miles from Sofia. After the ore from Jáchymov was analysed and found to be low in uranium content, Bukovo became the most important source of fissile material for the Soviet A-bomb.[7]

In whatever alphabet, Kimon Georgiev must have seen the writing on the wall. He was ousted from his party and political functions, which were taken over by Georgi Dimitrov the following year. Stalin's faithful follower, however, then tried to do a deal with Yugoslavia's Communist leader, Josip

Broz Tito, on the grounds that they were all 'southern Slavs', which is the meaning of Yugo-slavia. That failed because Tito was not interested in an equal union, only in absorbing Bulgaria as an additional republic in his Yugoslavian federation.

As in all the other satellite states, the pro-Moscow regime set up a KGB clone: Komitet za Darzhavna Sigurnost (KDS) or Committee of State Security. In line with the organisation of the 'mother house', so to speak, the First Chief Directorate was dedicated to foreign intelligence; the Second Chief Directorate was for counter-espionage; of the Sixth Chief Directorate, the first department organised and snooped on intellectuals and artists, the second spied on university staff and students, and the third kept watch on priests and 'unreliable elements' like Jews, Armenians and Turks. Early in 1945 a decree of Interior Minister Anton Yugov established the first of what would be a nationwide network of concentration camps for alleged enemies of the regime.

Nikola Petkov, leader of the Agrarian Party, was accused of being an 'agent of a foreign power'. He replied to the accusation in parliament by pointing out that Dimitrov had been a Soviet citizen until two days before taking office, and was obviously therefore an agent of a foreign power, whose capital was in Moscow. Spared until the peace treaty was signed in Paris in February 1947, he was then arrested in a fight with KDS men on the floor of parliament, given a fake trial and hanged as a traitor.[8]

Dimitrov was completely out of touch with his fellow Bulgarians, having lived in exile for twenty-two years, but that probably made it easier to turn the country of his birth into a carbon copy of Stalin's Russia. He brought with him a hard core of comrades who had spent years in the USSR, but they were already old men; the senior in-country politician was Traicho Kostov, who was considered likely to inherit Dimitrov's power. He showed his loyalty to Dimitrov by managing the Red Terror of 1944–6, but was himself purged in March of 1949 for stubbornly trying to prevent the wholesale post-war looting of Bulgaria to feed Soviet industry.

A visibly very sick man, Dimitrov travelled to Moscow for medical care and died there in July of the same year, prompting rumours that he had been quietly done away with because Stalin considered him too well known in the international Communist movement to be put on trial as a 'Titoist deviationist'. Dimitrov's brother-in-law Vulko Chervenkov – who had served in Russia as an agent of NKVD under the code-name 'Spartak' and been principal of Moscow's Marx–Lenin school for indoctrination of the foreign comrades – manoeuvred his way into the dual posts of General Secretary of BKP and prime minister, which gave him total power. He expelled 100,000 of the 460,000 party members to purge BKP of any non-Stalinist or nationalist influences which might impede his crash programme for the collectivisation of agriculture, rising from 12 per cent of the total arable area in 1950 to 61 per cent by 1953, with productivity dropping as a result. International trade was restricted to other members of the Soviet bloc.

By 1952 his repression was at its height, with a network of 100 concentration or forced labour camps in a population of only 8 million people. Run by the Interior Ministry, the Bulgarian Gulag was called Trudovo-Vazpritatelni Obshchezhitiya (TVO), echoing faithfully the deceptive title of the Soviet Gulag camps *ispravitelno-trudoviye lagery* or corrective labour camps. Tens of thousands of alleged 'counter-revolutionaries' were locked up and brutally treated by criminals working for the camp administration, as in the Allgemeine-SS camps. The most infamous Bulgarian camp was Belenè, on Pirin island, which lies in the middle of the Danube.

Starting in 1949 the Bulgarian state waged war on the Evangelical Church with what was called 'the Pastors' Trial', in which thirteen pastors were convicted of counter-revolutionary activities and received sentences of varying lengths in Belenè for proclaiming Christianity in an atheist state. Pastor Haralan Popov survived thirteen years in the camps and later published his autobiography, translated into English as *Tortured for His Faith*. At least the pastors knew why they were being punished; most detainees had no idea why they were there because, under Bulgarian law, *anyone* could be imprisoned for six months without trial. They were then released and immediately rearrested for another six months; in 1962 the period of incarceration without trial was increased to five years. Eventually Belenè held up to 7,000 inmates in grossly inadequate conditions, but while the pastors were there the camp already held seventy-five women and 2,248 male prisoners – which number included Konstantin Muraviev, the last non-Communist prime minister, who had surprisingly not been executed and would survive his incarceration.

The Belenè camp was closed officially after 1959, but used between 1985 and 1989 for Bulgarian Turks who refused to change their names and surnames to Bulgarian ones in a government 'programme of national unity'. Today Belenè is still a prison, but the other half of Pirin island is a nature reserve. Second for brutality to Belenè was the camp at Skravena, where 1,643 infants and children were held under the Russian system of *krugovaya poruka*, or collective responsibility, which punished the entire families of 'criminals'. Other notable concentration camps were at Kutsiyan, Rositsa, Bogdanov Dol and Bobov Dol, Nozharevo, Bosna and Chernevo, where what were called in the USSR *byvshye lyudi* or 'former people' – like army officers, landowners, Agrarian Party members, social democrats, anarchists and also Communist resistance heroes – were removed from the Stalinist society they might otherwise have 'polluted'. The camp at Lovech

in central Bulgaria was infamous throughout the eighteen years of its existence for the brutality of the guards, beating inmates working 18-hour days
and hired out as slave labour on nearby collective farms and construction sites until they died of malnutrition and abuse, the corpses piled up
by the latrines until there were enough to justify despatching a truckload
for burial in mass graves. So terrified were inmates of being reported by
a fellow prisoner for saying something that could be misinterpeted that
many spoke only when no one else was in earshot, just enough to make
sure they had not lost the power of speech.

In overall charge of the camps was Vice-Minister of the Interior Mircho
Spasov, who not only visited them, to see conditions for himself, but threatened guards whom he considered not to be brutal enough. Many infants
arrested with their parents were simply killed in transit or on arrival at
the camp; those who survived spent up to the first ten years of their lives
there, witnessing scenes of violence and murder. Many emerged with lifelong physical or psychological problems, to find themselves debarred from
higher education. Some of these victims later banded together under the
banner 'Children of the Camps' to demand compensation from the post-
Communist governments, but this has so far been refused on the grounds
that they were *too young to suffer from the experience.*[9]

In addition to those sent to the camps, some 25,000 people were forcibly
exiled to remote corners of the country. As to how so many 'enemies of
the people', and 'counter-revolutionary elements' were identified in the first
place, in 1972 the author was directing a BBC TV film in and around the
Black Sea resort of Slunchev Bryag – Sunny Beach, in English. Inside the
beautifully laid-out *turisticheski compleks* itself there were no indications
that one was in a country ruled by a totalitarian regime; indeed Bulgarian
law had wisely been suspended in the resort to encourage Western visitors
to come and enjoy themselves in an atmosphere without ubiquitous fear.
However, as the BBC team found when filming outside this privileged area,
life was very different for the locals. The film crew was accompanied everywhere by a French-speaking 'liaison producer' from Bulgarian Television,
who wrote a report of where we had been and what had been done at the
end of each day. I had a certain sympathy for him, trying not to be obstruc-
tive to us and yet please his masters. When setting up for a shot of the
endless sandy beaches, open sea and blue skies, he would say, 'Do not point
the camera north. That is forbidden,' or 'We cannot stop here. It is better
to drive on a few miles.' As to why filming to the north with a 20:1 zoom
lens was not a good idea, the reason may have been a forced-labour camp
reputed to be somewhere in that direction, whose 250 inmates worked and
died in a quarry, breaking rocks for the construction of a luxury villa for
party fat cats to take their holidays in. On another day, after recce-ing some

ancient ruins outside the resort, the author noticed a plaque on a house wall in the nearby village. Able to read Cyrillic script, he asked what exactly it meant. There was an embarrassed pause until the 'liaison producer' said, 'This is the house of a BKP member.'

'I understand that, but why does it need a plaque on it?'

Another embarrassed pause, then, 'So that people can tell him if their neighbour has done something wrong.'

... or thought or said 'something wrong', which might land them in a camp. The system was exactly like that of the *Blockleiter* in each city block of Nazi Germany, who snooped on everybody for the Gestapo. The 'crimes' that justified being sent to a labour camp included what the BKP regarded as cultural aberrations by the writer Dimiter Talev, the poet Yosif Petrov and the pianist Trifon Silyanovski. Internationally acclaimed jazz singer and recording artist Lea Ivanova was sent to a camp for allegedly promoting retrogressive sound and obscene behaviour on stage.[10]

After Stalin's death, Chervenkov's repressive regime weakened, amnestying 10,000 political prisoners in 1955 when the party denounced Stalinism and caused Chervenkov's resignation. Todor Zhivkov then took supreme power with a programme of 'modified socialism'. He was the epitome of the grey *apparatchik*, slavishly following the Moscow line and leading his country into economic meltdown with its Soviet-style central planning of everything from steel production to agriculture.

In 1964 a Bulgarian Smersh was formed, known as Service 7 and headed by Colonel Petko Kovachev, who despatched teams to assassinate or kidnap dissident Bulgarians living in Britain, France, Denmark, West Germany, Italy, Turkey, Sweden and Switzerland. The best-known example in Britain was that of 49-year-old playwright, novelist and broadcaster Georgi Markov, who was stabbed on Waterloo Bridge on 7 September 1978 with the point of a specially modified umbrella that injected a microscopic ricin pellet below the skin of his heel. This assassination on the sixty-seventh birthday of Todor Zhivkov was intended as a present for him. After walking across Waterloo Bridge on his way to Bush House, Markov felt a sharp pain like a wasp sting on his right heel. He looked round to see a man picking an umbrella off the ground and hurrying away. On arriving at work, Markov mentioned the incident to a colleague. That evening he was admitted to hospital with a raging fever, and died there three days later.

The assassination operation was overseen by KGB General Oleg Kalugin. The umbrella, the pellet and the ricin within were supplied by the KGB's high-security toxicology laboratory in Moscow, designated Laboratory X, which refined and supplied poisons for many other Smersh-type assassinations after first experimenting with them on condemned prisoners. This method of assassination being unknown in Britain, there was no antidote available. Markov died before any proper diagnosis could be made or any effective treatment given.

The 'crime' for which he had been condemned in Sofia was rejecting the invitations of party boss Todor Zhivkov – former head of Narodna Militsiya, the people's militia – to become a state-salaried 'socialist writer'. This was during the period when the Bulgarian Ministry of Culture was slavishly following the Moscow line of *zhdanovshchina* propounded by alcoholic Soviet Politburo member Andrei Zhdanov, which ruled that the only valid function for creative artists was to reflect an exclusively Marxist view of life and the world, as interpreted by the party. Like many self-taught people, Stalin was an avid reader and considered himself a discerning critic, sending handwritten notes to authors, composers and playwrights with advice they could hardly reject. On 26 October 1932 he had called a meeting of Russia's fifty most influential writers, including his favourite, Maxim Gorky. They were informed by him without equivocation, 'The artist ought to show life truthfully. And if he shows our life truthfully, he cannot fail to show it moving towards socialism. This is, and will be, Socialist-Realism.'[11]

The idea of becoming a BKP hack revolted Markov, who described Bulgarian society in terms that applied to a greater or lesser extent to all the satellite countries 1945–89:

> Today, we Bulgarians present a fine example of what it is to exist under a lid which we cannot lift and which we no longer believe someone else can lift ... And the unending slogan which millions of loudspeakers blare out is that everyone is fighting for the happiness of the others. Every word spoken under the lid constantly changes its meaning. Lies and truths swap their values with the frequency of an alternating current ... We have seen how personality vanishes, how individuality is destroyed, how the spiritual life of a whole people is corrupted in order to turn them into a listless flock of sheep. We have seen so many of those demonstrations which humiliate human dignity, where normal people are expected to applaud some paltry mediocrity who has proclaimed himself a demi-god and condescendingly waves to them from the heights of his inviolability.[12]

In 1969 Markov emigrated and satirised the communist regime of his country in many broadcasts over the BBC Bulgarian Service, RFE and Deutsche Welle, thinking himself safely beyond retribution. In 1972 Markov's membership of the Union of Bulgarian Writers was suspended and he was sentenced in absentia to six years and six months in prison for defection. His sense of humour still intact, Markov used *In absentia* as the title for his weekly broadcasts on RFE commenting on life in Bulgaria and criticising Zhivkov. As reward for the success of the joint KDS–KGB operation,

Kalugin was awarded a medal and received a Browning automatic pistol as a present from KDS. Since the whole story was well known in intelligence circles, when Kalugin visited London in 1993 he was arrested at Heathrow Airport and detained at Belgravia police station for twenty-four hours. He denied the charges of implication in Markov's murder and was released when the Crown Prosecution Service decided there was not enough evidence to begin proceedings against him in an English court.[13] What was not commonly known was that there had been two previous Service 7 attempts on Markov's life: to poison his coffee during a visit to RFE in Munich and a more dramatic scenario that had to be aborted while he and his family were holidaying on Corsica.

The murder of Markov was far from being the only KGB-style *mokroe dyelo* or 'wet job' undertaken against émigrés by KDS. Vladimir Kostov was posted to France in April 1974 as Paris correspondent of Bulgarian Radio and Television. He held the rank of major in KDS and the broadcasting role was a cover for his intelligence work. Three years later, in July 1977, he and his wife, Natalya, defected and were granted political asylum in France. He was immediately given the code-name 'Judas' in Sofia. In May 1978 he was sentenced to death in absentia; his wife, Natalia, was also sentenced to six and a half years' imprisonment as a 'traitor to the motherland'.

In order to have plausible denial, a French-speaking KDS Service 7 sleeper in Algeria was ordered to execute the sentence on her husband. On 26 August 1978 as Kostov was stepping off an escalator in a crowded Paris Metro station he felt a violent blow in the small of his back on the right side. Suspecting a KDS attack – had he already learned of this method of assassination in the course of his duties? – he consulted a doctor two hours later, but was told he might have been stung by a wasp. For two days, his condition steadily worsened with fever and a swelling where he had felt the blow. Kostov reported the incident and his suspicions to Direction de la Surveillance du Territoire (DST), the French counter-espionage service, but no trace of any toxin known to French doctors could be found in his body. After Markov died on 11 September, Kostov called a contact in the BBC Bulgarian Service, who told him Markov had repeatedly said in his last days that he had been poisoned by KDS.

Fortunately for Kostov, the 2mm pellet had in his case been lodged between layers of skin where there was little blood flow and the skin temperature was not high enough to melt the wax plugs in the pellet's microscopic holes, so the full effect of the ricin was never released. Scotland Yard detectives investigating the murder of Markov travelled to Paris, where a surgeon removed a thumbnail-sized piece of flesh from Kostov's back including the platinum and iridium pellet, which was taken back to London for analysis, to reveal the truth about Markov's death. Ricin was also the poison of choice used by the KDS against Vladimir Kostov, a Polish double agent in Virginia. Other assassinations attributed to the organisation were of a Bulgarian scientist working in Vienna and the editor of an émigré newspaper.[14]

Some stories never end. After Scotland Yard officers went to Sofia following the collapse of Communism, seeking information about Markov's death, on 21 September 2008 the London *Times* carried a story about 'a Danish-nationality petty crook [named Francesco Gullino and] code-named "Agent Piccadilly" [who] used to travel around Europe in a caravan pretending to be an antiques salesman'. He was said to be the prime suspect. Why would a KGB-linked state security organisation need to use a foreigner for such a job? The answer may lie in the *modus operandi* of a far higher-profile KDS assassination project.

This was the wounding of Polish-born Pope John Paul II at Vatican City on 13 May 1981 in an assassination attempt by convicted Turkish bank robber and hit-man Mehmet Ali Ağca. Ağca had 'previous form', as they say in police circles. On 1 February 1979 in Istanbul, with another member of the Grey Wolves Turkish terrorist organisation, he shot and killed Abdi Ipekçi, editor of the national daily *Milliyet.* He was caught and jailed, but escaped from a military prison with the help of the Grey Wolves and fled to Bulgaria. Before the attack on the pope, he travelled widely in the Mediterranean area to muddy his tracks.

Hit by four bullets in the attack, the pope lost much blood but survived. Ağca was sentenced to life in prison for the attempt; he was released in June 2010 and deported to Turkey, where he was imprisoned for the murder of Ipekçi and other crimes previously committed there. Although one theory about the assassination attempt was that the KDS had been ordered by the KGB to train a deniable assassin to kill the pope as punishment for his support for the Solidarność movement in Poland, for reasons of diplomacy the Vatican did not wish details of Ağca's connection with Service 7 to be publicly proven.

The umbrella murder on Waterloo Bridge was the most dramatic act of KDS in Britain, but at least some of the Bulgarian diplomats in London were also here for the purposes of collecting intelligence. The author's filming at the Black Sea coast song festival was made possible through the 'tourism counsellor' of the embassy. The image of that title conjures up a smiling, genial guy with a mission to make great holidays for people and earn foreign exchange for his country, but the reality was a hard-faced 'diplomat' who never smiled and was constantly looking behind him.

For many years before the end of Communism, KDS officers supplemented the organisation's funds by trafficking in arms, illicit drugs, cigarettes, precious metals and other commodities. Many people believe that after the end of communism in 1989 the same men who headed organised crime gangs grew rich on this trade and by money laundering. According to globe-trotting US author Jeffrey Robinson, for much of Zhivkov's year-long tenure of office the KDS ran an import–export company named Kintex, which laundered the proceeds of selling heroin and morphine base to Turkish drug rings and other illicit activities through Swiss banks and used the deposits to finance a large-scale illicit arms business that netted as much as $2 billion annually in much-needed hard currency.[15] Kintex was also thought to have discreetly supplied small clandestine mercenary units, modelled on the Soviet Spetnaz forces, to clients in a number of countries.

Although talking about *glasnost* and *perestroika* in line with Gorbachev's reforms, Zhivkov was overtaken by events, still stuck in the past, when a Human Rights Committee was formed in Sofia. This was in January 1989. Next came a Bulgarian 'Eco-Glasnost' movement protesting against the nationwide industrial pollution. In October 1989 and again in November, the KDS broke up their peaceful demonstrations – embarrassingly in the presence of foreign 'green' delegates. But the dam could not hold: on the day following the fall of the Wall, Zhivkov was ousted and charged with corruption, and the BKP changed 'Communist' in its title to 'Socialist'.

After the regime collapsed in January 1990, the official government line was that the KDS files had all been sealed and were open only to the new president's immediate staff, to be consulted before appointment of politicians and others to important positions, so that ex-secret policemen did not regain power. However, some people allege that KDS officers removed and destroyed many files that could have exposed them to prosecution. In particular, the former Interior Minister General Atanas Semerdzhiev was believed to have authorised destruction of 144,235 files from the KDS archives, to prevent prosecutions of officers who had simply 'done their patriotic duty'.

In January 2005 the Interior Ministry Chief Secretary Lieutenant-General Boyko Borissov – who later became prime minister – stated that many people in Bulgaria and outside the country were being blackmailed and manipulated under the threat that their KDS files would be made public. He said that the officers of KDS 1st Department (general espionage) and 4th Department (specialised industrial espionage) who died in the line of duty should be recognised as loyal servants of their country, and also maintained that those still alive should not be blackmailed by what he called 'the coyotes of the 6th Department [sic]' blowing their cover. Borissov said that it was necessary to destroy the KDS archives to put an end to this state of affairs. Well, maybe that has been done.

Notes

1. M. Gilbert, *The Routledge Atlas of the Holocaust*, London, Routledge 2009, p. 230
2. Dallas, *Poisoned Peace*, p. 361
3. Sudoplatov, *Special Tasks*, p. 233
4. T. Todorov, *Voices from the Gulag*, University Park, Pennsylvania State University Press 1999, pp. 39–40
5. Sudoplatov, *Special Tasks*, p. 233
6. Brogan, *Eastern Europe*, p. 197
7. Sudoplatov, *Special Tasks*, p. 198
8. Brogan, *Eastern Europe*, p. 198
9. Kassabova, *Street without a Name*, pp. 315–16 (author's italics)
10. See http://www.decommunization.org/Testimonies/Svideteli.htm. More eyewitness accounts may be found in E. Boncheva, E. Sugarev, S. Pytov and J. Solomon, eds, *The Bulgarian Gulag, Eye-Witnesses: A Collection of Documented Accounts of Camps in Bulgaria*, Sofia, 1991
11. Montefiore, *Stalin*, p. 96
12. G. Markov, *The Truth That Killed*, New York, Ticknor & Fields 1984
13. Sudoplatov, *Special Tasks*, pp. 282–3
14. Dobson and Payne, *Dictionary of Espionage*, pp. 214–15
15. For further details see 'Jeffrey Robinson', *Wikipedia*, http://en.wikipedia.org/wiki/Jeffrey_Robinson

20

A Different Umbrella in Bucharest

As historian Patrick Brogan once remarked, 'Romania had had territorial disputes with all its neighbours throughout its modern history.' One glance at the map explains why. Apart from 100 miles of Black Sea coastline, to the south is Bulgaria, then, clockwise, come Serbia, Hungary, Ukraine, Moldova and Ukraine again – the last three all part of USSR in 1945. On every border lies disputed territory and the dormant claims are reflected in the multiple names for major cities like Cluj, which is called Klausenburg in German and Kilosvár in Hungarian.

King Mihai I, a third cousin of Britain's Queen Elizabeth II, was the 22-year-old king of the troubled country who joined a number of pro-Allied politicians in the coup of 23 August 1944 which overthrew the pro-German regime of Marshal Ion Antonescu. After a series of typically Balkan 'misunderstandings', i.e. betrayals, Antonescu was handed over by Romanian Communists to the Soviets a week later. In a radio broadcast to the nation at 10.30 p.m. on 23 August the king announced over the state radio, 'Receive with confidence the soldiers of the Red Army. The United Nations have guaranteed the independence of the country and non-interference in our internal affairs.'

The broadcast was as far from reality as when his father, King Carol III, told the nation in 1939, 'Our soldiers will fight gloriously'. Within three weeks of 23 August, 165,000 officers and other ranks had been arrested as fascists and despatched by a number of the few serviceable trains to Gulag camps in Kazakhstan and Siberia.[1] Few returned home.

On 12 September an armistice was signed, which was in effect an unconditional surrender on Soviet terms. The Romanian Communist party Partidul Comunist Român (PCR) numbered fewer than 1,000 members, having enjoyed little support before the war because the country was largely a peasant economy with little concentration of workers in factories for activists to organise. It also supported Soviet plans to divest Romania of some border regions, which did not make it popular with the common people. However, with Soviet support, it now set about ensconcing itself until, in March of the following year, King Mihai was forced to accept a pro-Soviet coalition under Petru Groza, a lawyer and leader of the 'Ploughmen's Front' peasant movement, which had joined the PCR after King Mihai's coup. Even before the Potsdam Conference, some 70,000 ethnic Germans were driven out of Romania.

In November 1946 the so-called 'bloc of democratic parties' came to power after blatantly rigged elections,[2] confirming Groza's power – on the face of it, as leader of a democratic coalition. Behind the scenes two more of Stalin's puppets, named Anna Pauker and Gheorghiu Gheorghiu-Dej, both of whom had spent the war years in the USSR, were manoeuvring to build the political base of the PCR by supporting votes for women and land reform to win over the peasants. As one of the four members of the PCR's central committee, Pauker initiated a recruitment drive that netted a half-million new members without enquiring into their political ante-cedents. Despite this apparent liberalisation, mass arrests restarted in 1947 and many of Pauker's recruits would be purged between 1948 and 1950. In November 1947 she became the first woman in the world to hold a political post as high as Foreign Minister, and was hailed by *Time* magazine as the Iron Lady decades before Margaret Thatcher was given that accolade.

Paradoxically both a prime mover in the 1945 arrests of thousands of supporters of the Antonescu regime and an advocate of a Romanian path to socialism, Pauker was so much Stalin's creature that a newspaper car-toon – for which the cartoonist paid heavily – depicted her on a sunny day in Bucharest with her umbrella up. When a passer-by said, 'Anna, it's a lovely day, why the umbrella?' she replied, 'It's raining in Moscow'. Gallows humour? Probably, because the Romanian Iron Lady had had her own hus-band shot for Trotskyist deviation in Stalin's purges of the 1930s.[3]

King Mihai was now a figurehead without any real power, except briefly to refuse to sign Groza's decrees until forced by the UK, USA and USSR to 'behave' himself and accept the inevitable as PCR absorbed the other polit-ical parties. In November 1947 Mihai was allowed to travel to London for the wedding of Princess Elizabeth and Philip Mountbatten. Meeting at that assembly of European royalty his future wife Princess Anne of Bourbon-Parma, Mihai decided not to return to Romania, but was pressured to do so by Churchill, among others. On 30 December the king was summoned to Bucharest, where his palace was surrounded by pro-Communist troops of the Tudor Vladimirescu Division, blocking any communication with units loyal to the king. There, Groza and PCR boss Gheorghiu-Dej ordered

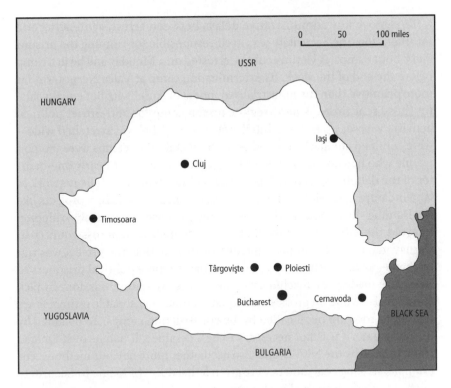

Romania after 1945.

him to sign an abdication already prepared for his signature and record an announcement of it to be broadcast later. Told they would execute 1,000 political prisoners if he refused, Mihai signed, which enabled them to proclaim a 'people's republic'. Four days later, Mihai was fortunate to be allowed to depart into exile with some personal possessions and a few members of his household – although government documents, which may be genuine, attest that the king was paid off with a half-million Swiss francs. According to Sudoplatov, Andrey Vyshinsky – the legally trained prosecutor at Stalin's show trials in the 1930s – laid down the terms of the abdication, agreeing that half of Mihai's pension would be paid to him in Mexico.[4]

Because of all these machinations, Romania did not get its Soviet-clone security police until the end of August 1948. Entitled Departamentul Securității Statului or Department of State Security, it was almost always called simply 'Securitate'. From its first day, it was 'guided' by MVD officers in the senior posts and employed many former officers of Siguranța Statului, the former royalist secret police, until they were all purged once it was up and running. Initially, its staff totalled 4,641 officers, rising to 11,000 officers controlling a half-million coerced informers in a population of 22 million people.

To remove any administrative delays between arrest, sentencing and incarceration, the Securitate was itself responsible for running the prisons and labour camps. A victim could be arrested on a Monday and be in a camp before the end of the week. Its extermination camp at Valea Neagra was far more primitive than the industrialised model of Auschwitz but equally fatal for those sent there. A hard-regime prison camp for anti-Soviet political activists was set up at Aiud. Intellectuals – the label was stretched wide – were confined at Gherla. Locked away in several other camps were 180,000 people who had committed no crime; 40,000 of them, or nearly one-quarter of the detainees, were women.[5] The regime created a whole network of labour camps ostensibly to fulfil central planning construction projects like the Danube–Black Sea canal, whose stated purpose was to enable shipping to avoid the difficult Danube delta by cutting straight across country to Cernavoda. For much of the interrupted construction, the project was run by the Securitate, using convicted criminals to force political prisoners to work with inadequate machinery – most of the excavation was done by pick and shovel – while on grossly inadequate rations. Reasonable estimates are that up to 100,000 people died in the construction camps. To be killed by the Securitate, it was not necessary to be a detainee. It had its own Smersh team, trained by the NKVD, and also used other more devious methods. For example, striking coal miners were given lethal doses of X-rays by Securitate doctors under the guise of health checks.

Pauker, herself from a religious Jewish family, also made possible the emigration to Israel of some 100,000 Romanian Jews – including her own parents – between 1950 and 1952, which was not in line with Stalin's 'anti-cosmopolitan' views on Soviet Jews. In the summer of 1950, undergoing surgery for breast cancer in Moscow, she also resisted Stalin's orders for collectivisation in Romania, releasing the conscripted peasants on her return and encouraging a market economy for their produce, which earned her Moscow's rebuke that she had drifted into non-Marxist policies. In the bloc-wide purges of 1950, Foreign Minister Anna Pauker was denounced and removed from power; she died in 1961.

After Gheorghiu-Dej dropped dead in March 1965 a physically unimpressive grey figure emerged from the shadows behind him. The 47-year-old Nicolae Ceaușescu and his previously unknown wife, Elena – who would manoeuvre her way to become the second most-important person in the country – were to govern Romania until their grisly end on Christmas Day of 1989. Initially acclaimed for his independent line in foreign affairs, Ceaușescu even condemned the Warsaw Pact invasion of Czechoslovakia in 1968. Internally, however, he pursued a personality cult, claiming titles like 'Great Genius of the Carpathians', placing family members in positions of power and razing one-third of central Bucharest to make a parade ground like Moscow's Red Square, flanked by an enormous palace seven storeys high that would have delighted Hitler's architect Albert Speer. He made *any* contact with foreigners illegal, limited electricity consumption for each house to one 6-watt bulb – for which there was power between two and four hours a day – and required every woman to produce five children. In this last connection, contraception and abortion were forbidden under a law that obliged women to undergo regular gynaecological examinations to ensure compliance. All internal and international mail, telephone calls and faxes were intercepted. While neither as ubiquitous or efficient as the Stasi, the Securitate did have thousands of informers known as *sicuristi* – roughly one for every forty-three people – so that no one could trust any friend or even a relative in the deliberately manipulated paranoia.

The external intelligence operation of Securitate was unimpressive, compared with that of other satellite states, but it did exist. The first time that this came to general attention in the West was in July 1978, when 50-year-old General Ion Pacepa was on a duty visit in Bonn to deliver a message from Ceauşescu to Chancellor Helmut Schmidt. Arriving at the US embassy, he requested and was immediately granted political asylum. The Romanian espionage chief, who was also a confidant of Nicolae Ceauşescu, was an important catch for the CIA, which whisked him off to Andrews Air Force base outside Washington in a military aircraft. He was already known to Western services, having served in Germany from 1972 to 1978, and had no reservations about telling all he knew during debriefing. In an attempt to prevent this, he was condemned to death in absentia with a price of $2 million on his head, to which Yasser Arafat and Muammar Al-Gaddafi reportedly each added another million dollars.

Working in France at the time of Pacepa's defection was a 30-year-old agent of the Direcţia Informaţii Externe (Foreign Intelligence Directorate of the Securitate). Born Matei Hirsch, but using the name of Matei Haiducu, he was the privileged son of a high official in Ceauşescu's Interior Ministry, whose task was to steal French technology, especially in the realm of nuclear research. However, in January 1981, Haiducu received an order from Bucharest to assassinate two Romanian émigré writers living in France named Virgil Tănase and Paul Goma. In a sense it was a repeat of the Markov murder, with a different method, because the two intended victims had irritated Ceauşescu – in Tănase's case by describing the dictator as 'His Majesty Ceauşescu the First'. Instead of doing that, Haiducu reported his orders to DST, the French counter-espionage service. With Gallic subtlety, they let him squirt poison from an adapted fountain pen into a drink that was to be swallowed by Goma, but he 'accidentally' spilled the poisoned chalice. They then assisted Haiducu to stage the kidnapping of Tănase in front of witnesses on 20 May 1982, after which he was spirited away to a quiet hotel in Britanny with Goma. With French President François Mitterrand in on the act, a press conference was called to protest at the flagrant outrage, and Mitterrand cancelled a scheduled visit to Romania to add verisimilitude. This enabled Haiducu to return as a hero to Bucharest and be rewarded with promotion and the rare privilege of a holiday abroad with his family, from which they did not return home.[6]

By the 1980s Romania had the lowest standard of living and the most appalling food shortages of the satellite countries. In an attempt to pass the buck, the Securitate arrested 80,000 peasants as 'saboteurs' who had obstructed the infallible dictates of the government.[7] Photographs of the time show peasants in shabby clothes riding on horse-drawn carts along unmade roads in scenes where little had changed since the previous century. Nothing worked. No home was anyone's castle: forcible entry was routine, as was the planting of hidden microphones.

The collapse of the regime was inevitable in 1989. It began on 14 December in Timisoara, a major city in the west of the country, where Securitate officers attempted to arrest a Hungarian pastor named László Tokes. Encouraged by the news from the other satellite states, his parishioners made a human chain around his house. Most unusually, local Romanians joined in the struggle until it seemed the whole population was engaged. After three days, Ceaușescu ordered soldiers and police to shoot the demonstrators to 'restore order'. The Securitate and some soldiers did so; other soldiers refused to obey the order. Tokes was arrested after 100-plus people had been killed and many wounded. Returning from a state visit to Iran on 21 December, Ceaușescu ordered a massive rally in Bucharest to endorse his authority. Televised live, its great surprise was the booing from younger people in the crowd, swiftly followed by a roar of anger from most of the people. The screen faded to black as Securitate snatch squads dived into the crowd to arrest the ringleaders. Incredulous at meeting resistance, they began shooting wildly, reportedly killing several hundred people. Ceaușescu ordered Minister of Defence General Vasile Milea to send troops against the people. Milea refused and committed suicide, or was murdered. The army then went openly over to the side of the protesters.

On 22 December an enormous crowd stormed the Central Committee building in Bucharest. The president and his wife escaped from the roof in a helicopter that landed about 60 miles to the north-west, near Târgoviște, where they were recognised and arrested by soldiers. Meanwhile Securitate riot police were launching three days of civil war against the people and army units, in which 1,140 people were killed and more than 3,000 wounded. Their main target was the state television building, where the National Salvation Council of dissidents, students and officials who had fallen foul of the dictator was announcing live to Romanians and the world what was happening.

On 25 December a show trial was filmed, with the president and his wife helped from an armoured car in which they had been held for three days, moving continuously from place to place to prevent a rescue by Securitate shock troops. The kangaroo court, held in a barracks at Târgoviște, heard no witnesses, just a succession of accusations. Ceaușescu seemed too stunned to protest much, in contrast to his wife, who screamed at the guards when the impromptu court, after a 90-minute deliberation, ordered a squad of paras to execute the couple immediately. Caught on film, they were shot in a courtyard and shown lying in pools of their own blood. The film was repeatedly broadcast on television, and may be viewed on YouTube. In one Western television interview, several respectable-looking ladies in Bucharest said that they had watched it many times in the days following the execution. The site of the execution – bullet holes still visible in the wall – is now a tourist attraction.

Such was the speed of this bloody revolution that many people believed it must all have been agreed in advance with Moscow. The Securitate snipers stopped shooting people after a few days, but that the organisation was merely dormant – even continuing to occupy the same premises as before the revolution – became clear in June 1990 when the new government ordered Securitate units into the streets again to beat up students occupying Bucharest's University Square. Scuffles turned into a riot, with cars set on fire and overturned, windows smashed and public buildings occupied. Figures of those killed and wounded vary widely. The government then sent trains to ferry Ceaușescu's rent-a-mob of miners to the capital, so they could teach the students a lesson. The miners ran wild for three days of terror, beating up intellectuals, students and people with foreign contacts.

As in the other former satellites, one difficult problem for the new government was what to do with the Securitate archive containing millions of files. The majority were placed in the care of the new internal security service Serviciul Rôman de Informații (SRI) and some, presumably relating to foreign espionage of the Ceaușescu years, given to Serviciul de Informații Externe (SIE), the new foreign intelligence service. This proved not to be a good idea: many files were leaked for political reasons or in return for favours or protection, and so the archives were deposited in a specially created body, Conciliul Național pentru Studearea Archivelor Securitâții (CNSAS). Theoretically, this body works like the BStU in Berlin, granting access to personal files for Romanian citizens who can prove their identity and entitlement to see them. It is, however, widely believed that, like Orwell's pigs, some politicians and officials have more rights to poke their snouts into the archive trough than has the general population.

Notes

1. Dallas, *Poisoned Peace*, p. 360
2. This shocked Western leaders, who were still expecting Stalin to abide by the terms of the Yalta conference
3. Brogan, *Eastern Europe*, p. 220
4. Sudoplatov, *Special Tasks*, p. 232
5. Applebaum, *Iron Curtain*, p. 296
6. Dobson and Payne, *Dictionary of Espionage*, pp. 347–8
7. Brogan, *Eastern Europe*, p. 220

21

ALBANIA

FROM SERFDOM TO THE SIGURIMI SECRET POLICE

The break-up of the Ottoman Empire after the First World War has had long-term impact throughout the Balkans, where the mutual hatred of population groups defined by language or religion had been held in check by Constantinople's hegemony. It unleashed a struggle which still continues a century later with minorities fighting to join their kindred in neighbouring countries, to dominate their ethnic or religious enemies and/ or fight off attempts by other peoples to take them over. Nowhere were the consequences worse than in ancient Illyria – modern Albania, whose native name, Shqipēria, is translated as 'land of eagles' – which has all the ingredients of medieval struggle and bloodshed.

After the First World War, attempts by its immediate neighbours Yugoslavia and Greece to bite off respectively the northern and southern provinces were frustrated by US President Wilson's policy of national independence. National integrity notwithstanding, Albania was the most backward and undeveloped country in Europe. Its mountainous terrain made the construction of a modern infrastructure of roads and railways virtually impossible, given the resources available at the time. Outside the capital, Tirana, and the main port, Durrës, much of the land remained the legendary 'land of eagles', where peasants laboured in medieval serfdom on estates owned by local lordlings, who pursued blood feuds known as *gjakmarrja* through the generations. Although a superficial semblance of parliamentary democracy existed in the main cities, even in the corri-dors of government buildings assassins lurked and claimed their victims. A member of a wealthy land-owning family, educated in Istanbul, Ahmet Muhtar Bej Zogolli was elected prime minister in 1922. In 1923 he was shot and wounded in the parliament building by a man whose death he arranged shortly afterwards. After another enemy was assassinated, Zogu – the prime minister had modified his name to make it sound more Albanian – and his followers were forced to leave the country by a leftist uprising. They returned to grab power with help from White Russian troops of General Pyotr Wrangel and the government of neighbouring Yugoslavia, which was rewarded for its help with some frontier adjustments. Surviving some fifty assassination attempts, Zogu was understandably paranoid and never seen in public unless surrounded by bodyguards. Preparation of all his food was in the hands of his mother, the only cook he trusted.

On 1 February 1925 Zogu's political astuteness and ruthlessness saw him installed as Albania's first president. Three years after that he was named King Zog I – modifying his name again to the Albanian for 'bird', so that his full title read 'Bird I, King of the Sons of the Eagle'. As king, he reigned for eleven years, until driven out by Mussolini's invasion of 1939. Having stashed at least $2 million in accounts at Chase Manhattan Bank, Zog and his Hungarian-American consort left the country, taking care to remove a disputed amount of portable valuables from the royal palace and bullion from the state treasury. Probably no one except their immediate household mourned their departure. In keeping with the prevailing political climate, on arrival in Britain they and their infant son – they had left within hours of his birth – were hailed as victims of fascism, which, in the commentary of a contemporary newsreel, was 'defiling civilisation'.

However, during Zog's presidency and reign some attempts at modernisation had taken place with the aid of Italian loans; serfdom was eliminated and Albanians *began* to think of themselves as citizens of a nation, rather than as subjects of a local lordling. To force these measures through against the resistance of landlords, Zog did not need to suspend civil liberties, because they had never existed in Albania, so there was nothing to stop him installing a nationwide secret police. With himself as supreme commander of the armed forces, his country was a military dictatorship, with all political opponents driven abroad, incarcerated or executed. So the scene was set for what happened after the Second World War, during which there was internecine fighting between the communist and other resistance organisations fighting at first the Italian occupation and then the Germans, who were finally driven out in November 1944.

The seed was sown in November 1941 when Yugoslav Communist partisan chief Josip Broz Tito was ordered by Moscow to send two party commissars into occupied Albania, where they formally established Partia Komuniste e Shqipërisë (PKSh) – the Albanian Communist Party – under the leadership of Enver Hoxha, a teacher from Korçë in the south-east of the country, near the Yugoslav border. He, ironically, had become a Communist when sent by his wealthy father to study in France in 1930, at the age of 18. Literally from the last day of the German occupation, Albania had its new dictator.

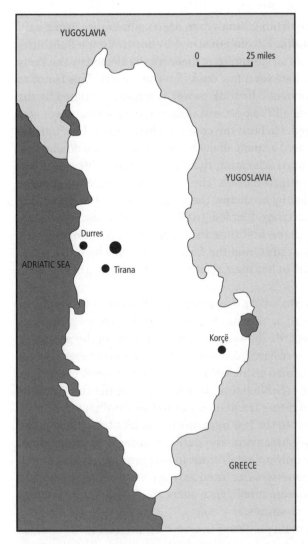

Albania after 1945.

The title of PKSh was changed in 1948 to Partia e Punës e Shqipërisë (PPSh) or Albanian Workers' Party, but the name was unimportant since all other parties were swiftly banned. Unlike in the Central European satellite states, which had enjoyed strong commercial and cultural links with Western Europe before the war, there was no need to pretend democracy in a country that had never known it, but Hoxha took the title of prime minister, later adding those of foreign minister and defence minister – and governed what vaguely resembled a coalition until only the PPSh was left.

Until his death in 1985, Hoxha controlled his police state on Stalinist lines, breaking with Moscow and leaving the Warsaw Pact to espouse 'the Chinese way to Communism' when Khrushchev denounced Stalinism;

Hoxha later broke away from China when Mao's successors 'went soft' after his death. Like Stalin, Hoxha governed by controlling a Politburo, which controlled the Central Committee, theoretically elected by the Party Congress, which assembled for a few days every five years. This is not to belittle Hoxha's achievements: he took power in a country ruined by the dual occupations, where all the port installations, mines and power stations had been destroyed. He built the country's first railway line, opened its first university, imposed a single dialect – his own – as the official language and introduced mass education that brought adult illiteracy down close to the levels in Western Europe. The former near-endemic scourge of malaria was eradicated by medicine, the spraying of DDT and draining of swampland. Life expectancy doubled, tripling the population during his four decades of rule. For the first time in this formerly Muslim country, women were given legal rights, and the *Lekë Dukagjini*, which had made every woman the chattel of her male relatives, to do with as they wished, was abolished.

The dark side of Hoxha's rule was internal repression of thought or action that was perceived as threatening the Party. In the first purges of 1944 and 1945 official records showed that 2,000 'enemies of the people' or 'war criminals' – there were hardly any war crimes committed there – were tried and executed.[1] Informed estimates are that 15,000–20,000 executions in this period is a more reliable figure. In 1951 and 1952 the small groups of Albanian freedom fighters trained, equipped and infiltrated by CIA and MI6 were wiped out to the last man due to Philby's treachery, but so also were any in-country Albanians who dared disagree with government policy. Nor was that the only political crime: in his purge of 1981 Hoxha had several of his closest associates executed as 'traitors to Albania who had been in the service of foreign intelligence agencies' – a rigmarole familiar from other Communist countries.

In addition to the six main political prisons and fourteen most-infamous labour camps, where political prisoners and common criminals were confined together, with convicted criminals running the camp for the uniformed personnel, the government admitted in 1990 that there had been seventy-one other labour camps, making a total of 30,000–50,000 people imprisoned for political reasons in Albania at any one time. Article 47 of the criminal code stated that attempting to flee the fatherland was a crime punishable by a minimum sentence of ten years or death, as was the failure of any person allowed to travel abroad to return when he or she was ordered to. Material evidence of the regime's paranoia is everywhere: the countryside is still disfigured by 100,000 concrete pill-boxes and bunkers of all sizes for defence against a foreign invader. To prevent Albanians escaping, the borders were defended by mine fields, electrified fences, trip-flares and guard towers at 1km intervals. Every morning the guards checked the 2m strip of raked soil on either side of the fence for footprints. Religion was banned, with every church and mosque closed or demolished and a list of permitted names drawn up which made it a crime to name an infant after any religious figure. Ironically, Hoxha's own name – pronounced 'hodja' – was cognate with *hadji* and had been an honorific given to an ancestor who taught the Koran. The dictator himself was often referred to as 'Dullah', a shortened form of Abdullah, meaning 'slave of God'.

The main instrument of internal repression was the Drejtoria e Sigurimit të Shtetit, or Directorate of State Security, usually abbreviated to 'Sigurimi'. This organisation was founded in March 1943, before the German forces left Albania, and eventually numbered 30,000 uniformed officers under 800 senior personnel. The Sigurimi had local headquarters in each of the twenty-six administrative districts, as well as an HQ in Tirana opening mail, monitoring telephone conversations, censoring all media and infiltrating every cultural society and educational establishment. Its effectiveness was considerably enhanced by a nationwide network of coerced and unpaid informers that was said to include one person in every four or five citizens, informing on family, friends and neighbours. In addition, 7,500 'riot police' were formed into five regiments of mechanised infantry held ready across the country to quell any civil disturbance. As in the other Eastern-bloc countries during the Cold War, all these personnel were positively vetted as loyal PPSh members, kept under perpetual surveillance and allowed many privileges in accommodation and ration entitlement denied to the rest of the population.

The Sigurimi was also responsible for many functions of a civil service, including the state archives. It provided armed bodyguards for leading political figures, but also spied on them. There were nearly 200 executions of Central Committee and Politburo members. The counter-espionage section was responsible for neutralising foreign intelligence operations in Albania and anti-party activity by Albanians. Of the work of Sigurimi officers abroad, little is definitely known, except that Albanian diplomats exercised the usually tolerated intelligence-gathering functions. Although the Albanian diaspora numbers several millions, in Yugoslavia, the United States and other countries, it would have been difficult to recruit many sleepers because of the expats' hostility to the Hoxha regime.

Yet, strangely, one of the most famous spies of the twentieth century was Albanian Elyesa Bazna, a locksmith and small-time criminal who was employed as valet by British Ambassador Sir Hugh Knatchbull-Huguesson in Ankara during the Second World War. After making duplicate keys to the ambassador's safe, he regularly removed and photographed confidential papers, selling the prints to Counsellor Ludwig Moyzisch in the Nazi

German embassy. The saying that there is no honour among thieves also covers intelligence officers: Bazna, code-named 'Cicero', was paid in forged notes produced by prisoners in Sachsenhausen concentration camp. When he tried to cash them, they were revealed as worthless counterfeit and his attempt to sue the post-war German government for their replacement with genuine notes failed.

As when fellow dictator Tito died in neighbouring Yugoslavia, after Hoxha's death in 1985 his system collapsed. The first free elections were held in April 1991. The Interior Ministry controlled the three branches of state security: the Sigurimi, the frontier guards and the so-called people's police. Whereas in the Sigurimi *all* personnel were Party members, in the other two services some of the lower ranks were not. In July of that year the still-Communist-dominated parliament abolished the Sigurimi, replacing it with Shërbimi Informativ Kombëtar (ShIK), or State Intelligence Committee, which was in turn replaced by Shërbimi Informativ Shtetëror (ShISh), or State Intelligence Service, in 1997. In October of that year the CIA sent a management team to set up the staffing of ShISh, with Italian help in training the frontier guards and internal police. In addition to intelligence-gathering abroad, the new service oversees internal security and counter-espionage and is responsible for suppressing organised crime and drug-trafficking and -transiting networks, the last of which particularly affects Italy.

Unprovable allegations were made that many former Sigurimi personnel were employed in its successor agencies – unprovable because all archives were held by them. As to the vexed question of opening those files, which were used to vet all candidates in the 1996 and subsequent elections, it appears that some have already been destroyed. Also, while certain members of parliament, some of whom spent ten years and more in Hoxha's prisons for a single indiscreet remark, want to reveal everything, others consider that this would lead to revenge and blood feuds in the rural population.

When the author was recovering his Stasi file from the BStU, in the same reading room was a thin elderly man holding his head in his hands and moaning, '*Wir waren nur arme Menschen.*' We were only poor people. God knows what awful secret he had just learned from his file. The point of stating that here is that the people who suffered under the KGB-clone secret police services in Central and Eastern Europe were not only the intellectuals, educated dissidents and politicians. Many of those locked away from their families for years, even decades, were ordinary men and women whose whole lives were ruined for reasons unknown or so slight that they would not merit even a cautionary warning in any democracy.

When someone is released after a long stay in even the most enlightened form of incarceration, he or she has become institutionalised and may never lead a normal life again for that simple reason. Most of those released after long confinement in a Gulag-type camp have in addition to cope with severe physical and mental health problems. After the initial euphoria of release, many found they could not adjust to the disorientating chaos of the post-Communist era, and committed suicide. In Albania, from a population of only 3 million, an estimated 200,000 people were locked away in Enver Hoxha's Gulag at one time or another, labouring in mines and construction projects with inadequate food and clothing and no safety precautions. So, almost every family has or had a relative or friend whose life was ruined by Communism in this way. A quarter-century after the end of Hoxha's 45-year dictatorship, fewer than 3,000 of the former political prisoners are still alive.

Lavdrim Ndreu spent most of his life in a prison camp. For the past twenty years, he has lived in part of a derelict former football stadium with other homeless men he calls 'my cousins from the camp'. They have been promised compensation for the time spent in labour camps and prisons. A law passed in 2007 entitled former political prisoners to compensation of €14.30 for every day they had spent incarcerated, but even this was to be paid in eight instalments because it amounted to around €400m – a considerable item in the Albanian budget. A cynic might say the delays in payment are deliberate because ex-detainees are dying earlier than the rest of the population, so with every year that passes, the government is saving money. Protests have included ex-prisoners dying on hunger strikes and at least two setting themselves on fire in Tirana. According to a welfare organisation that attempts to rehabilitate the ex-detainees, many of them suffer chronic ill-health. Others, released younger, have married much later than they would have in normal times and are struggling to support their children, who themselves suffer the delayed-action effect of Albania's Communist era.[2]

The Balkan Investigative Reporting Network (BIRN) learned that, of the hundreds of thousands of files in the Sigurimi archives, only 14,000 have been conserved and many of these show signs of having been crudely sanitised in the last days of the Sigurimi. A few individuals were able to find information about their own cases. Aged 23 in 1974, Fatos Lubonja was locked away for seventeen years – the best part of his adult life – his identity reduced to a number in the notorious prison camp at Spac. After serving five years for having kept a hidden diary which included unwise criticism of the regime, he was informed that his sentence had been extended on the grounds that he had become a dissident in the camp. He was freed when Communism collapsed in 1991.

BIRN was able to trace a thick Sigurimi file dealing with Lubonja's case that included reports of handwriting experts tying Lubonja to the diaries, statements by friends and family members produced at the trial, photocopies of pages from the diaries and transcripts of his interrogations – all this for keeping a diary! There was, however, no indication of who had betrayed him. After his release, Lubonja was constantly tormented by that question. He eventually managed to find the name of an ex-Sigurimi officer who had signed one paper in his file and traced that man's telephone number in a local directory. The former secret policeman, named Lambi Kote, at first refused to meet him. By the time they finally met, Lubonja was in his early sixties and Kote was in his seventies – two old men whose battle was not yet over. Kote refused to answer any questions, except by posing his own, alleging that he had fallen out of favour and also been punished. After they parted, Lubonja said, 'I was terrified that he [still] had power over me. He knew what had happened, and I didn't.'[3]

Knowledge is power. Will the remaining archives, kept in the Interior Ministry building in Tirana, ever be made public? It seems unlikely because both the ruling Democratic party and the opposition Socialists each accuse the other of blocking this, which smells of conspiracy. As BIRN comments, there are former Communists in the leadership of both parties who have personal reasons not to wish their past to be exposed.

And so it is. In Albania, Bulgaria, Czech and Slovak Republics, Hungary, Poland and Romania – different countries with very different people, languages and cultures – Stalin's and Lenin's lethal legacies linger on in the unmarked forest graves and the ruined lives of hundreds of thousands of people – and in the ballot boxes too, which is why so many surviving victims are denied the closure that might come from knowing *why* and *by whom* a relative was executed or they themselves imprisoned, tortured or deported.

Notes

1. Ibid, pp. 196–7
2. More on www.balkaninsight.com
3. Ibid

Author Note

All translations are by the author, unless otherwise attributed.

All illustrations are from the author's collection.

Every effort has been made to trace copyright owners. In the event of any infringement, please communicate with the author, care of the publisher.

INDEX